DEVELOPMENT OF INDIA'S URBAN, RURAL AND REGIONAL PLANNING IN 21ST CENTURY: POLICY PERSPECTIVE

Gopal Bhargava

Foreword by

JAGMOHAN

GYAN PUBLISHING HOUSE

NEW DELHI-110 002

DEVELOPMENT OF INDIA'S URBAN, RURAL AND REGIONAL PLANNING IN 21ST CENTURY: POLICY PERSPECTIVE

ISBN: 81-212-0714-2

Published in 2001 in India by
Gyan Publishing House
5, Ansari Road,
New Delhi-110 002
Phone : 3282060, 3261060 Fax : 3285914
E-mail: gyanbook@del2.vsnl.del.in

Laser Typesetting at: Power Photocomposers, New Delhi-110 002
Printed at: Mehra Offset Printers, Delhi-110 002

way, pushing down the old cities in the growth of total population. By 1950, there were six larger cities in the developed region and four in the developing region. During that year, there was no city with eight million people in the developing region. Moreover, the growth of urban population was mainly controlled in the context of developed region. Therefore, in 1990, out of ten largest urban conglomerations, seven emerged in the developing region.

In the year 2001, out of 28 cities with eight million and more people, 22 cities are likely to be in the developing countries. In the same year, 24 cities are likely to emerge as "mega cities" with population in excess of 10 million; 18 of these mega cities would be confined in the developing countries of Asia, Africa and Latin America. Surprisingly, the larger growth of urban population in the developing countries will take place in the already overcrowded and unmanageable cities. Subsequently, in the 21st century these mega cities would rise to gigantic size of population and thus would become unmanageable in terms of law and order, administration and provision of public utility services.

In the urban governing system in Asia, the challenge thrown by the emergence of mega cities is severe in magnitude as it has to cater to almost two-third of the total urban population of the world. Asia in 2001, would have five mega cities as against none in Africa. Thus, India too is going to be confronted with greater intensity of the city problems with the emergence of large number of mega cities. As against four mega cities—Bangalore, Mumbai, Calcutta, Delhi—in India; there will be three mega cities—Beijing, Shanghai and Tinjin—in China; and only two in Los Angles and New York in the USA. According to the projections of the United Nations, the countries in Asia, namely Thailand (Bangkok), Egypt (Cairo), Bangladesh (Dhaka), Turkey (Istanbul), Indonesia (Jakarta), Pakistan (Karachi), Nigeria (Lagos), Philippines (Metro Manila), South Korea (Seoul) and Iran (Teheran) will have only one mega city each.

Interestingly, the 20th century has been called the age of urbanization. In 1900, about eight per cent of the world population lived in urban areas. In 2001, this percentage is likely to rise to 50 and about three billion people will be living in cities of the world. Out of these three billion people, 66 per cent will be in inhabitant cities of the developing countries.

The question arises as to whether the cities of new millennium will grow haphazardly without the basic amenities or otherwise.

Traffic and Transport Bottlenecks in a Metropolitan City

Courtesy: Photo Section, Delhi Development Authority (DDA), Ministry of Urban Development, Government of India.

Courtesy: Photo Section, DDA,

TABLE 1
Urban Agglomerations/Cities having Population more than a Million in 1991 and Projected Figures of 2001 (in million)

Rank in 1991		*U.A./City 1,000,000 + Population*	*1951*	*1961*	*1971*	*1981*	*1991*	*2001**	*2011**	*2021**	*2031**
1.	Greater Bombay	UA	2.97	4.15	5.97	8.24	12.57	13.95	18.27	23.39	30.81
2.	Calcutta	UA	4.67	5.98	7.42	9.19	10.91	12.93	14.22	16.18	19.09
3.	Delhi	UA	1.44	2.36	3.65	5.73	8.38	12.90	16.78	22.22	31.08
4.	Madras	UA	1.54	1.94	3.17	4.29	5.36	7.37	9.31	11.07	12.95
5.	Hyderabad	UA	1.13	1.25	1.80	2.55	4.28	4.62	5.98	7.18	9.11
6.	Bangalore	UA	0.79	1.21	1.66	2.92	4.09	7.63	10.26	14.82	19.55
7.	Ahmedabad	UA	0.88	1.21	1.75	2.55	3.30	4.55	6.23	7.71	9.43
8.	Pune	UA	0.61	0.80	1.14	1.69	4.49	3.31	4.27	6.11	7.57
9.	Kanpur	UA	0.70	0.97	1.28	1.64	2.11	2.57	3.33	4.75	6.51
10.	Nagpur	UA	0.49	0.69	0.93	1.30	1.66	2.27	3.44	4.81	6.43
11.	Lucknow	UA	0.50	0.66	0.81	1.01	1.64	1.46	1.97	2.53	3.18
12.	Surat	UA	0.24	0.32	0.49	0.91	1.52	2.59	3.71	5.27	7.13
13.	Jaipur	UA	0.30	0.41	0.64	1.02	1.51	2.38	3.98	5.51	7.21
14.	Kochi	UA	0.18	0.29	0.51	0.69	1.14	1.19	1.53	1.88	2.32
15.	Coimbatore	UA	0.29	0.45	0.74	0.92	1.14	1.36	1.91	2.62	3.96
16.	Vadodara	UA	0.21	0.31	0.47	0.74	1.16	1.58	2.08	3.31	4.78
17.	Indore	UA	0.31	0.39	0.56	0.83	1.11	1.77	2.31	3.69	5.11
18.	Patna	UA	0.33	0.41	0.55	0.92	1.10	2.50	3.92	5.27	6.89
19.	Madurai	UA	0.37	0.49	0.71	0.91	1.09	1.39	1.92	2.87	3.53
20.	Bhopal	MC	0.10	0.22	0.38	0.67	1.06	3.07	4.87	6.38	8.27
21.	Vishakhapatnam	UA	0.11	0.21	0.36	0.60	1.05	1.50	2.09	2.88	3.65
22.	Varanasi	UA	0.37	0.51	0.64	0.80	1.03	1.31	1.90	2.66	3.47
23.	Ludhiana	MC	0.15	0.24	0.40	0.61	1.01	1.18	1.78	2.27	3.18

Note: Population for the years 1951 to 1981 is for the jurisdiction which prevailed in 1981 and has not been adjusted for the 1991 set up. In other words, 1991 population includes component attributable to inclusion of new areas in the urban agglomeration or expansion of jurisdiction of the 1981 census.

Source: Census of India, 1991 Series I India, paper 2 of 1991, Government of India.

India's Explosive Urban Population

India is experiencing a significant phenomenon in its demographic structure, namely massive growth of pupulation, urbanization, metropolitanization and megalopolitanization. The last two decades have witnessed a large number of metropolitan cities of India. It is visualized that the 21st century will be marked by the dominance of mega cities, several of which will be state capitals.

In 1991 census, India had recorded a population of 844.3 million, out of which 25.76 per cent i.e. 217 million was in urban settlements. The level of urbanization is expected to rise to 30 to 32 per cent by the year 2001 urbanities ranging from 290 to 310 million. The growth rate of urban population was 4.61 per cent per annum during the decennial period 1971–81 and 3.62 per cent during 1981–91. The number of urban settlements in India is too small and not commensurate with its population and area. Too many people and too few cities, sums up the haphazard demographic and settlement structure of India.

The growth pattern of the urban centres in India is imbalanced. Bulk of the urban population is concentrated in a few large cities—most of them states capitals—and they are growing much faster than the smaller towns. In 1991, class I cities accounted for 65 per cent of the urban population; class V towns only three per cent and class VI towns held less than one per cent of the total urban population of India. Some class V and VI towns showed a declining trend or they had been stagnant.

Out of the 23 metropolises (population: one million plus each) four urban agglomerations (Calcutta, Greater Mumbai, Delhi and Chennai—all capital complexes) accounted for one-third of the urban population of India, and nearly one-fourth of the population living in class I urban agglomerations.

Cities, with a million plus population, have continued to dominate the urban scene, accounting for 82 per cent of the urban population in West Bengal, 77 per cent in Maharashtra and over 66 per cent in Gujarat, Tamil Nadu and Karnataka. In 1951, there were only five mega cities—all state capitals Calcutta, Greater Mumbai, Delhi, Chennai and Hyderabad. In 1961, two more cities had joined the mega cities rank, namely Bangalore and Ahmedabad. By 1971, the number of cities had rose to nine, with the addition of Pune and Kanpur to this category.

In 1981, the number of mega cities in India reached 12, by the addition of—three more cities to such a size group Lucknow, Nagpur and Jaipur. During the decennial period, 1981–91, an unprecedented number attained the status of the mega city, by the addition of Surat, Coimbatore, Cochin, Vadodara, Indore, Patna, Mumbai, Bhopal, Vishakhapatnam, Varanasi and Ludhiana. It has been projected that by the year 2001, the number of metropolitan cities in India may rise to about 35.

Mumbai overtook Calcutta in population growth between 1981 and 1991 and Bangalore outstripped Ahmedabad during the decade 1971–81. The population of Bangalore was almost equal to that of Hyderabad in 1991. By the year 2001, Bangalore may have a population of about 7.0 million and is likely to overtake both Hyderabad and Chennai, to claim the rank of the fourth largest city in India.

India's population dynamics has been characterized by a small number of mega cities with heavy concentration of population and a large number of medium and small-size towns with meagre population base. Such a process of imbalanced urban population distribution and distorted settlement structure has the serious implications for generating employment, creating thereby a sustainable economic base and delivering adequate urban infrastructure at affordable prices.

Another feature of urbanization in India is that the cities which are seats of the state governments are growing much faster than other cities. Even the district headquarters and taluka centres have registered faster growth rates than other towns, as they are the centres of administration. The non-administrative urban centres have generally been recording slower growth rates.

TABLE 2

Urbanization Trends and Projections: India (1901-2021)

Census year	*Population (in '000)* *Total*	*Urban*	*Urban as Percentage of Total*	*Per cent annual increase in urban population in the previous decade*
1	2	3	4	5
1901	238,396	25,852	10.84	-
1911	252,093	25,942	10.29	0.03
1921	251,321	28,086	11.18	0.79
1931	278,977	33,456	11.99	1.75
1941	318,661	44,153	13.86	2.77
1951	361,088	62,444	17.29	3.47
1961	439,235	78,937	17.97	2.34
1971	548,160	109,114	19.91	3.21
1981	633,329	159,462	23.34	3.83
1991	844,324	217,178	25.72	3.09
2001	1,032,452	341,330	33.06	-
2011	1,185,606	453,850	38.28	-
2021	1,328,337	577,830	43.76	-

Note: Actual census figures 1901-91; projections based on final totals of the 1981 census and preliminary census figures for 1991, including projected figures for Jammu-Kashmir where the census was not conducted.

Source: India, Registrar General (1991); projections by India Planning Commission (1989); cited from paper of Dr. K. Srinivasan and Dr. Sanjay Kumar; India's Urbanization and Health Conditions: Some Observations.

Most of the capital cities are growing fast and are not able to provide the adequate public utilities, municipal services and community facilities to their exploding population. However, such a situation has resulted into the proliferation of slums, deficiencies in water supply, sewerage and power, encroachment on open spaces and public land, increasing inefficiency in management, deterioration of the central areas and aimless sprawl in the peripheries of the capital cities. The capital cities of the states reflect the variations in the social, cultural, economic, administrative, political and environmental conditions.

In the span of less than fifty years, India has evolved from a backward colonial economy with all its associated limitations to a country which is likely to have one of the highest urban population in the world. The urban scenario of India has been grim. It is visualized that in the beginning of the 21st century India's urban population is likely to be more than 350 million. Therefore, such a situation necessitates an appropriate approach to planning, administrative and legal controls for managing the urban settlements, particularly the metropolitan and large cities. The pertinent question arises as to how will the already strained urban conditions of the nineties respond to the demographic explosion which is likely to emerge in the 21st century.

The deteriorating situation of metropolitan cities like Ahmedabad, Calcutta, Chennai, Delhi, Mumbai, Pune, Hyderabad, Kanpur, and so on, have become a serious threat for the inhabitants with reference to the provision of public utility services. In the 21st century each of these urban nuclei will be subjected to an alarming magnitude of air, water and noise pollution. As a result of such a phenomenon, the quality of life in these cities is likely to deteriorate miserably. Further, coupled with such urban degradation, not only will housing for the vast population projected for these cities will be inadequate, but also the power and water supply will be unsatisfactory in terms of per capita population. The educational and medical facilities, which are presently confronted with acute shortage, are also likely to suffer further.

Aforesaid are the elements of urban framework in the new millennium and present projections are indication of what lies in store for the burgeoning urban segment of the Indian population. Hence, the urban planning during the forthcoming years should be managed effectively.

The unmanageable growth of Indian cities to a large extent has been due to the excessive concentration of economic and industrial activities in the Indian metropolises. These cities have become the sole urban units that provide the necessary financial and infrastructural facilities for development.

The challenging task of India's urbanization has resulted in the emergence of unauthorized slum settlements, the well-known *jhopadpatties* and *jhuggi-jhompris* in the cities like Mumbai, Calcutta, Delhi and Chennai. Such a situation has resulted from the large-scale migration to these metropolises from rural hinterlands and adjoining small towns where the employment opportunities are unsatisfactory. The alarming number of migrants to the cities are unable to afford the rental value of a proper habitation and they are forced to live in unhygienic conditions of slums and squatter settlements. In the 21st century, the unhygienic of the slums living conditions in the Urban centres of India are likely to worsen. This may cause the spread of diseases.

TABLE 3

Projected Urban Population of India as on 1st March, 1996-2016

(in '000)

Year	*Male*		*Female*		*Total*	*Annual Growth*
	No.	*%age*	*No.*	*%age*	*No.*	*Rate*
1996	133661	52.5	120745	47.5	254406	-
1997	137163	52.4	124387	47.6	261550	2.8
1998	140738	52.3	128092	47.7	268830	2.8
1999	144373	52.3	131849	47.7	276222	2.7
2000	148060	52.2	135646	47.8	283706	2.7
2001	151796	52.1	139460	47.9	291256	2.6
2002	155532	52.0	143327	48.0	298859	2.6
2003	159420	52.0	147367	48.0	306787	2.7
2004	163442	51.9	151563	48.1	315005	2.7
2005	167579	51.8	155896	48.2	323475	2.7
2006	171814	51.7	160347	48.3	332161	2.7
2007	176119	51.6	164901	48.4	341020	2.7
2008	180463	51.7	169488	48.3	349951	2.6
2009	184849	51.5	174110	48.5	358959	2.6
2010	189277	51.4	178770	48.6	368047	2.5
2011	193749	41.3	183466	48.7	377215	2.5
2012	198173	51.3	188194	48.7	386367	2.4
2013	202724	51.2	193053	48.8	395777	2.4
2014	207404	51.1	198046	48.9	405450	2.4
2015	212215	51.1	203174	48.9	415389	2.5
2016	217160	51.0	208441	49.0	425601	2.5

Source: Report of the Technical Committee on Population Projections constituted by Planning Commission 1996, Registrar General of India.
Cited from Ninth Five Year Plan 1997–2002, Volume II, Thematic Issues and Sectoral Programmes, Planning Commission, Goverment of India.

Such a phenomenon is not peculiar to India alone, but has manifested itself globally in every country of the Third World. It indicates the failures of urban planning and policy directives. The haphazard growth of urbanization has become an evident fact. These multiplying challenges of the problems will be a threat in the 21st century.

The former chief of World Bank, Robert McNamara had highlighted the plight of the urban poor who lived in thoroughly squalid conditions, afflicted by malnutrition and devoid of rudimentary sanitary facilities, employment and minimum shelter facility. Surprisingly, no corrective measures have been adopted to check this trend. In 1980, there were only 40 million urban poor. However, there is an apprehension that by 2000, the urban poverty would increase by 76 per cent to count 72 million urban poor. Confronted with hyper-inflationary situation, the debt burden and the structural adjustment imposed by the International Monetary Fund (IMF) and the World Bank are likely to multiply in an alarming proportion. The government policies are increasingly going to reduce the welfare assistance in terms of subsidies and further bring down the per capita expenditure on water and sewerage in the context of urban settlements. There are over three million people in Calcutta who live in shanty towns without potable water. Ironically, taps often go dry in summers in major parts of Delhi. Aprodicio Laquian, an expert of the United Nations (UN) population fund has emphatically pointed out that the cumulative effects of poverty and structural adjustments would make the urban survival a challenging task. Further, the situation demands the changing concepts of transport system and housing fulfilments which seem to be the fundamental basis for realizing a balanced process of urban growth and an effective governing system.

The abnormal growth of urbanization in different parts of India has been attributed not only to an increase in population growth but also to the various policies of the government industrial, licensing, which encourage the existing industrialized areas to grow even faster, transportation policies which favour the movement of goods and people in concentrated spatial urban directions. In the 21st century, the alarming migration in the metropolitan cities like Ahmedabad, Mumbai, Bangalore, Calcutta, Chennai and Delhi will be unmanageable. Thus, in the new millennium, the Indian metropolitan cities would lead to disaster due to population explosion.

The total poulation of India in 1991 increased from 683 million, as a result of 2.16 per cent per annum growth of population. It is believed that the overall population growth rate in India will significantly come down in the coming decades. Based on the various estimates worked out by different experts and agencies (Hashim 1996, United Nations Conference on Human Settlements 1996), concerned with the population growth in the country, we have assumed that this rate will be 1.9 per cent per year in the present decade. This will further decline in the next two decades to 1.6 and 1.2 per cent per annum respectively.

It is widely recognized that the urban population will continue to grow at the same rate or even at a higher rate than that achieved during 1971-91 (Hasim 1996, Alag 1996, Bhatnagar et. al. 1996). Considering the decline in the natural growth rate, that will be significant in urban areas in the next three decades, we have assumed that the overall growth rate, including the growth due to natural increase, in-migration and increase in the number and spatial spread of the urban areas, will be 3.16, 3.15 and 3.10 per cent respectively, in the next three decades.

TABLE 4
Total and Urban Population Projections, 1997-2021

Population/Growth Rate Total Population %	*1997*	*2001*	*2011*	*2021*
Assumed Growth Rate Total (million)	1.9	1.9	1.6	1.2
Total Population	962.07	1021.56	1197.29	1348.98
Assumed Growth Rate	3.16	3.16	3.15	3.10
Urban Population	262.27	297.02	405.02	549.62
Per cent Urban to Total Population	27.26	29.09	33.83	40.74

Source: V.K. Tewari, Urbanization in India: Patterns and Perspective, paper presented at national seminar on future cities - Urban Vision: 2021, October 6-7, 1997, New Delhi, organized by the Ministry of Urban Affairs, Government of India.

The urban population in 2001 is estimated to be 297 million which is likely to increase to 549 million in 2021. However, with these projected population figures, the level of urbanization in the country is expected to increase from 25.71 per cent in 1991 to 40.47 per cent in 2021.

An attempt has also been made here to project the urban population of different States. These projections are presented in Table 5. In this analysis, statewise urban population growth rates are estimated by dividing the assumed all-India growth for each decade, in proportion to the growth rates of the states during the previous decades. These projections are based on the past trend of urbanization in different states. The projections show that the state of Kerala will emerge as the most urbanized state in the country and by 2021, Kerala will continue to be the most urbanized state, followed by Maharashtra, Gujarat, Andhra Pradesh and Karnataka. At the lower end of the scale of urbanization, Bihar is likely to remain as the least urbanized state. Other states that will have less percentage of urban population than the all India average are Assam, Orissa, Uttar Pradesh, Rajasthan and West Bengal.

Overall states with progressive economic development would follow the higher process of urban development. This would lead to an uncontrollable situation of civic amenities with unmatched per capita requirement of population growth.

TABLE 5
Statewise Projected Urban Population (1997-2021)

States	*Urban Population (in million)*			*Percentage Urban Population to Total*			*Rank % Urban*		
	2001	*2011*	*2021*	*2001*	*2011*	*2021*	*2001*	*2011*	*2021*
Andhra Pradesh	25.62	36.66	52.16	31.83	38.77	48.88	7	4	4
Assam	3.48	4.87	6.77	12.84	15.27	18.81	16	16	15
Bihar	14.77	19.27	24.88	14.20	15.78	18.17	15	15	16
Gujarat	19.16	25.73	34.40	39.13	45.53	54.66	2	3	3
Haryana	5.80	8.29	11.78	28.45	33.97	42.18	10	8	7
Karnataka	18.03	23.36	30.13	33.87	38.05	44.12	5	6	5
Kerala	12.37	19.88	31.73	37.76	54.96	81.41	3	1	1
Madhya Pradesh	22.22	32.15	46.25	27.23	33.02	41.60	11	10	8
Maharashtra	42.41	58.85	81.23	43.91	51.39	62.42	1	2	2
Orissa	5.75	7.82	10.57	15.47	18.35	22.41	14	14	14
Punjab	7.72	9.93	12.73	32.22	36.04	41.59	6	7	9
Rajasthan	14.06	19.62	27.24	25.63	29.69	35.83	12	12	12
Tamil Nadu	22.82	27.29	32.53	36.02	38.73	42.63	4	5	6
Uttar Pradesh	38.31	53.09	73.22	22.55	26.40	32.07	13	13	13
West Bengal	24.23	31.34	40.39	29.29	32.16	36.63	8	11	11
All India*	296.97	404.87	549.31	29.06	33.80	40.70	9	9	10

* Including all States and Union Territories.

Source: V.K. Tewari, Urbanization in India: Patterns and Perspective, paper presented at national seminar on future cities - Urban Vision: 2021, October 6–7, 1997.

The excessive growth of urban population will also give rise to a larger number of million-plus cities. Using an average growth rate of 3.15 per cent per year, based on the growth during the decade 1981-91, the population of towns in the 50,000 to one million class are projected for the years 2001, 2011 and 2021. It has been estimated that at least 14 more cities, viz. Agra, Jabalpur, Meerut, Vijaywada, Jamshedpur, Thiruvananthapuram, Dhanbad, Kozhikode, Asansol, Nasik, Gwalior, Tiruchirapalli and Amritsar, are likely to be added to the group by 2001. The number of such cities is estimated to be 52 by 2011 and 75 by 2021.

At the outset, it seems that if present trend of urbanization continues in India, the future perspective will be disastrous, if not catastrophic. However, there is need for an inquiry into and questioning of the basic premises of the present urban life to improve living conditions in India's urban settlements in the 21st century. The urban crisis of India is neither merely the manifestation of the problems of habitating a vast number of people with provision of basic amenities of life, like adequate water supply, electricity and transport facilities, nor is it the incarnation of the problems of growing metropolies with the exhausted urban infrastructure. Rather reflection of a deep rooted crisis emanating from the absence of rapid economic development, essential for meeting population, the challenges of the growing both quantitatively and qualitatively; expansion of employment opportunities together with a rise in standard of living of the masses. However, the urban problem involves difficulty arising out of the small and medium town settlements, thereby leading to stagnation of the economy together with a low rate of increase in the levels of investments. Surprisingly, urbanization has not been able to promote adequate production, income and employment prospects which needs to be visualized in context of the small and medium town settlements. Only then the process of urbanization in India in the 21st century would become balanced in terms of spatial and demographic development.

Scenario of Delhi in the 21st Century

With present population of over 10 million, Delhi, the national Capital, can easily be described as a mini state. With the unchecked process of migration, phenomenal influx of people from different parts of the country and with city's own annual natural growth, eventually the population of Delhi is likely to cross 11.15 million mark even before the beginning of the 21st century. With the paucity of basic civic resources and absence of a long-term policy with regard to the planned development in Delhi, the prevailing as well as the likely future scenario is not optimistic. According to the statistics of a conservative estimate, Delhi's peak consumption of electricity is 1450 mw during the summer months. Though the official sources indicate that the peak load requirement is in fact, around 1700 mw. In the 21st century, the estimated demand for electricity is likely to be around 4000 mw, but the question arises as to whether the demand requirement would be met. This is a serious challenge for the planners.

According to the 1991 census, Delhi's water requirement was 535 MGD as against the installed capacity of Delhi Water Supply and Sewage Disposal Undertaking is 470 MGD.

The actual water availability in Delhi has been restricted to 455 MGD due to the large scale operational losses. From 2001 onwards, the water supply scarcity will assume an alarming proportion and would become a challenging task to accomplished.

Strain on economic resources is likely to reduce the quality and quantity of services in urban areas. The excessive process of population growth in Delhi will continue undaunted, encompassing the large number of people within its fold in the new millennium. If we are not to be knocked down by the fatal blows of powerful forces such as misery, poverty, hunger and death due to mysterious diseases, we should be prepared for developing the National Capital Region (NCR) in terms of viable rural, small and medium town settlements. The decentralised housing, medical and educational activities and job opportunities can only relieve Delhi from public utility threats in the 21st century.

According to a survey conducted by the Delhi Water Supply and Sewage Disposal Undertaking (DWSSDU), and recommendations made by various expert groups, by 2000, the population in Delhi would go up to 1.28 crores. If the present rate of migration remains unchecked, Delhi would need a water supply of 900 MGD. This would be a situation of an acute water crisis.

Delhi is being confronted with gigantic problems of air, water and noise pollutions. Fast shrinking of green areas and insanitary conditions prevailing in most parts of the city have virtually worsened the increasing problem of pollution. Air, water and noise pollution levels are also adding to the serious health hazards for the inhabitants of Delhi. The scenario for Delhi in the 21st century does not seem to be encouraging; unhygienic and overcrowded living environment will present a disastrous confrontation.

Delhi has the notoriety of facing the pollution menace from more than 2000 industrial units. It is likely to increase to 2500 by the beginning of the 21 century. The emergence of enormous unauthorized industrial units and rising number of motor vehicles have aggravated the environment pollution, thereby making Delhi a choking city. Even though the civic administration decided the unauthorized industrial units from non-conforming areas to conforrning areas, the result has not been satisfactory.

Everyday about 200 metric tonnes of pollutants are injected into Delhi's atmosphere. About 64 per cent of these pollutants are caused by the motorized vehicles; 16 per cent by the two thermal power stations, 13 per cent by the industries and seven per cent by the residential colonies, particularly the *jhuggi jhopris*. Every day, about 6000 tonnes of flyash and about 4750 tonnes of garbage get deposited on its surface. Such a trend will assume a gigantic proportion in the 21st century perspective.

The vehicular traffic in Delhi is around 20 lakhs which has added to pollution in the air—carbon monoxide and hydrocarbons. At the major road junctions, the carbon monoxide and hydrocarbon levels in the air exceed the prescribed limits. According to a study as a result of rise in consumption of petrol, diesel, furnace oil and lubricants, the vehicular pollution has increased by one and-a-half times during last five years. However, what is causing an alarm is the sharply rising vehicular population estimated to reach about 40 lakh in 2001. A study has revealed that in Delhi about 620 tonnes of pollutants are released into atmosphere every day by the motor vehicles which was about 13 lakh until a few years ago. Out of this 45.5 tonnes per day is emitted from diesel and steam locomotives of the railways.

In the 21st century, Delhi is likely to become number one polluted city of the world. Innumerable diseases like tuberculosis, lung cancer, asthma and bronchitis are likely to threaten the health of Delhi's inhabitants. With the alarming growth of vehicles, Delhi would be confronted with enormous numbers of accidents.

The vehicular pollution in Delhi largely constitutes air pollutants like carbon dioxide, oxide of nitrogen and lead. If, such a trend continues, the vehicular smoke will become gaseous poison for the inhabitants of Delhi in the 21st century.

According to an estimate, about 15 per cent of Delhi's sub-soil water is contaminated. Subsequently, with the growing search for more water, there is likelihood of the entire sub-soil water, both at the deeper level and closer to surface, to be contaminated by 2001. The large scale open defecation and improper treatment of sullage is also one of the main reasons for the sub-soil water contamination. The situation would be aggravated in the new millennium.

In slums, besides sub-soil water residents also drink from the public hydrants and tankers. A survey in Delhi had revealed that 45 per cent of water that slum dwellers take is unfit for drinking purpose. Nearly 18 per cent of tap water was found contaminated. Presently the water in Delhi is polluted. With the result, water borne diseases are widespread, like typhoid, dysentery, diarrhoea and jaundice.

Mumbai's Challenging Problems

In this narrow strip of island-city of 437 square kilometres, nearly 8.3 million people live. The experts have visualized that with over 500 families coming in daily for settling in the metropolises, the future megapolis would be bursting at the seams with about 12 to 14 million people by the year 2001.

There are nearly 300,000 vehicles running on Mumbai's road with a length of 1,400 kilometres. Besides these, a number of trucks, cars and buses enter the city every day in a big way. The projected number of vehicles on roads of Mumbai in the 21st century would be enormous.

Mumbai is one of the fastest growing metropolises rates; in neck and neck with the front runner cities like Mexico, Cairo and Caracus. It will be one of the 15 largest cities of the world by 2001. However, Mumbai in the 21st century is going to be one of the biggest slum-metropolises.

Calcutta's Confrontation

Presently Calcutta is confronted with a severe shortage of water, housing, medical and educational facilities. Further, the city in the 21st century will witness a population explosion, alarming unemployment situation and serious environmental hazards, with an acute shortage of basic socio-economic and infrastructural facilities.

The variations in the estimates of urban India and its spatial distributions in 21st century, however, will depend upon, amongst other factors, squarely on the fact that, how much more employment is going to be generated both in rural and urban areas and at what rate. Besides a natural or normal process of urbanization due to the agricultural prosperity and the consequent demand on a variety of consumption goods and services, rural to urban migration (even urban to urban migration) will continue to be significant casual factor for urbanization in the 21st century. The 'gravitational' pull towards on major metro cities and their region will continue for sometime, though trend of growth of middle level centres (of which most are district headquarters) will accelerate in a significant manner.

Presently, designated a lean or poorly urbanized (less than 10 per cent urbanization) areas will catch up significantly with higher level of urbanization. However, this is likely to continue in the 21st century. Either way, urbanization levels and patterns will be linked with the level of agricultural prosperity, as nearly 65 per cent of the population would still be dependent on agriculture.

The lesser urban areas of eastern Uttar Pradesh and eastern Madhya Pradesh are included in the zone. The northern zone, which includes agriculturally prosperous areas of Punjab, Haryana and northern Rajasthan has shown a significant increase in urbanization and as is expected to further increase by the year 2001. The existing urban settlements are likely to grow in population size. Within the same larger northern region, intra-regional variations in urbanization will widen. As such, the growth of urbanization in the states of Jammu and Kashmir, Himachal Pradesh and arid areas of Rajasthan are likely to remain low even in the next two decades.

It is worthwhile to point out that, the western zone, constituting Gujarat and Maharashtra, will almost double its urban population to reach above 60 million by 2001. But again the intra-zone spatial variation is very significant. The Vidarbha and northern Gujarat areas are the lean areas of urbanization.

With the advent of industrialization India's metropolitan centres have developed from small towns into teeming cities, burdened by the constant influx of people from rural areas, mainly in search of employment opportunities. As a result, the human beings are struggling for a roof over the head and for the provision of basic civic amenities. Without the cohesive and coordinated planning, Calcutta and Mumbai and to a lesser extent Delhi and Chennai, will soon present a picture of filth and congestion. Further, all the remedial measures will prove futile in the context of the 21st century perspective.

The net consequence of the absence of a positive attitude on the subject of urbanization has been an unregulated and imbalanced growth in urban population, without corresponding resource allocation for urban population, for urban civic bodies, to meet the needs of the growing population. The deterioration in the quality of life has been the characteristics of nearly all cities which have crossed the one million mark. It has become an uphill task for the planners provide the basic public utility services in relation to per capita population.

All over the world, the metropolitan cities are posed with a serious threat of survival. The problem as to how to deal with the large urban concentrations of the modern world has not yet been solved. Further, it is likely to promote and advanced process of population growth and consequently the emergence of big urban centres. In the 21st century, the metropolitan and large cities in a worldwide perspective would become a challenging threat to the environmental pollution. Thus, living in the metropolitan and large cities will be come a nightmare in the new millennium.

The urban population is likely to increase in leaps and bounds in the 21st century. Table 6 highlights the urban population situation since 1961 to 2001. As such, during the last two decades there has been spectacular growth of urban population in the Indian scenario.

TABLE 6
Growth and Distribution of Urban Population During 1961-2001

Year	*Population (in million)*	*Scenario 'A' Total Urban population present urban*	*Present Growth Rate*	*Population (in million)*	*Scenario 'B' Total Urban population present urban*	*Present Growth Rate*
1961	79	18.0	26.0	79	19.0	26.4
1971	109	19.9	38.2	109	19.9	38.2
1981	150	22.5	37.5	165	24.7	51.3
1991	205	25.6	36.7	265	33.1	60.6
2001	278	29.4	35.6	445	47.1	67.0

Source: Scenario 'A' Government of India, Registrar General of India, 1974. World Population Year.

Note: The estimates of urban population by the Government organization is on a lower side as natural growth and immigration from Bangladesh has been in an alarming proportion.

The total population of India, the figures for 1961 and 1971 are actuals. Scenario 'B' Government of India, Town and Country Planning Organization : A Model for India's Urbanization Pattern for 2000, December, 1975. Cited From: Towards a Human Settlement Policy in India 2001, Town and Country Planning Organization, September, 1975.

The projected population indicates that India's urban population is likely to grow beyond 350 million by 2001. Consequently, the rural areas will be absorbed as urban settlements in a big way. There is likely to be a decline in the rural areas by 2001. Thus, the ecological balance will be disturbed with vanishing of rural areas due to excessive process of urbanization.

Large areas of the Indian cities are confronted with the dangers and nuisances of motor traffic. The rush hour congestion in the streets and lack of proper public transport movements has led to the haphazard development in the context of India's urban settlements. The defective system of economic base of towns, leading to rising unemployment and insufficient opportunities, is indeed a challenging task for settlement planning.

The shortage of basic services and amenities like water, power, housing, problems of slums and squatters, traffic congestion and unhygienic conditions are ugly manifestations of explosive growth of the Indian metropolitan and large cities. Small and medium town settlements on the contrary, suffer from demographic and economic stagnation, and in some cases also from population decline. Both the explosion as well as the stagnation are vital symptoms of economic maladies. The remedies of these problems lie in the purposeful approach of urban development programmes which should include the creation and strengthening of economic and infrastructural base in small and medium town settlements.

Alarming Migration Chaos

Excessive concentration of few metropolitan and large cities has attracted a large number of people to migrate to these cities. It may be pointed out that the process of urbanization means the rising population, consequently, the per capita needs of population in terms of public utility services is unsatisfactory. The slow rate of growth of small and medium town settlements has not provided the adequate production, income and employment prospects for rural inhabitants. With the result, it is presumed that in the 21st century, the vast rural hinterland is likely to be converted into big urban settlements. Thus, the urban scenario in the new millennium perspective will add to the miseries of with inadequate public utility services, with a serious threat to the living environment.

Over the decades, the flow of migration has been directed towards the urban settlements from small, medium and rural settlements, in an alarming proportion. To a large extent, the illiterates have migrated to the metropolitan and large cities and the main reason has been the employment opportunities. The migration phenomenon from rural areas, particularly the educated professionals an skilled workers from small and medium town settlements to the metropolitan and other large cities has been mainly due to the better employment and income prospects. Such a trend is likely to rise in multiple proportion in the 21st century.

The migrant population consists of individuals who in a large number, enter the cities and are placed at the lowest level of the economic hierarchy. As such, they are not the groups that contribute to the cities resources. The civic administrations are unable to cope up with the additional demands created by these groups. The result is general shortage and lower efficiency in nearly all the municipal services.

The process of urbanization involves massive movement of people from smaller to larger communities. However, this has resulted into the concentration of population in a given space which has assumed the role of economic specialization. India's per capita rural income is extremely low. Thus, in these circumstances, the appropriate approach to urbanization is to develop the intermediate towns, called the growth-centres, and they should be identified and developed. These should be designated for future public investments in the context of India's urban planning in the 21st century perspective, such should be India's approach of balanced development and equitable growth phenomenon. There is an imperative need for coordinating the rural-urban continuum, inter linkages of spatial and economic development in the context of the 21st century.

In 1981, there were 160 million people living in India's urban settlements and by 2001 is expected to be more than 350 million. The migration phenomenon from rural areas has speeded up the process of urbanization and simultaneously the contribution of urban areas to the national economy has shown a spectacular growth phenomenon. In 1950-51, India's urban contribution to the net domestic product was 29 per cent, by 1970-71 it was 37 per cent, and by 2001 it could rise to 60 per cent. While, the urban contribution to the economy grows, what city governments provide to keep the services going is negligible. Indeed such are the burdens and the deep-seated neglect, that what is needed is not merely a greater share of resources, but the massive doses of funds to make good the *backlog* of several decades.

Beyond the major metropolitan centres are smaller towns and other nodes which have to be kept alive to take the burden off the bigger centres. All these have to come from within an encompassing policy, if long-term solutions are to be found to the problems of urban India in the context of the 21st century planning and development perspective.

It can be surmised that urban population in different regions and among different size of towns and cities has been growing at differential rates. Should such an imbalance be permitted? The condition of Indian cities today clearly indicate that suitable measures must be taken for ensuring a balanced process of urban planning and development. Today, the Indian cities are characterized by the inadequacy of public utilities and services like drainage, sewerage, drinking water, electricity and so on.

In urban areas of India, the housing shortage and its unaffordability has led to the haphazard growth of slums and squatter colonies. Even in planned towns and housing estates, the number of people who have been provided decent housing and plots is less than the number of people who have settled in slums, squatter colonies or simple on the pavements. Still, we know for sure that urbanization is bound to grow at an accelerated rate beyond the unmanageable limit in the year 2001. Thus, at best what we can do, therefore, is to devise means for enabling the process of urbanization along the right lines, by developing the small and medium town settlements and viable rural growth-centres in a comprehensive statewise perspective.

It is visualized that in the beginning of the 21st century there will be 20 cities with population of one million each and at least 600 cities with population of 50,00,000. The smaller towns will continue to decline or they will be absorbed by the larger metropolitan cities of India. Large masses of people, about 40 per cent now and 65 per cent at the end of the century, will live only a marginal existence. In Mumbai, in the year 2001, there will be at least 16 million people, almost 72 per cent of them living in slums, with an acute water shortage in the order of 400 million gallons and the housing shortage of nearly two million units.

Those who know and understand the potentials of good urban life can observe the failure of Indian cities even today. With the rapidly expanding cities and subsequently the increasing demand for basic urban infrastructure there is an urgent need for creation of a climate of effective metropolitan administration and financial management. As 'prevention is better than cure' there is need to frame a comprehensive urban plan and to subsequently formulate a sound national urbanization policy for a balanced urban growth. The policy innovations should aim for a much closer interaction between urban development policy and national development planning, and must give less emphasis to an independently conceived spatial policy. The national urban policy must not be treated as any other traditional vertical sector within national system, such as, national industrial policy, transport policy, water policy, national power policy, and so on. Instead, it should be conceptualized as a horizontal slice cutting across almost all other sectors. This is because of the fact that in many sectors of urban areas the investment has taken place in a spectacular way.

There is absence of an effective urban development administration in a statewise perspective. In India alone thousands of master plans are being developed but lack of right approach to urban land, finance and material has made them redundant. Necessarily, it has to be understood in the light of emerging trend of urbanization and the need for shelter. Basic services have affected the existing urban landuse pattern of development. The growing menace of slums, which are ubiquitous at least in the case of metropolitan and large cities, are throwing big challenge to urban land acquisition and development.

It needs to be underlined that the urban development problems are complex and require a package of policies to manage issues of varied nature and character. One has to further refine one's own vision in the context of the fact that the urban development and policies are framed and implemented through a mix of local, state and national agencies. Therefore the inter governmental relations, institutional arrangements and mechanisms are important to be viewed as effective tools of planning.

There is need to have a positive urban policy in the context of the 21st century which could eventually lead to the purposeful utilization of human resources. However, this can only be done if the rate and volume of economic development in cities are kept near the level of urban growth.

A glance at the economic structure of Indian cities and towns is likely to indicate a distressing situation. It is officially estimated that the urban housing shortage is about eight million dwelling units. In the nine metropolises, more than 66 per cent of the population live in one room tenements and the average number of persons per tenement is four. Of the rest, 25 per cent of the population live in slums or *jhopadpattis* and many of them sleep on footpaths. However, the luxurious flats and big houses which occupy enormous land do not house even five per cent of the population. Due to the alarming poverty, it is visualized that in 2001, the urban settlements, particularly the metropolitan and other large cities, would witness the degradation in the slum living conditions.

The shortage of basic services is also appalling in the context of urban settlements. The Research Programme Committee on the Planning Commission has found out that after a survey of 20 big cities, on an average, only 25 to 45 per cent of the families have water connection in their houses and only 30 per cent have independent latrines. In some areas of Calcutta, for instance, one latrine is shared by 30 persons. The percentage of families having drainage connections to sewer in Hyderabad, Kanpur and Lucknow is 25, 30 and 45 respectively. The position in regard to public latrines, parks and gardens is most unsatisfactory; such amenities are conspicuously lacking in Mumbai. Such a confrontation would be widespread in the entire urban settlements during 2001.

Urban Chaos in the 21st Century

In the beginning of the present century, the urban scenario will have the following implications. The spectacular growth of population, especially in urban areas, will strain all the resources and social institutions of the country beyond any Malthusian calculations.

Even if the food production in India was doubled by the end of the previous century to 200 million tonnes per year, there will be still a deficit of at least 30 million tonnes per year from the beginning of this century. This implies two basic difficulties for the Indian economy. On the one hand, India will be dependent on other countries for its basic needs and on the other hand, the rural economy will remain weak and saturated, forcing the excess number of people to migrate to the urban areas, causing a challenging threat to human survival in the present century.

It is visualized that if the economic growth picks up, again then the per capita Gross National Product (GNP) will increase at the rate of two per cent a year on average over the $100 GNP per capita of today; it would hardly be $160 GNP per capita. However, this will not take the mass of people above the poverty line. On the contrary, since much of the surplus will be absorbed by the increasing population, at least 65 per cent of the urban population will be living below minimum standard of living. As such, the urban poverty index will increase by at least 10 per cent. Thus urbanization, will lead to crisis, affecting thereby every aspect of urban life with severe and chronic deficits and innumerable other difficulties.

It is probable that with the application of an effective approach of population control and better means of communication in urban areas that the natural growth of population may decline marginally. However, this will not affect the total growth of urban population significantly since the immigration from rural areas will continue and will record an alarming proportion in the 21st century.

Urbanization Policy Resolution

The Town and Country Planning Organization (Government of India) in its National Urbanization Policy Resolution, has highlighted the following main recommendations for ensuring the rural-urban integrated settlement planning:

(i) Evolving a spatial pattern of economic development and location of a hierarchy of human settlements, consistent with the exploitation of the natural and human resources of the region, thereby promoting the functional linkages.

(ii) Securing the optimum distribution of population between rural and urban settlements within each region and also among the towns of various sizes.

(iii) Securing the distribution of economic activities in small and medium sized towns and in growth centres in order to achieve maximum economic growth for the future.

(iv) Controlling and arresting the future growth of metropolitan cities by dispersal of economic activities, legislative measures and establishment of new counter-magnets in the region.

(v) Providing maximum level of services for improving the quality of life in rural and urban areas and reducing gradually the difference between the rural and urban living.

In the present century, there is likely to be a wide gap of economic variations in the rural and urban settlements. Thus, the national urbanization policy should be formulated accordingly.

The recommendations of the seminar on national policy on urbanization held by National Institute of Urban Affairs, New Delhi, had rightly observed the outline of National Urbanization Policy:

1. Formulation of a feasible national urbanization policy with clear indication as to its various dimensions in the short and long range.
2. In the context of the constraints especially due to energy which aims to give a positive relationship between the shelter and work, it is looking for urban land policy which would ensure the optimum use of land and avoid wastage.
3. Formulation of Planning design standards to ensure a minimum living environment for majority of people in various community types, rural or whether urban in different regions of India.
4. Recognition of positive role of the informal sector in cities and towns with a view to boost the optimal employment opportunities

for this vital sector as a positive element in the community planning efforts.

5. While there are large number of small and medium towns, it is important to identify the potentially viable centres for development, and it should be linked with the view for servicing the agricultural hinterland.
6. In the formulation of developing city plans, a specific emphasis must be given to landuse and density pattern for minimizing the transport needs.
7. More innovative approach is required than has yet been attempted, particularly in the planning of large urban settlements and metropolitan centres. Due regard must be paid to alternatives of development choices.
8. Conservation of environment and natural landscape as also manmade resources so far. Planning efforts have lacked pertinent measures for adequate protection for environment.
9. Multiple use of open space in and around cities and towns. Environmental impact studies outlining therein measures to conserve environment (natural and manmade) must be an essential pre-requisite of all major projects in the country before they are taken up for execution.
10. For recognizing the dynamics of urban process, it would be necessary to envisage a well conceived programme for recycling. In fact, it should be possible to plan building for several uses in mind.

The positive governmental intervention is vital in the process of urban planning and development. It is therefore imperative that a national policy be evolved not only to tackle urban problems but also to make positive use of urban growth, so as to foster economic and social development. The formulation and implementation of a national urbanization policy pre-supposes the existence of a competitive administrative machinery at all levels.

Action Approach

The natural urban policy must take into account the following factors which are likely to raise the challenging problems in the context of the 21st century perspective.

(i) The increasing drift from villages and towns.

(ii) The need to provide adequate funds for the creation of a minimum urban infrastructure.

(iii) A greater emphasis on the development of middle level towns independent of metropolitan areas.
(iv) An attempt to create inter-relationship between villages, service towns and middle level towns.
(v) The need to plan cities in terms of space rather than structure.
(vi) A recognition of the fact that compartmentalization of land-use on the pattern of modern, Western cities has no relevance to the Indian context; individual planning units have to be self-contained in terms of employment opportunities, residential facilities and shopping.

Undoubtedly, the metropolitan cities like Ahmedabad, Mumbai, Bangalore, Calcutta, Lucknow, Kanpur, Pune and so on have created enormous economic activities adding thereby the huge employment opportunities. Consequently, the population growth has assumed an increasing phenomenon added to the haphazard growth of industrial developments. India's urbanization policy in the context of 2001 perspective should be confined to (i) slum environmental programmes, (ii) large scale planning of the low cost housing scheme, (iii) a quick and cheap transport service, (iv) cheap rate plots, (v) decentralizing urban economic planning, and above all spread of industrial and economic activities for checking the environmental pollution.

The excessive growth of industrialization, automobiles and population in Indian cities would create a problem of air pollution by 2001. Already in metropolitan and other large cities like Ahmedabad, Calcutta, Delhi, Chennai, Kanpur, so on, the industrial waste has become a serious health hazard to the inhabitants. A proper legislation is called to have an appropriate treatment of the industrial waste in the urban areas. Such an action plan policy would be able to save our cities in 2001 from the challenging confrontation of air and water pollution, and create thereby through proper legal measures, a congenial urban environment. Then only, the urbanization policy would become meaningful in India and subsequently the proper spill over of population would be possible with the balanced regional development in the spatial and economic framework in rural and urban settlements.

There is a vital need for the approach of a new balanced human activities and settlement patterns by dispersal of employment opportunities and population over wider areas. This has to be visualized now by considering the urban challenges and suitable planning and development perspective of the 21st century.

During the new millennium, the predominantly rural character of India will drastically change and thus, the process of urbanization will gather momentum. India's policies and programmes on population, urbanization and settlement structure should, therefore, be based on the realization that neither sustainable economic growth nor social eduity can be achieved without a demographic balance. This depends on planned population growth, balanced population distribution, balance between urban and rural areas, and an equilibrium within the urban order, comprising capital cities, metropolitan complexes, small and medium-size settlements.

Regional planning and development of backward areas has received increasing attention. But the methods and techniques for a systematic approach to settlement planning are yet to be evolved. A social system, an economic system, a political administration system and an environmental system have got to be worked out, not only in relation to city in terms of its hierarchy of institutional levels of human settlements, but seen and planned for development in a totality. These micro-regions in turn have to be linked up with macro-regions and perhaps with some metropolitan, highly urbanized regions having national impacts and implications in the field of techno-economic specialization.

Appendix I

State Legislations Relating to Urban Development Planning in India

	Area Level		*Act Name and Year*
1.	Andhra Pradesh	(i)	The Andhra Pradesh (Andhra area) Town Planning Act, 1920.
		(ii)	The Andhra Pradesh Urban Areas Development Act, 1975.
		(iii)	The Andhra Pradesh Slum Improvement (Acquisition of Land) Act, 1956.
		(iv)	The Andhra Pradesh Cooperative Societies Act, 1964.
2.	Assam	(i)	The Assam Town and Country Planning Act, 1959.
		(ii)	The Assam Slum Areas (Improvement and Clearance) Act, 1959.
		(iii)	The Assam State Cooperative Act, 1950.
3.	Bihar	(i)	The Bihar Town Planning and Improvement Trust Act, 1975.

	(ii) The Bihar Regional Development Authority Act, 1951.
	(iii) The Chotanagpur and Santhal Parganas Autonomous Authorities Act, 1971.
	(iv) The Bihar Restriction of Use of Land Act, 1948.
	(v) The Bihar and Orissa Cooperative Act, 1935.
4. Gujarat	(i) The Gujarat Town Planning and Development, 1976.
	(ii) The Gujarat Slum (Improvement/ Clearance/Re-development) Act, 1973.
	(iii) The Gujarat State Cooperative Act, 1961.
5. Goa	(i) The Goa, Daman and Diu Town and Country Planning Act, 1974.
	(ii) The Maharashtra Cooperative Societies Act, 1960.
6. Haryana	(i) The Faridabad Complex Development and Regulation Act, 1971.
	(ii) The Haryana Development and Regulation of Urban Areas Act, 1975.
	(iii) The Punjab Improvement Act, 1922.
	(iv) The Haryana Urban Development Authority Act, 1977.
	(v) The Punjab New Mandies Township (Development and Regulation) Act, 1960.
	(vi) The Punjab Seheduled Roads and Controlled Areas Restriction of Unregulated Development Act, 1963.
	(vii) The Haryana Cooperative Societies Act, 1984.

7.	Himachal Pradesh	(i)	The Himachal Pradesh Town and Country Planning Act, 1977.
		(ii)	The Himachal Pradesh Cooperative Societies Act, 1968.
8.	Jammu and Kashmir	(i)	The Jammu and Kashmir Town Planning Act, 1963.
		(ii)	The Jammu and Kashmir Development Act, 1963.
		(iii)	The Jammu and Kashmir Town Area Act.
		(iv)	The Jammu and Kashmir Prevention of Ribbon Development Act, 1950.
		(v)	The Jammu and Kashmir Cooperative Societies Act, 1969.
9.	Karnataka	(i)	The City of Mysore Improvement Act, 1903.
		(ii)	The Karnataka Town and Country Planning Act, 1961.
		(iii)	The Karnataka Improvement Boards Act, 1976.
		(iv)	The Bangalore Development Authority Act, 1976.
		(v)	The Karnataka Slum Areas (Clearance and Improvement) Act.
		(vi)	The Karnataka State Cooperative Societies Act, 1969.
10.	Kerala	(i)	The Travancore Town Planning Act, 1945.
		(ii)	The Travancore Town and Country Planning Act, 1945.
		(iii)	The Madras Town Planning Act, 1920.
		(iv)	The Guruvaryur Township Act, 1961.
		(v)	The Kerala State Cooperative Societies Act, 1959.

11. Madhya Pradesh	(i)	The M.P. Town Improvement Trusts Act, 1960.
	(ii)	The M.P. Slum Improvement (Acquisition of Land) Act, 1956.
	(iii)	The M.P. Regulation of Use of Land Act, 1948.
	(iv)	The M.P. Town (Periphery) Control Act, 1960.
	(v)	The Madhya Pradesh Cooperative Societies Act, 1960.
12. Maharashtra	(i)	The Maharashtra Regional and Town Planning Act, 1966.
	(ii)	The Maharashtra Housing and Area Development Act, 1976.
	(iii)	The Bombay Metropolitan Region Development Authority Act, 1974.
	(iv)	The Maharashtra Slum Areas (Improvement Clearance and Redevelopment) Act, 1971.
	(v)	The Maharashtra Cooperative Societies Act, 1976.
13. Manipur	(i)	The Manipur Town and Country Planning Act, 1975.
	(ii)	The Manipur Cooperative Societies Act, 1976.
14. Meghalaya	(i)	The Assam Town and Country Planning Act, 1959.
	(ii)	The Assam State Cooperative Societies Act, 1950.
15. Nagaland	(i)	The Nagaland Town and Country Planning Act, 1966.
16. Orissa	(i)	The Orissa Town Planning and Improvement Trust Act, 1951.
	(ii)	The Orissa Cooperative Societies Act, 1962.

17. Punjab
(i) The Punjab Town Improvement Act, 1951.
(ii) The Punjab Slum Areas (Improvement and Clearance) Act, 1961.
(iii) The Punjab Development of Damaged Areas Act, 1951.
(iv) The Punjab Urban Estates (Development and Regulation) Act, 1964.
(v) The Punjab Scheduled Roads and Controlled Areas (Restricted of unregulated Development) Act, 1963.
(vi) The Punjab Regulation of Colonies Act, 1975.
(vii) The Capital of Punjab (Development and Regulation) Act, 1956.
(viii) The Punjab New Capital (Periphery) Control Act, 1952.
(ix) The Punjab Nangal Township (Periphery) Control Act, 1958.
(x) The Punjab Talwara Township (Periphery) Control Act, 1961.
(xi) The Punjab State Cooperative Societies Act, 1961.

18. Rajasthan
(i) The Rajasthan Urban Improvement Act, 1959.
(ii) The Rajasthan State Cooperative Societies Act, 1965.

19. Tamil Nadu
(i) The Tamil Nadu Town and Country Planning Act, 1971.
(ii) The Tamil Nadu Slum Clearance and Improvement (Acquisition of Land) Act, 1959.
(iii) Tamil Nadu Slum Areas (Improvement and Clearance) Act, 1971.

	(iv)	The Tamil Nadu Parks Play fields and Open Spaces (Preservation and Regulation) Act, 1960.
	(v)	The Tamil Nadu Urban Land Tax Act, 1966.
	(vi)	The Tamil Nadu State Cooperative Societies Act, 1983.
20. Tripura	(i)	The Tripura Town and Country Planning Act, 1973.
21. Uttar Pradesh	(i)	The U.P. Urban Planning and Development Act, 1973.
	(ii)	The U.P. Slum Area (Improvement and Clearance) Act, 1962.
	(iii)	The U.P. (Regulation of Building Operations) Act, 1958.
	(iv)	The U.P. Roadside Land Control Act, 1945.
	(v)	The U.P. Cooperative Societies Act, 1965.
22. West Bengal	(i)	The West Bengal Town and Country Planning and Development Act, 1979.
	(ii)	The Calcutta Metropolitan Development Authority Act, 1972.
	(iii)	The Durgapur (Development and Control of Building Operations Act, 1958.
	(iv)	The Calcutta Improvement Act, 1911.
	(v)	The West Bengal and Development and Planning Act, 1948.
	(vi)	The Howrah Improvement Act, 1956.
	(vii)	The West Bengal Comprehensive Area Development Act, 1974.
	(viii)	The West Bengal Slum Areas (Improvement and Clearance) Act, 1972.
	(ix)	The Calcutta Metropolitan Water and Sanitation Authority Act, 1966.

		(x) The West Bengal Township (extension of civic amenities) Act, 1975.
		(xi) The Calcutta Metropolitan Planning Area (Use and Development Land) Control Act, 1965 (repealed).
		(xii) The West Bengal Land (Requisition and Acquisition) Act, 1948.
		(xiii) The West Bengal Cooperative Societies Act, 1973.

Union Territories:

1.	Andaman and Nicobar Islands	(i) There is no planning legislation in existence at present. (ii) The Andaman and Nicobar Cooperative Societies Act.
2.	Arunachal Pradesh	There is no planning legislation in existence at present.
3.	Chandigarh	(i) The Capital of Punjab (Development and Regulation) Act, 1952. (ii) The Punjab Capital (Development and Regulation) Building Rules, 1952. (iii) The Chandigarh (Sale of Sites) Rules, 1952. (iv) The Chandigarh Tree Preservation Development Control Order, 1952. (v) The Punjab State Cooperative Act, 1961.
4.	Dadar and Nagar Haveli	There is no planning legislation in existence at present.
5.	Delhi	(i) Delhi Development Act, 1957. (ii) The Slum Areas (Improvement and Clearance) Act, 1956. (iii) The Delhi Cooperative Societies Act, 1961.
6.	Daman and Diu	(i) The Goa, Daman and Diu Town and Country Planning Act, 1974.
7.	Pondicherry	(i) Pondicherry Town and Country Planning Act, 1969. (ii) The Pondicherry Cooperative Societies Act, 1972.

(C) Environmental Laws in India

Directly Related Acts:

(i) The Water (Prevention and Control of Pollution) Act, 1974.

(ii) The Water (Prevention and Control of Pollution) Cess, Act, 1977.

(iii) The Water (Prevention and Control of Pollution) Cess, Rules, 1978.

(iv) The Air (Prevention and Control of Pollution) Act, 1981.

(v) The Indian Forest Act, 1927.

(vi) The Forest (Conservation) Act, 1980.

(vii) The Wild Life (Protection) Act, 1972.

General Acts

(i) The Indian Penal Code, 1860 which deals with water pollution, atmosphere pollution and general pollution.

(ii) The Code of Criminal Procedure, 1973.

(iii) The Police Act, 1861.

(iv) The Code of Civil Procedure, 1908.

Special Laws

(i) The Factories Act, 1948.

(ii) The Insecticides Act, 1968.

(iii) The Motor Vehicle Act, 1939.

Source: Report of the National Commission on Urbanization, Volume V, Research Study Reports, Part-I, August 1988.

REFERENCES

1. Bhargava, Gopal: Pressures on Cities of the Future, *Business Standard*, November 18, 1980.

2. Buchanan, Colin: Cities in Crisis: An Overview, *The Planner Journal of the Royal Town Planning Institute*, Volume 61, July-August, 1975.

3. Buch, M.N.: Towards a National Urban Policy, *Journal of the Institute of Town Planners*, India, Number 83, November, 1974.

4. Chandreshwar, Prasad Narain: Inaugural Address, 20th Annual and Country Planning Seminar, Lucknow, March 18-20, 1980, *Journal of Institute of Town Planners*, India, Volume Numbers 105 and 106.

5. Editorial: Urban Development, *The Economic Times*, 5th February, 1981.

6. *Economic and Political Weekly*, Volume X, Number 4, January 25, 1975. Social Development and Strategy for Urbanization: Absence of a Positive Approach to Urbanization.

7. Ghosh, S.: No Sign yet of Urban Strategy, *The Economic Times*, October 6, 1991.
8. Indian Society for Agro-Asian Studies Foundation, 13th Foundation Day Seminar, held on January 28. Paper presented: Problems of Urban Governance in a Comparative Perspective.
9. Jagmohan: Delhi 2001, *The National Herald*, October 2, 1983.
10. Jagmohan: Cities and Civilization; Delhi: A Case Study, *The Hindustan Times*, March, 1955.
11. Link: November 10, 1985, India 2001, The Urban Scenario.
12. Mayur, Rashmi: A Presage of Urban Decay More Less Life, *Femina*, January 28—February 10, 1977.
13. Mayur, Rashmi: Urbanization in India in the year 2000 (cyclostyle paper) May 21, 1974.
14. Mayur, Rashmi: Man, City and Future Civic Affairs, Volume 27, Number 6, January, 1980.
15. Maudgal, S.: An outlook for India's Future (2000 AD) Interim Report on Urbanology (National Committee on Science and Technology), Government of India, September 15, 1975.
16. Mohanty, Manoranjan, Expanding Million Cities and Urban Future of India by 2000 A.D. Problems and Prospects in the book, *India's Land Policy and Development Finance*, edited by R.C. Sharma, published by Seema Publications, Delhi 1988.
17. Mazumdar, Atreyi: Problems of Urbanization in India by 2001 AD. Demographic View, paper presented in the Seminar organized by the National Institute of Urban Affairs and Town and Country Planning Organization, New Delhi.
18. Mahapatra, Satyen: Delhi 2001, Delhites Gasping for Breath, *The Hindustan Times*, September 27, 1991.
19. Meeting of Expert Group on National Planning Organization, held on January 28, 1975, New Delhi: National Urbanization Policy Proceeding.
20. Pal Anjali: Nightmare in Stinking Cities, Civic Affairs, Volume 20, December, 1972.
21. Raj, Deva: Some Factors in National Urbanization Policy, Nagarlok, Volume VII, Number 19, January-March, 1975.
22. Rao, M. Koteswara: Trends and Patterns of Urbanization in India, The Civic Affairs, April, 1989.
23. Report of the National Commission on Urbanization, Volume V, 1988.
24. Sadhu, Arun: Bombay, the Big Cities in a Mess, *The Sunday Statesman*, November 29, 1981.
25. Sharma, R.C.: India's Urban Land Policy and Development Finances, Seema Publications, Delhi.
26. Special Monograph, Number 1, Census 1971. Birth Place Migration in India.

27. Shah, S.M.: Urbanization Emerging Problems, *Journal of the Institute of Town Planners*, India, Number 83, November, 1974.

28. Tewari, V.K.: Urbanization in India: Patterns and Perspective, paper presented at National Seminar on Future Cities—Urban Vision: 2021, October 6-7, 1997, organized by the Ministry of Urban Affairs and Employment, Government of India.

29. *The Hindu,* October 6, 1991: Meeting the Challenge.

30. Thiagarajan, D.: Need for a National Policy on Urbanization, Social Welfare, Volume XXIX, Number 3, June, 1982.

31. Vagale, L.R.: State Capital of India: Planning Imperatives for Sustainable Development, paper presented at 45th National Town and Country Planners Congress on Planning and Development of State Capitals held at Thiruvananthapuram and organized by The Institute of Town Planners, India.

32. Wig, A.R.: Delhi Faces A Grim Future, The Hindustan Times, October 13, 1991.

33. Zaidi, S.T.H: Planning and Development, Civic Affairs, Volume 26, Number 8, March, 1979.

34. Zakaria, Rafiq: Urban Chaos, *The Illustrated Weekly of India*, Volume XCV (27) September 1, 1974.

CHAPTER 2

HOUSING PLAN FOR THE MASSES INNOVATIVE TECHNIQUES AND POLICY PERSPECTIVE

Housing is one of the requirements of human beings. To provide housing has been accepted as the responsibility of a welfare state. Yet a substantial proportion of the world's population in urban settlements, especially in the third world countries, live in sub-standard dwellings and unhealthy environments. As such, housing constitutes an important part of the social environment, where an individual is nurtured and where he grows and matures as a member of society. It plays a significant role by improving the national economy for maintaining the social health, stability and ensuring a decent life for the people.

Shelter as a basic human need ranks next only to food and clothing. Shelter does not simply mean protection from the vagaries of nature but also requires a series of services that are essential for the specific location and dwelling. It requires not only adequate water supply, but also arrangements for the disposal of human waste and refuse that must be taken into consideration in the provision of healthy, environmentally sustainable shelter. Housing as an activity contributes significantly to the generation of employment and works as a stimulator of dormant savings. It is a major indicator of the growth-path of the nation and the quality of life it bestows on its citizens.

The housing and shelter concerns the living accommodation of people. Housing connotes well-planned, built up tenements, having the aesthetic and architectural designing. It is either through construction of housing by public agencies/boards or through private developers and builders. Within the housing planning, economic affordability, public utility requirements and landscaping assumes importance. The huge housing complex has become a prerequisite for planning the socio-economic and public utility services. The rich housing is linked with luxurious bungalows and for the middle and low income groups it is a bare necessity of a shelter. Housing is a fundamental prerequisite for a healthy living in a society.

Housing Profile

TABLE 1

Housing Stock : Residential Buildings (in millions)

	1971	*1981*	*1991*	*2001**	*2011*	*2021*	*2031*	*2041*
Urban	18.5	28.0	39.3	59.4	80.7	105.8	117.0	126.7
Rural	74.5	88.7	108.7	119.7	131.4	141.6	153.1	162.0
Total	93.0	116.7	148.0	179.1	212.1	247.4	270.1	288.7

Source: Prominent Facts on Housing, 1997 document of National Building Organization, Government of India.

Note: *Projections from 2001 to 2041.

TABLE 2

Usable Housing Stock (in millions)

	1971	*1981*	*1991*	*2001**	*2011*	*2021*	*2031*	*2041*
Urban	16.1	23.7	36.0	55.9	66.2	75.4	83.8	91.6
Rural	66.4	77.8	97.8	108.2	120.2	130.8	140.4	149.3
Total	82.5	101.5	133.8	164.1	186.4	206.2	224.2	240.9

Source: Ibid.

Note: *Projections from 2001 to 2041.

Table 3

Households (in millions)

	1971	*1981*	*1991*	*2001**	*2011*	*2021*	*2031*	*2041*
Urban	19.1	29.3	40.7	59.4	68.8	80.2	89.3	97.9
Rural	78.0	94.1	112.5	121.0	130.7	136.7	142.1	145.6
Total	97.1	123.4	153.2	178.5	199.5	216.9	231.4	243.5

Source: Ibid

Note: *Projections from 2001 to 2041.

The problem mainly is to meet the tremendous housing backlog and to ensure an ever increasing demand of population in the 21st century perspective. The magnitude of the problems at a given place is the number of households who are either houseless or who live in substandard, dilapidated houses in sub-human conditions of slums and squatter settlements. The deficiency in numbers is found out by subtracting the number of dwellings from the number of households.

The acute shortage of housing is created by a number of factors, like paucity of funds and high cost of land, increasing cost of construction, low incomes, inadequate participation of the public sector, lack of improvement of the people, lack of liquidity support for long-term housing from financial institutions, and so on.

The housing finance system consists of two distinct components: (i) formal and (ii) informal. The formal sector includes: (a) budgetary allocations of Central and State Governments, (b) financial institutions like the Housing Development Finance Corporation (HDFC), Life Insurance Company of India (LIC), General Insurance Company (GIC), Commercial Banks and Provident Funds and (c) specialized housing finance institutions, namely, National Housing Bank (NHB), Housing and Urban Development Corporation, apex and primarily cooperative housing finance societies and Housing Finance Institutions. The informal sector includes households and private sector employees providing housing loans to their employees.

The households in urban areas during 1991 have largely been confined to the rented premises which constitute 36.9 per cent, whereas the owned premises constitute 63.1 per cent. This indicates that the accommodations in urban areas for rental purposes are not significant. There is a tendency not to rent (by the owners of property) as the Rent Control Legislation are cumbersome and do not guarantee back the rented premises to the landlord. Thus in metropolitan and large cities the newly built houses are locked and not rented in a big way. Hence there is scarcity of houses in an alarming proportion. (Prominent Facts on Housing, 1997 Document of National Buildings Organization, Government of India).

Presently housing at an affordable price is a major issue which has been agitating the minds of the public with reference to spiralling construction cost of flats in major cities, rapid growth of slums, overcrowding and congestion. It will aggravate the severe shortage of shelter and basic services and would lead to strains in the political and social fabric of the cities.

It is emphatically pointed out that being a capital intensive industry, the housing sector has been accorded a low priority in development by the government, unlike agriculture and industry. The total investment in housing has increased from Rs 1,150 crore (First Plan) to Rs 31,458 crore in the Seventh Plan. However, the share of housing to total investment has decreased from 34 per cent in the First Five Year Plan to 19 per cent in Second Plan, 15 per cent in Third Plan, 12 per cent in Fourth Plan, 9.3 per cent in Fifth Plan, 12.5 per cent in Sixth Plan, 9 per cent in Seventh Plan and 1.5 per cent in Eighth Plan. Thus, the percentage of investment during the Five Year periods has not been significant compared to the total outlay of investment. It is evident that in India in the Five Year Plans the housing sector has been neglected and thus the problem of investment in shelter has been hampered in a big way.

TABLE 4

Investment on Housing in Different Five Year Plans

Plan Period	*Investment in Housing* *Public*	*Private* *(Rs in crore)*	*Total*	*Percent of Investment in Housing of Total Investment in Economy*
1st	250	900	1150	34
2nd	300	1000	1300	19
3rd	425	1125	1550	15
4th	625	2175	2800	12
5th	796	3640	4436	9.3
6th	1491	18000	19491	12.3
7th	2458	29000	31458	9
8th	6377* +25000 (Institutional)	Not ascertain		around 1.5

*Hence it is given as the plan outlay.

Source: Ministry of Urban Development.

Note: Though the total investment in housing has been declining in percentage terms, in absolute terms, in the Five Year Plan periods, but the financial outlay figure is showing an increasing trend. However, it may be observed that the total investment in the housing sector has not been adequate to wipe out the housing shortage prevailing in the country. Cited from Ansari, P.N., Housing Situation: The Malaise and Some Suggestions, Yojana, March, 1999.

Slum Flats at Sarai Rohilla

Courtesy: Photo Section, Delhi Development Authority, Ministry of Urban Development, Government of India.

Low Income Group Flats

Courtesy: Photo Section, Delhi Development Authority, Ministry of Urban Development, Government of India.

The rate of construction of houses is not keeping pace with the requirements of the population. In India, the rate of construction of houses is about three to four houses per thousand population. But the United Nations norms suggest that the rate of construction should be such that housing needs of all segments of the population will have to be met. Ninth Five Year Plan, 1997–2002 has focused the special attention to the households at the lower end of the housing market, the priority groups identified for such support are people below the poverty line, scheduled castes scheduled tribes, disabled, free bonded labourers, slum dwellers and women-headed households. The government as a facilitator will create an environment in which access to all the requisite inputs will be in time, in adequate quantum and in appropriate quality and standards.

The Ninth Plan visualizes the provision for more direct intervention by the government in case of lower segments of the housing market and select disadvantaged groups. In the Plan period a package of incentives and concessions to attract private sectors will be introduced to shoulder the task of housing the poor.

The housing shortage has been a serious problem in the urban areas. Particularly in the cities, due to the scarcity of land, housing has become an uphill task. Too many people have led to the acute housing shortage in the metropolitan and other large cities. Table 5 indicates the housing shortage scenario in India from 1991–2001. Every year the cities are confronted with housing crisis as larger number of people are showing the need for rising trends of accommodation in accordance with the various income groups.

TABLE 5

Housing Shortage in India

(In millions)

Year	*Rural*	*Urban*	*Total*
1991	14.67	8.23	22.90
1992	14.53	8.01	22.54
1993	14.37	7.97	22.34
1994	14.21	7.91	22.12
1995	14.04	7.82	21.86
1996	13.85	7.71	21.56
1997	13.66	7.57	21.23
1998	13.45	7.36	20.81
1999	13.23	7.18	20.41
2000	13.00	6.93	19.93
2001	12.76	6.64	19.40

Source : National Buildings Organization.

Cited from Ansari, P.N., Housing Situation: The Malaise and Some Suggestions, Yojana, Volume 43, No. 43, March, 1999.

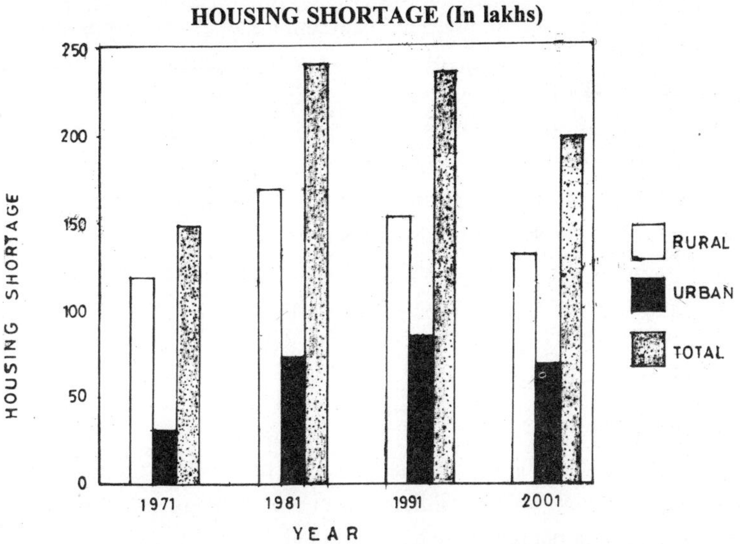

Source: Prominent Facts on Housing 1997, National Building Organization, Ministry of Urban Affairs, Government of India.

In a developing country like India, housing is a challenging phenomenon, because of both exponentially increasing construction cost and deteriorating quality of life in congested urban pockets. The meagre number of additional housing required to meet the needs of the growing urban population presumes a formidable task. If we add to this the housing stock in rural areas, it assumes frightening proportions. This would become an uphill task in the 21st century. The problem of housing seems to be a planning challenge in the context of the new millennium. This is mainly due to the non-availability of land, mainly in the rural and urban areas. In the 21st century the gravity of housing crisis is likely to increase in a gigantic proportion, particularly in the urban settlements. As such, housing has to be tuned to show progressive results of housing construction with the effective utilization of land acquired. The competitive housing organizations in the states have not taken the prompt initiative in policy measures for accelerating the tempo of construction activities.

The urban housing market is imperfect and beset with several constraints. It is imperfect because in the market there is limited information and the activities of the producers and contractors are generally supplied in an informal manner. The conversion of housing activity from raw agricultural land is assuming an alarming proportion. In this process, there is involvement of many agencies and there are cumbersome procedural and regulatory constraints.

The role of government is crucial at different levels. It is not only confined to building houses but to make an appropriate investment and create conditions where all women and men, especially the poor may gain and secure adequate housing and remove the impediments to housing activity. With the result, in the new millennium, the acute housing shortages in the urban settlements would become unmanageable due to the non-availability of land. Accordingly, the strategy of planning and development of housing schemes has to be visualized.

Emerging Issues

Land is a state subject and has become a profiteering proposition in which the different house building agencies of state are being involved. As such, the rich people are in a position to bargain for the land through auction. Such a process has given rise to the enormous rental value in metropolitan and large cities. The poor are forced to live in unauthorized colonies, slums, squatter settlements and even as pavement dwellers. The housing problem for the urban poor has become a serious, challenging task. The backlog of housing shortages should be dealt effectively on the basis of mass scale construction activities through the national housing policy approach and strategies.

TABLE 6

Household Occupying Number of Rooms

	1981		*1991*		*2001**		*2011**		*2021**		*2031**	
	Urban	*Rural*	*Urban*	*Rural*	*Urban*	*Rural*	*Urban*	*Rural*	*Urban*	*Rural*	*Urban*	*Rural*
One Room	45.8	44.3	39.6	40.8	33.4	37.3	26.3	32.2	20.1	25.4	14.3	18.7
Two Rooms	27.8	28.9	30.4	30.6	33.0	32.3	37.2	35.1	42.0	37.9	46.3	41.3
Three Rooms	12.2	12.3	14.8	13.5	17.4	14.7	20.5	10.1	24.2	17.7	27.7	19.2
Four or More Rooms	2.1	2.4	0.5	1.1	0.1	0.4	0.03	0.05	0.008	0.009	0.001	0.001

Note: It is observed that in urban areas the larger number of people are living in one room tenement due to the exorbitant rent. Due to scarcity of housing the inhabitants of urban areas are deprived of adequate housing facility.

* Projected Figures

Source: Prominent Facts on Housing, 1997 document of National Building Organization, New Delhi.

In the 21st century the affordability of housing, even of one room tenement would become a costly affair.

Middle Income Groups Flats

Courtesy: Photo Section, Delhi Development Authority, Ministry of Urban Development, Government of India.

Self Financing Houses

Courtesy: Photo Section, Delhi Development Authority, Ministry of Urban Development, Government of India.

The Directive Principles of the Constitution of India reflect the Government's desire to improve the conditions of the low income groups (constituting the weaker sections of the community, Scheduled Castes and Scheduled Tribes). Major thrust of state housing policy has been towards the weakest section. During 1950–60, more than 85 per cent of the population lived in rural areas, but there was no specific mention in the First Five Year Plan for improving rural housing or providing house sites to the rural shelterless whose number was quite large during this decade.

During the First Five Year Plan, the government had been confined to providing housing to the low income groups, most of which were located in the urban areas. However, in 1952 a subsidized housing scheme for urban industrial workers was initiated. Consequently it can be concluded that from the state's earliest intervention in housing, the focus was on the urban population, in spite of the fact that more than three-quarters of the total population lived in rural areas. However, in the later decades, due to an emphasis on investment in industry, the farmers in big numbers started migrating to the urban centres and found shelter in the shanty towns, thus creating congestion and unhygienic slums which also includes *bustees, jhopries, zopadpatties*. These settlements were the breeding grounds of disease and social unrest. Consequently, the government in order to prevent civil disturbance and/or a major epidemic, deemed it fit to intervene to improve the slums. Thus, slum clearance and improvement schemes were included in the Second Five Year Plan.

In view of the prevailing acute housing shortage to the middle income sector, the Government decided to intervene (as otherwise it would have faced severe criticism from the most vociferous group) by directing the Government-sponsored Life Insurance Corporation of India to provide housing finance to the middle income groups. In reality, the selective financing policy of the LIC has been responsible for preventing the majority of middle income families from taking advantage of housing finance provided by the Corporation. The Government's unwillingness to intervene on a large-scale was reflected in the Third Five Year Plan, when assistance for the middle income group was to be operative only in the Union Territories.

The Government's emphasis on supporting housing in urban areas was once again reflected in the Fourth Five Year Plan when schemes for the slum clearance, housing for industrial workers and dock labour housing were undertaken. There was investment in rural areas for the weaker sections of the community however, expenditure on rural housing was low. It is important to mention the fact that the low income groups could not financially participate in the public or private housing market.

In the Fifth Five Year Plan finding of sites and housing for the landless rural labourers and weaker sections of the community continued with vigour as this formed part of the government's programme for eliminating poverty in the context of the Minimum Needs Programme. The state institutions and housing board had channelled the limited finance for housing the low and middle income groups. The terms and conditions of the financial institutions were so rigid that the low and middle income groups were frightened away. In their absence the loans were usually disbursed to those who could better afford them; these groups mostly belonged to the higher middle income groups.

The Sixth Five Year Plan perpetuated the former social injustice; public housing built for low-income groups (LIG) was being occupied to pay the monthly instalments. The Government instead of finding a way to bring down the cost of housing in order to make it available to the lowest income level population, imposed restriction on those families whose earning was less than Rs 700 per month. LIG houses were available to those whose earning ranged from Rs 7700 – Rs 1,500 per month. The government thus excluded and deprived millions of low-income households from public housing; these groups would now have to face the competition of the private housing market in slums and shanty towns. The Plan had recognised the need for reducing the cost of houses by reducing the standards of building construction and the application of using cheaper materials. While the Plan document advocated the use of cheap construction materials, the local municipalities in urban areas had enforced the building standards and codes established by the British engineers and architects, suitable to the developed Western countries.

In the Seventh Five Year Plan, the Government of India for the first time realized the specific contribution made by the public housing with respect to the total housing investment in the country (about three quarters of investment being made by the private sector) and advocated that the major responsibility for house construction, in particular the household sector should be left to the private sector. A similar sentiment had also been expressed in the 'National Housing Policy' (NHP) (1988) where the government saw its role as that of a initiator rather than a builder of houses. The item 2.1 of the NHP stated as follows: 'To motivate and help all people and, in particular, the homeless and the inadequately housed, to secure for themselves affordable shelter through access of land, materials, technology and finance.' Such policy approach has already created a lot of controversy. Some critics feel that this is a part policy to privatize public agencies and to leave the low-income families as well as the weaker sections of the community at the mercy of market forces. The long-term impact of such a policy will mean a further growth of slums, shanty towns and squatter settlements as the low-income families will be completely priced out of the open housing market; they will have no access to developed land (freehold/leasehold/tenureship) on account of high land prices.

Innovative Technologies

Efforts should be made in the overpopulated India to bring a large number of people under the low cost housing scheme. This is no doubt an uphill task for any government. During the last two decades, the housing conditions in India's metropolitan and other large cities have deteriorated in an alarming proportion. The rapid process of population growth has been a responsible factor for aggravating the acute housing crisis in the Indian urban settlements. To a large extent, the low and middle-income groups are unable to afford an exorbitant rent and *pugree* (security money) which is prevalent in India's metropolitan and other large cities. Therefore, the urban poor are forced to live in sub-standard houses, slums and squatter settlements. Keeping this fact in view, the housing scenario in the new millennium would be disappointing. There is a fear that the 21st century would witness an alarming magnitude of slum and squatter settlements in the urban areas.

Planning mass scale housing programmes necessitates an inexpensive substitute for building materials. However, there is need for a rational utilization of space and design of the construction outlay with an appropriate application of architectural use of building materials for the urban poor.

The government agencies like the PWD, Housing Boards, Development Authorities etc., are still shy of using low-cost techniques, for their own reasons. This needs to be changed, especially when there are many techniques, tested and proved to be strong and safe. The new experiment of low-cost housing technology should be evolved in the 21st century by the governmental housing agencies.

Enormous effort and experience is required to construct houses with maximum convenience at minimum cost. Even today many engineers shy about low-cost housing because of the misconception that such houses are neither durable nor safe. In spite of the fact that many cost-efficient techniques, having proved their credibility and reliability, the engineers have not acquired necessary courage to adopt the same. One reason for this malady may be the absence of cost-efficient techniques in the curriculum of engineering courses. This important drawback needs to be mitigated as early as possible. Further, those who are already in service should be given training through short-term training courses in the technical institutions.

Planning houses for the 21st century necessitates the cost optimization which can be achieved in a variety of ways such as avoiding wastage, adopting appropriate technology, evolving innovative designs, achieving efficient construction management, effective programming of works and efficient monitoring. In fact, in the developing countries, all housing should be formulated on the basis of low-cost housing programmes, whether it is for the poor or for the rich. What happens otherwise is wastage of valuable resources—money, materials and manpower. It is gratifying that many innovative construction techniques and improved building materials already have been discovered and put to use. But sincere efforts to make use of such innovative techniques in an extensive manner are lacking. This needs to be contemplated in the new millennium.

At present the building materials like iron, cement, bricks and wood have become a costly proposition. There is an imperative need for research and development innovations, so as to device the appropriate substitutes for the building materials. Thus, comprehensive analytically oriented technologies will have to be emphasized in the 21st century. Instead of the traditional use of cement in the building structures, the application of flyash as a substitute for the cement has got to be recognized. In India's urban areas, due to presence of the thermal power stations flyash is available and can be collected. Innovations in building technology can help in providing mass scale housing facilities to an alarming urban population. Such a strategy has to be emphasized in planning and developing the housing schemes in urban settlements in the 21st century perspective.

The housing programmes should not be vested in a monopolistic governmental housing agency alone. The approach of *laissez-faire* in low-çost housing competition will give a better layout in housing designing and eventually reduce costs. The prefabrication process of mechanization has to be encouraged for building houses for the masses in a short span of time. It is possible to build houses quickly through the application of prefabricated materials. The prefabricated material constitutes the concrete structure of building block formulations of cement and iron. Therefore, the prefabricated building material blocks are easily accountable and the chances of corruption is ruled out by the contractors and officials of the housing agencies in a statewise perspective. The greater use of prefabricated material for housing the masses should be the watchword in the new millennium.

The layout for low-cost housing is an important factor for achieving the optimal utilization of space at a minimum cost. In a paper on housing approach, Mr Jagmohan, the Union Minister for Urban Development has rightly pointed out that our policy should clearly specify that we have problem not of housing in the conventional sense, but that of shelter, not of luxurious living but of roof over the head.

It is learnt that the cost of roofing can be reduced by the use of asphaltic corrugated sheets and cement pulp roofing sheets which have been recently made use of with advantage in constructing the low-cost housing structures. The use of plastic pipes and fittings would also add to the specific amount of savings in the context of internal and external plumbing services. However, there is also scope for cost reduction in foundation work of under piles, a product developed by the Central Building Research Institute and has been found suitable for low-cost housing under certain soil conditions.

The National Buildings Organization (NBO) had suggested 'several measures for reducing the consumption of deformed bars, tubular structure, light gauged structural sections and substitute materials like reinforcement cement, concrete and timber'. These measures are increasingly used in the process of construction. To expedite its low-cost housing schemes, the government should evolve a rational land acquisition policy.

It is recommended that 'the under-reamed piles and hyperbolic paraboloid footings are suggested for foundations in the case of poor bearing capacity soils. Brick cavity walls, thin load bearing walls, stone blocks, flyash-gypsum bricks, stabilized and blocks (SBM) are suggested for masonry to reduce the construction cost. In the place of scarce and expensive materials (like steel, cement and timber) alternate building materials such as hydrated lime, cement pozzuolana mix and flyash cement are suggested without any compromise on performance'.

Boosting Housing Activities

Over a decade, the cost of housing construction has registered a considerable slow progress due to the alarming prices of building materials. The cost of land construction has shown a rising trend over the decades. However, the cost reduction technique and availability of cheap building material require an extensive innovative application of research technology. Such a possibility needs to be duly recognized while evolving an effective national housing policy and a strategy approach for the Ninth Five Year Plan.

The housing policy should treat the housing sector as an industry in the new millennium. The necessary incentives and loan concessions would be able to enhance the possibility for boosting the housing activities. Thus, such an approach should be given appropriate importance in the national housing policy of the 21st century. If housing is treated as an industry, it will have a specific orientation of tax relief and greater technical know-how for accelerating the pace of housing development on a nationwide basis. Further, the credit worthiness for the housing sector should become an indication of a progressive development through the active participation of financial institutions. Then only the housing activities, both in rural and urban areas, can boost the construction activities in the new millennium.

Financial Institutions : Critical Appraisal

The HDFC surprisingly charges a high rate of interest on the financial assistance granted to the house builders. The mode of loan repayment of the HDFC is that a large portion of interest is recovered every year on a subsequently nominal principal amount. This indicates there is no proportionate balancing of the principal amount and interest payment. Such is the cumbersome procedure and it discourages the housing construction activities. It is suggested that the financial institutions, through the credit policy should encourage the housing construction activities in a big way and recovery should be made in a proportionate ratio to the principal amount and interest. To boost the housing activities in the new millennium, the financial institutions' credit policy should rationalize a low rate of interest over a long time period.

The Housing and Urban Development Corporation (HUDA) has not been able to induce the mass scale financial benefits to house builders on a statewise basis.

Availability of housing finance from the housing institutions like HDFC and LIC at astronomical interest rates (15-16 per cent) has been an inhibiting factor in the larger participation of private builders in housing activity. Housing finance in New York and London is available at 4 to 5 per cent interest rate against fixed assets and securities and at 10 per cent against movable property.

At present, the acute scarcity of finances has hard hit the housing sector in nearly all the states. There is an imperative need in the context of national housing policy perspective to evolve the cooperative and commercial banks for providing the required housing financial assistance at a reasonable rate of interest for the housing sector on a nationwide basis. Then only the housing activities would be accelerated with the suitable incentives in the context of the Ninth Five Year Plan perspective.

The legal provisions are also one of the constraints in the flow of institutional finance. They affect funds flow in two major ways: (a) raise the transaction cost and (b) affect the recovery process. The existing system of registration of deeds and documents is time consuming and cost prohibitive.

The stamp duty and registration charges for transfer of immovable property in most of the states are quite exorbitant. It ranges between 8 to 15 per cent. Similarly, municipal taxes and other taxes are also substantial and all these factors dissuade an investor from participating in housing sector. There is need to rationalize the Land Acquisition Act 1894, Transfer of Property Act 1882, Indian Stamp Act 1899 and Registration Act 1908, which seem to have outlived their utility. Simplification of laws concerning transfer of property would facilitate creation of secondary mortgage market intended to provide the requisite housing finance requirements in the country.

Housing Policy

The National Housing Policy document has laid its basic objectives as (i) to assist all people and in particular the houseless, the inadequately housed and the vulnerable sections, to secure for themselves affordable shelter through access to developed land, building materials, finance and technology; (ii) to create an enabling environment for housing activity by various sections by eliminating constraints and enabling an efficient and equitable system for the delivery of housing inputs; (iii) to expand the provision of infrastructure facilities in rural and urban areas in order to improve the environment of human settlements, increase the access of poorer households to basic services, and to increase the supply of developed land for housing; (iv) to help mobilize and facilitate the expansion of investment in housing sector in order to meet the need of housing construction and upgradation and augmentation of infrastructure; (v) to provide larger supply of developed land and finances to different income groups and (vi) to promote use of appropriate and energy saving building materials and cost effectiveness in construction technologies.

The national housing policy of the new millennium should stress the importance of participation of different housing agencies in a statewise perspective by emphasizing the construction of durable houses. By providing greater opportunities to the people with shelter and housing facilities, they would be able to ensure a higher level of efficiency in their work performance. Further, the productivity of the workers can be increased if suitable accommodation is provided. This aspect needs to be emphasized in the national housing policy framework.

At present, the industrial schemes of housing for workers have not been encouraging as the rents charged are not economical and, therefore, the workers continue to live in slum and squatter settlements. This is the reason why too many slums have come up in haphazard manner in India's metropolitan and other large cities. While formulating a national housing policy, the mass scale housing schemes must ensure the maximum social advantage for a large number of people. The comprehensive research should be conducted for reducing the cost of construction of housing, both in rural and urban settlements. It is only then that India's approach to national housing policy will promote a mass scale housing programme for the urban poor.

The key objective of the NHP, 1994 is to provide access to adequate shelter to all. There is an enormous shortage in the housing sector and major deficiencies in the housing and related infrastructure. The government has been progressively adopting the role of an enabler rather than a direct provider. However, this necessitated a policy shift to encourage private and cooperative sector to play a major role in housing sector, modifying the existing legal and regulatory regime. Keeping in view the above government has since adopted a new Housing and Habitat Policy (approved by the Cabinet in July, 1998).

Public housing thrust is directed towards social housing to reach out housing solutions to priority groups. An equally important activity is to provide a policy framework and a legislative, fiscal and financial system that would put into effect the enabling role of the government in stimulating, supporting and promoting other actors to play direct roles in the housing sector. These two activities have been the pillars of the Eighth Plan approach and will continue in the Ninth Plan.

The NHP highlights that the suitable measures for devising an efficient use of land and also to prevent diversion of scarce resources in luxurious construction will be prescribed by incorporating them in the lending norms of housing finance institutions as also in building regulations.

Building Technology Approach

The NHP document of Government of India has advocated the importance of building materials and technology with the following considerations. (1) Selection, extension and promotion of proven technology and building materials, and the use of materials conforming to standards and quality construction through the efforts of Building Materials and Technology Promotion Council and State Governments and to provide financial and other assistance to entrepreneurs for the manufacture and marketing of appropriate and innovative materials. (2) Encourage the use of materials based on industrial and agricultural wastes by public and private construction agencies, and also those based on local resources and alternate appropriate technologies. (3) Incorporating the low-cost technologies and materials in the national standards and specifications laid down by state agencies, and further requiring the public construction agencies to draw up plans for the use of cost effective technologies and materials to the extent of at least 10 per cent of the total annual construction. (4) Training, technology extension and skill upgradation through a network of Building Centres in urban and rural areas set up by state agencies, research bodies and voluntary agencies and dissemination of information to the actual users and communities. (5) Building up an extension of network for the spread of information on housing schemes inputs and low-cost technology, shelter guidance centres, retail outlets for materials. (6) Strengthening the existing research and development (R & D) institutions and promoting the setting up of R & D facilities in other suitable institutions by necessary financial support, by obliging all public and private construction agencies to set apart at least 1% of their annual expenditure for R & D in housing sector.

Cooperative Housing Sector

The cooperative sector forms a prominent actor in the delivery system in urban centres, especially the metropolitan centres which face the problem of availability of serviced land. This sector had a vast network of 85,000 primary housing cooperatives with 5 million membership in 1992-93. These primary cooperatives are part of the institutional infrastructure at the state level operationalized through 25 apex cooperative housing federations, all of them being members of the National Cooperative Housing Federation (NCHF), which is the umbrella organization of the cooperative housing movement in the country.

The cooperative sector's contribution has been 1.4 million housing units, and as many as 0.54 million dwelling units have been developed during the period 1989-90 to 1994-95. The cooperatives cater mostly to the economically weaker section and the low-income group households, that account for the three-fifths of the housing stock of this sector. The middle income group (MIG) households account for two-fifths of the cooperative housing stock. The cooperative housing constructions necessitates to have a higher satisfaction level in terms of design, quality of structure, services and cost, than other actors. The achievement is mainly due to the participatory endeavour of the members, who become effective 'watchdogs' of the construction and development processes. In

Mumbai, cooperative housing societies of slum community have been formed in about 1,500 settlements consisting of 100 to 500 households in each of the slum settlements. The NHP recognizes cooperatives activity as the principal form of housing activity in large urban areas facing acute shortage of land.

Role of Private Developers

The NHP has rightly emphasized the need for motivating and helping all people for the provision of housing facilities. The National Commission of Urbanization (NCU) has pointed out that the elimination of private enterprise from estate development is one of the major reasons for the current housing shortage. NCU has recommended to the government that the role of housing agencies and development authorities should be that of a facilitator and not that of delivering finished houses.

Presently, the private developers have not been involved in the Delhi Development Authority (DDA) housing construction schemes. Consequently, there has been an enormous backlog of housing in national capital, Delhi. To boost the mass scale housing scheme in Delhi, the involvement of private developers has become a vital necessity. The private developers will be required to ensure competitive rates and speedy construction with the regulated control of the competent authority.

Prior to the existence of DDA, private developers had already built innumerable colonies which were affordable in residential areas like Hauz Khas, Green Park Extension, Greater Kailash, South Extension, Qutab Enclave, also on.

Interestingly, in Haryana the private developers have come up with mini city complexes like Palam Vihar, Sushant Lok, South City, and Aravali Enclave. The private developers have also participated in the construction of housing complexes in the satellite towns around Delhi, like Ghaziabad, Meerut and NOIDA. Housing in these townships has developed at an accelerated pace because these places are close to Delhi.

A document by DDA—Role of Private Developers in the Context of Delhi, 2001 has rightly laid down guidelines for the involvement of private developers in Delhi's housing schemes. Due to the acute shortage of housing caused by enormous influx of migrants into the city, there is an imperative need to involve the private builders to supplement the government's efforts to boost the construction of houses in Delhi.

For attracting private builders in a big way, the scheme must have adequate incentives by way of return on the capital invested by them. The scheme must also have an effective built in system of free and fair competition among the prospective private builders. A select list of reputed builders needs to be prepared after inviting applications through wide publicity in the press, so that DDA is assured of speedy completion of the schemes entrusted to the private builders.

In view of the acute paucity and scattered nature of land available with the DDA for development, it has been felt that the plot size allotted in each case to private builders for construction of houses should not exceed five to ten acres. For the optimum utilization of land, a minimum density of 60 dwelling units per acre with a maximum floor area ratio (FAR) of 1.75 has been prescribed by DDA, within these parameters DDA provides full freedom to the builder to evolve combinations of different types of houses.

DDA's main objective has been to increase the housing stock in Delhi as rapidly as possible. As such, for attracking the maximum number of builders and removing any possible complications and bottlenecks during the process of implementation, maximum possible freedom should be allowed to the builders with minimum restrictions. Keeping this in mind, it has been felt that there should be no restriction on builders for building some minimum percentage of MIG, Janata/Economically Weaker Section (EWS) schemes and making the same available to DDA at a fixed price (which will necessarily involve number of complications such as approval of detailed drawings, designs and specifications, supervision of works, checking of structural designs). Builders should be allowed to construct any type of house they think fit, within the limits of maximum FAR and minimum density and they should also be free to sell these houses at market rates to any person without any restrictions, except that the buyer or his wife or dependent children should not own any residential plot or house in Delhi.

The DDA document suggests that four or five suitable housing pockets (of size five to ten acres) should be identified within the urban limits of Delhi for development and construction through the involvement of private builders. Thereafter, these pockets could be disposed of either by auction among the select list of reputed builders or by calling tenders.

As a policy decision DDA document reveals that builders should be allowed to make advance bookings from prospective buyers for financing the project. Further, the builders themselves should be fully responsible for the design, structural safety, execution of work as per the specifications and rectification of defects without any supervision or inspection by DDA.

In the matter of calling tenders a set of detailed terms and conditions have been framed by DDA. These cover aspects like responsibilities of developers, maximum FAR and minimum density to be achieved, time for completion of the project in all respects and penalties for its unnecessary delay.

Other terms and conditions include, ground rent and instalments in which the tendered price has to be paid, guarantees and securities to be furnished by the builders for performance of the contract and other normal contract provisions applicable in such cases.

Involvement of private developers by DDA seems to be commendable proposal which needs to be strictly administered. However, their proper supervision is required in terms of pricing and effective use of the durable construction material.

The DDA should provide private developers with technical knowledge, easy availability of building material, financial and institutional facilities. This would promote mass scale housing programmes in Delhi in a big way.

Haryana Experiment: Private Developers

Haryana has broken new ground by enacting the Haryana Development and Regulations of Urban Areas Act, which permits a land owner to assume the role of a colonizer within the strictly controlled parameters. Though the law was enacted in 1975, its meaningful implementation started only in mid-eighties and came into action after a careful preparation. The private colonizers are working side by side with the Haryana Urban Development Authority (HUDA) in developing residential areas with commercial components. This has created not only a choice for the plot buyers between the official and private agencies, but also a keen competition among private colonizers.

The colonies are already been developed near the Indira Gandhi International Airport on NH-8 and Mehrauli-Gurgaon Road. Besides the residential areas, clubs, educational institutions and commercial complexes have come up on an area of over 4,000 acres.

Though not stipulated by law, the private colonizers have earmarked a minimum percentage of plots/flats for the low income/weaker sections of the society, which are subsidized/sold on 'no profit no loss' basis. For the inter-colony roads, drainage, and trunk sewer, water and electric lines, being laid by the HUDA, the private colonizers have contributed proportionately.

For the benefit of plot holders, a fund has been created with contribution @ Re 1 per sq. mt. of the plots disposed of by the private and official agencies. The private enterprise has generated funds of Rs 10,000 million in 6-8 years, of which about Rs 5,000 million are claimed to have been contributed to the HUDA's consolidated fund for the external development.

A private colonizer has to funish bank guarantee equal to 25 per cent of total cost of the internal and external development in the beginning, and keep 30 per cent of the inflow of funds from the plot buyers in a separate bank account for the internal development. The private colonizer's operations are closely monitored and necessary correctives are applied by the Director, Town and Country Planning, Haryana for which he has extensive powers under the Haryana Development and Regulation of Urban Areas Act, 1975, and Rules, 1976. The main factors, contributing to the physical and financial success of the private enterprise in this area are:

Instead of only developing land, an all-round development, including commercial, educational and social infrastructure, has been undertaken which has attracted the new settlers more.

The land for colonization has been assembled through outright purchases from the farmers, avoiding difficulties and delays in the acquisition process. The buyers get free-hold rights. The plots and flats are easily transferable.

The colonies developed by a private developer have a larger mix of plot-housing, group-housing and town houses, which suit the middle and higher income groups better.

Some of the cultivators have declined to sell their land. These small pockets here and there, being eyesores in the private colonies, need to be legally acquired. Provisions of bulk services and sector roads, though paid for, has been delayed, retarding the progress of habitation. The HUDA should gear up the external development, which may as well help the colonies developed by itself. Several multi-storeyed complexes of upto 200 ft. height have came up in the area, needing strengthening of fire-fighting arrangements.

The provisions of the Haryana Development and Regulation of Urban Areas Act, 1975 and Rules, 1976 need to be revised and strengthened in the light of the experience gained. The particular items which need attention are, namely, limit the period of licensing under section 3 from two to five years, a single window system for sanction of layout and building plans, setting up a local authority to take over the maintenance of the colonies, conferment of legal ownership rights on flat holders in multi-storeyed buildings, and a machinery to resolve disputes between colonizers and the plot/flat buyers.

Private Housing Scheme

The role of private developers, at present, stands confined to houses for middle income group and high income group families, no doubt because of the profits involved. The tendency has to be checked through the application of legal and administrative actions. If effectively tackled, private agencies can play a significant role in providing housing to a large number of the urban poor. A few broad suggestions are highlighted as follow:

1. The private developers may be required to construct at least 25 per cent of the housing units they undertake, as low cost houses, within prices affordable by the LIG and EWS. This condition can be imposed when the private developers apply for approval of plans and projects to the financial agencies.
2. Encouragement may be given to private developers by making available to them cash loans at reasonable rates of interest.
3. Loan upto 75 or 80 per cent of all conclusive cost may be offered to LIG and EWS families for outright purchase of houses from the private developers.
4. Non-refundable withdrawals from Provident Fund Accounts may be sanctioned to the employees, exclusively for purchase of low-cost houses.

Housing is a state subject. Given the wide variation in the housing needs, State Governments and Union Territories would have to play a crucial role in formulating plans and programmes suited to local needs and conditions in consultation with the local bodies. State governments would need to identify the specific agencies for implementation of the action plan. Development of housing infrastructure and services has not kept in tune with the growth of housing. The problem of upgradation and renewal of basic services like potable drinking water and sanitation is serious. An integrated programme for land assembly and infrastructure development, particularly water supply, sanitation, drainage and electric supply would be required to be taken up on a priority basis. Action of the state government would need to take into account the resource flow from the private, cooperative and public sectors. The role of the Central Government would be to guide and facilitate the implementation of action plan. The synergy created with efficiency of private sector and experience of the public agencies would ensure that the overall costs is kept at minimum.

Governmental Role

The public housing thrust is directed towards social housing to reach out housing solutions to priority groups. An equally important activity is to provide a policy framework and a legislative, fiscal and financial system that would put into effect the enabling role of the government in stimulating, supporting and promoting other actors to play direct roles in the housing delivery system. These two activities have been the pillars to the Eighth Plan approach and would continue in the Ninth Plan, 1997–2002.

Integrated Settlement Planning

The NHP should be directed to promote the mass scale scheme for housing in its regional perspective. The significant importance has to be given for decentralizing the urban economy in the small town and village settlements. Such a process would be able to check the concentration of population growth in metropolitan and other large cities and the housing planning could be spread out in a regional perspective.

A vital need for planning the housing schemes is to provide an effective transport network system between the peripheral areas of urban settlements. With the provision of adequate socio-economic facilities people should be persuaded to live outside the city limits and thereby the strain of housing on cities can be eased. As land is available at a reasonable rate in the peripheral areas, a comprehensive housing plan has to be contemplated in a regional perspective. The proper peripheral planning of transportation and socio-economic facilities is planned in Western countries in an effective manner. In London, people like to stay outside the city limits and come for work in the city as the electric transport operates in an efficient manner. Such an approach of planning needs to be streamlined in our country. The national housing policy should visualize the decentralization of urban economic activities.

The NHP should adopt a guideline for the effective technological innovation of research and development for ensuring low-cost programmes on a massive scale. Further, the rural land within the city limits should not be directed for the housing activities keeping in view the disastrous effects of ecological imbalance. The NHP should also be directed at preserving landscape particularly in the metropolitan and large cities.

As such, the NHP should emphasize the promotion of large-scale housing activities, with a speedy technology of prefabrication in its construction for increasing the flow of funds for the purpose. The participative process of land development by corporate sector needs to be encouraged.

Fiscal incentives is required to be devised for increasing the rate of savings at the household level and also the need is to encourage the savings for house construction in a big way.

The appropriate changes in the approach of existing financial institutions will be required to make them more responsive and to increase the access of the households excluded currently from their operations.

A suitable mortgage insurance scheme under appropriate legislation needs to be enacted to provide insurance cover to lender against non-payment by the borrower.

Secondary mortgage market to enable the holders of mortgage and mortgage-based securities to obtain cash from them by passing them to other holders, should be created. The upgradation of old building materials and techniques needs to be intensified.

The government should address itself to remove the constraints in the legal framework, which inhibits the investment in housing by private sector, by amending the Rent Control Act, by linking rents with cost of living index, delinking non-residential from residential accommodation and by enabling tenant cooperatives to secure ownership rights of old premises development. In this connection, specific attention should be provided to research and development of cost reduction technique of prefabricated building material. However, there is slow progress of house building activities and rampant corruption prevails in the housing agencies in urban areas. The inferior building material has to be discouraged and the comprehensive prefabricated building material component should be emphasized for promoting durability and the mass scale housing programmes in the urban settlements. Housing is the basic social need and it should be recognized while evolving the NHP.

For any physical development (housing construction, improvement of slums, laying of roads, etc.) proper site, prevailing laws of the land such as provisions laid down under the Town and Country Planning Act, building bye-laws, and construction standards, need to be compiled. The provisions of zoning, landuse, the control of development, and the use of land are covered by the Town Planning Act. These Acts and Laws are impediments to an accelerated development of housing stock within the country; they are based on colonial concepts and standards and hence they are irrelevant today—their practice, at present, makes the majority of housing construction illegal.

Although relaxation of standards to suit the circumstances of weaker sections has been often recommended, it is seen that the progress has been slow. In the absence of essential and urgent reform, even minimum housing continues to be beyond the reach of the majority of the urban poor. Consequently, a good proposition of popular housing also continues to be technically illegal.

REFERENCES

1. Ansari, P.N.: Housing Situation: the Malaise and some suggestions, Yojana, March, 1999.
2. Bhargava, Gopal: Housing the Urban Poor, Evening News, *The Hindustan Times*, June 1, 1995.
3. Bhargava, Gopal: Socio-Economic and Legal Implications of Urban Land (Ceiling and Regulation) Act, 1976, published by Abhinav Publisher Private Limited, New Delhi.
4. Bhattacharya, K.P.: Housing in India—Observation on the Governmental Intervention Policies. Edited by Gil Shidlo, published by Routledge, London.

5. Delhi Development Authority: Document cyclostyle 'Role of Private Developers in the context of Delhi 2001.
6. Federation of Indian Chamber of Commerce and Industry, Background Paper: Seminar on Housing and Urban Development, February 5, 1996, New Delhi.
7. Government of India, Planning Commission: Ninth Five Year Plan, 1997-2000 Thematic Issues and Sectoral Programmes.
8. Ministry of Urban Development: National Housing Policy, 1992.
9. Ministry of Urban Development: Task Force on Housing and Urban Development.
10. Lal, A.K.: Urban Housing, Post Reforms Scenario, Yojana, Volume 43, Number 3, March, 1999.
11. Murthy, M. Krishna: Alternate Building Technologies and Materials for Housing, paper presented at the International Symposium on Housing, Energy and Environment, organized by Shelter Promotion Council (India) held at New Delhi, January 27–29, 1996.
12. Pratap Krishan: Alternative Models for Assemblage of Land for Development of the NCR Towns, Spatio-Economic Development Record, Volume 1, Number 5, November-December, 1994.
13. Sengupta, B.K.: Financial and Technological innovations for Cost Optimized Housing Key Note addressed for presentation in the International Symposium on Housing, Energy and Environment organized by Shelter Promotion Council (India) held at New Delhi, January 27–29, 1996.
14. Suresh V., Singh, T.N. and Singh: Kulwant Paper presented in the National Seminar on Future Cities Urban Vision 2021, organized by the Ministry of Urban Development.
15. Sunderam, P.S.A.: Housing Needs in Urban India, Social Welfare, Volume XXXVIII, No. 11, February, 1987.
16. *The Financial Express,* February 25, 1993.

CHAPTER 3

URBAN SLUMS AND SQUATTER SETTLEMENTS PLANNING AND POLICY ISSUES

The Indian cities like Ahmedabad, Mumbai, Bangalore, Calcutta, Delhi, Chennai, Pune, Kanpur, Lucknow, so on, have witnessed an excessive inflow of migrants. The reasons for the alarming phenomenon of migration have gathered momentum as the large scale economic, infrastructural and industrial activities are mainly concentrated in the urban centres. In view of the exorbitant land prices and lack of low-cost shelter constructions, the migrants are being forced to squat on public land or land which is unfit for the human habitation. Thus, the urban poor usually occupy the low lying areas and are prone to floods during the rainy seasons. However, such a situation is mainly true to the urban settlements. The haphazard growth of slums has been a forceful encroachment phenomenon on vacant land. There is an uncontrollable growth of slums, unauthorized colonies and squatter settlements in the context of metropolitan and other large cities. If such a trend continues then the Indian urban settlements in the 21st century would become uninhabitable and unmanageable.

Emerging Issues

The poor cannot afford to pay the growing market prices of pucca shelter or buy land at the sky-rocketing prices near their work place. They are unable to afford the cost of transporting themselves or their stock for trade over long distances and therefore, they settle near their work places, which are otherwise considered unfit for habitation. The notable examples are, namely, near river banks, *nallas* and drainage canals, marginal railways lands and swamps. Their constructions are of cheap scrap and salvaged material—gunny bags, tarpaulin, scrap tin sheets, wooden planks, etc. The civic amenities are inadequate. As a result, the public sanitation and personal hygienic breaks down.

It is realized that, 'the growth of slums is therefore a symptom of the inability of people to procure land and shelter through market transaction, in which they find themselves out priced since government has failed to regulate urban land resources in such a way that poor can have equitable access to them.'

The haphazard growth of urbanization has not followed a systematic process of balanced development. With the result the excessive growth of population, slums and migration have become unmanageable crises.

It is 'generally observed that the small to medium towns have a lower percentage of squatter and slum inhabitants. Mumbai is estimated to have the highest number of slum dwellers followed by Calcutta, Delhi and Chennai (3.3 million, 3.2 million, 2.6 million and 1.3 million respectively). Among the other cities, Kanpur has 680,000 and Bangalore 510,000 slum dwellers'. The trend of slum growth in the Indian cities has caused a serious concern to the city planners, administrators and policy makers.

The slum population of India in relation to total population in cities has shown an increasing trend since 1981. It is likely to multiply by the year 2000. The table below indicates the slum population in India during the period 1981–2000.

TABLE 1
Slum Population in India
1981–2000 A.D.

(Percentage of Slum Population)

Year	*Urban Population*	*Percentage of Slum Population*	
		**Low Estimates*	***High Estimates*
1981	162	32 (20%)	42 (24.7%)
1985	188	38 (20.2%)	47 (25%)
1990	225	45 (20%)	56 (24.9%)
2000	310	62 (20%)	78 (25.2%)

Source: Task Force on Planning for Urban Development, Planning Commission, Government of India.

Estimates Cited from Sudesh Nangia, 'Slum of Urban India: Planning and Policy Actions', The Civic Affairs, December, 1987.

Notes: *All India Low Estimate assuming 20% of additional urban population will be in slums, squatter settlements.

**High estimates assuming 25% of additional urban population will be in slum and squatter settlements.

Emerging Issues

The *jhuggi-jhopri* (JJ) clusters of Delhi, the *bustees* of Calcutta, the *cheries* of Chennai, *zopadpatties cum chawls* of Mumbai depict the unhygienic way of urban poor living conditions. The lack of civic amenities like drinking water and latrine facilities in the slums and squatter settlements in the Indian cities have become a serious challenging problem for the planners and policy makers. Due to the deteriorating slum environment, the anti-social activities have emerged in a big way.

Half of Indian city population in the 21st century will be living in slum and squatter settlements. Thus, there is likely to be the rise of large scale encroachments in India's metropolitan and other large cities.

Slums of Delhi: Challenges

Types of slums vary from place to place. But as far as the national capital. Delhi is concerned, slums can be classified broadly in two categories. In the first category comes the notified areas of Slum Areas (Improvement and Clearance) Act, 1956. Few examples of notified slums are—Chawri Bazar, Chandni Chowk, Sadar Bazar and Katras, so on. The second category of slums constitute this JJ clusters which possess the sub-human living standards and lack even the minimum basic civic amenities. Few examples of JJ clusters are specified as Shadipur JJ clusters, Arjan Dass JJ Camp and JJ cluster at Mayapuri Chowk and so on.

It is evident that the slums of Delhi are increasing in an alarming proportion and this increase has many causes to its accountability. Some of the causes are spelt out as follow:

(i) The influx of more than two lakh migrants which come to Delhi every year in search of livelihood as well as other socio-economic reasons like homelessness, poverty, ignorance, hunger and social discrimination. These migrants, in order to get settled in Delhi, involve themselves in low paid jobs, like shoe polishing, rag picking, coolie and likewise, and encroach the land (both private as well as public) near their place of employment.

(ii) The poor people, due to an acute shortage of sufficient money for survival, just cannot afford the luxury of having a shelter of their own and are forced to live in the shanty townships.

(iii) Crores of rupees are spent by the government on the rehabilitation of these migrants. It cures the poor people living in other parts of India to migrate to Delhi, which in turn, results in increasing the number of slums in Delhi.

(iv) The political rallies are also one of the causes for increase in the number of slums in Delhi, as a large number of people of the country come from every nook and corner of the country to attend the various political rallies. But unfortunately, one-fourth of them do not go back to their respective places and try to get themselves settled in Delhi.

(v) Mushrooming of a large number of government offices and other economic activities is another cause of enormous flow of migrants to Delhi in search of livelihood etc.

(vi) These slum dwellers generally have to live in the congested areas lacking even the minimum civic amenities like water, electricity and sewer and are compelled to defecate in the open. As a result of this, unhygienic conditions prevail in these slum areas and often take the shape of an epidemic.

The government policies have priced out most of the poor from the formal housing market, confining them to slum settlements. Keeping this fact in view, a three-pronged strategy has been developed for dealing with the problems faced by the slum population, namely (i) relocation, (ii) environmental upgradation with the necessary restructuring of the layout and (iii) extension of minimum basic community services where neither of the above mentioned approaches are possible.

With regard to the first approach, the city of Delhi had initiated one of the largest programmes of resettlement, covering about 2.5 lakh households. However, unlike in many other states in the country, the second approach of in-situ upgradation has not been favoured; only three to four slum settlements, involving less than 800 families have been covered. Most of the other remaining clusters are covered under the scheme for the provision of basic community services. While considerable involvement of financial resources, amounting to several crores of rupees, are being poured into these settlements, there is need to promote an integrated strategy of planning and development.

In Delhi, the phenomenon of slums had commenced since the sixties. It was in the seventies that the resettlement colonies were constituted by rehabilitating more than 10 lakh people. New *bustees* of Delhi have

Jhuggi Jhopri Clusters of Delhi

Courtesy: Photo Section, Delhi Development Authority, Ministry of Urban Development, Government of India.

Slums Around the Housing Complex of Urban Delhi

Courtesy: Photo Section, Delhi Development Authority, Ministry of Urban Development, Government of India.

come up after the establishment of 44 JJ resettlement colonies, where more than two lakh JJ plots of 25 square yards each were allotted in which more than 15 lakh people live today. In spite of such a scheme it seems that in the 21st century a large number of pople are likely to live in slum and squatter settlements.

Delhi has become a vital source of attraction for migrants in terms of providing adequate employment opportunities in the formal, informal and service sectors. The income factor too has played a significant role in attracting the migrants towards Delhi in an alarming proportion.

In the recent past, Delhi has witnessed an excessive growth of slum and all around squatter settlements, the city. It is estimated that there are more than 1,080 JJ clusters in Delhi with a population of 22 lakh; 20 lakh living in slums and 15 lakh in unauthorized construction. Out of Delhi's population of more than a billion, three-fourths are living in slums and squatter settlements.

According to the 'Review of the Provision in Slums and Squatter Settlements in Urban India' by E.F. Ribeiro, there are two types of slums in the national capital, Delhi i.e. the *katras* and open plots, former dating back to the time before Delhi became the capital of the British India in 1911, remaining largely unattended with only marginal improvements undertaken by the Municipal Corporation. The squatter resettlement was a major operation, related to the city's tremendous growth rate after independence and the government's inability in keeping pace with the housing needs of new residents. This slowness has also resulted in unauthorized construction on the notified land. A major defect of the Delhi Master Plan was that it had not taken into account the adequate housing needs of a large number of low-income workers in government service and in the informal sector.

A survey of slum dwellers plight has revealed that in Delhi, apart from some major slum colonies in the trans Yamuna area, most of the small slums have come up around new and major construction sites. The contractors exploit the labourers and pay meagre wages. After the construction of a building complex, the labourers eventually stay on permanently near the complex looking for other works. Thus, more and more slum and squatter settlements have emerged in and around Delhi.

During the Seventh Plan, in Delhi, initially the expenditure for slum and squatter settlement was Rs 20 crores raised to about Rs 48 crore. In the Eighth Five Year Plan, the provision of financial outlay had been raised to Rs 36.25 crore. The items covered were street lighting, water supply, paved pathways and drainage. An amount of Rs 9 crore had been provided for latrine facilities under the 'Sulabh Sauchalaya' and other Delhi Administration departments.

The 22 lakh population of JJ clusters in Delhi are without adequate drinking water supply and toilet facilities. As such, a large percentage of the population has been deprived of privacy and they defecate in the open and on a vast tract of land. This has resulted into spread of serious diseases amongst the inhabitants.

Surprisingly, the politicians of Delhi are sponsoring the growth of slums and squatter settlements in a big way as a vote bank, yet doing nothing for providing basic services to the inhabitants.

There is need for assessing the essential public utility services and civic amenities in the context of slum and squatter settlements. The better provisions of services like drinking water and toilet facilities have to be considered as a prerequisite of a congenial living environment in the JJ clusters.

The socio-economic living standard of slums dwellers in Delhi is unsatisfactory. The income level does not allow the inhabitants to afford a decent accommodation. Therefore, they prefer to get a job and remain without a shelter, such a situation coupled with the exorbitant rental rates is responsible for excessive trend of homelessness.

It is realized that 'the situation is further complicated by the continued concentration of industries and commercial establishments in the few metropolitan areas alone. A balanced and harmonious development of every region should be ensured. Carefully selected core villages, small and medium size towns should be developed to serve, on the one hand as nerve centres of agro-industrial activity and on the other, to prevent the growth of unmanageable cities.'

There is an urgency to check the enormous flow of migrants towards Delhi. The National Capital Region (NCR) should emphasize planning as a regional process of balanced development by providing the employment and income opportunities in the context of small and medium town settlements. Thus, the shifting of Central Government's offices and wholesale trade should be undertaken far away from Delhi with an adoption of action-oriented planning and policy perspective. A top priority has to be given the power development, so that people are induced to promote industrial development along with the adequate sources of employment and income prospects in the entire rural and small town settlements of NCR.

It is visualized that if the migration to Delhi is not checked then Delhi's entire vacant land, including parks and open spaces, will be occupied by the slum and squatter population by the 21st century.

Mumbai's Slums

In the city of Mumbai, the suburban railway stations have acted as a reception centre for the rural migrants. Gradually, two to three days' stay at the platform is purely temporary while the other place of shelter for the rural migrants, for 10 to 12 days, is in the loading and unloading shunting railway sheds. Subsequently, the acquaintance of the rural migrants with the slum-dwellers of Mumbai adds to the number of slum population, particularly in the context of *zopadpatties* clusters. Eventually, the rural migrants have become a part of slum settlement. To demolish a few huts is easy but the same becomes impossible when it multiplies in an alarming proportion over a period of time, with the political support.

According to the Government's estimates the State of Maharashtra has the highest percentage of its population living in slums among the Indian states. Mumbai tops the list beyond 4.5 million slum inhabitants. In fact, in size, density and living conditions, the slums of Mumbai are considered to be among the worst slums in the entire world.

The Mumbai's slums have grown in an haphazard manner. In fact, in squalor, poverty, disease and anti-social activities the slums of Dharavi stand unmatched in Asia and possibly in the entire world. Over 50 per cent of the families that live in Mumbai slums have a monthly income of less than Rs 1000 per month. The slum dwellers include a few reasonably well-off persons with skilled or white collar jobs, a large number of people are in blue collar permanent jobs and an overwhelming number are in unprotected jobs or just unemployed rural refugees.

The city of Mumbai is being confronted with slums of *zopadpatties* and *chawls*; its inhabitants are living in the congested unhygienic environment.

The unhygienic conditions of *zopadpatties* and slums speak about the horrible life of the inhabitants. Dirt and filth has become a serious health hazard for the inhabitants of *zopadpatties*. Moreover, the dilapidated buildings are a serious threat to the life of the inhabitants.

One of the challenging problems of Mumbai slums embodies the clusters of *zopadpatties* and *chawls* which are deprived of water and latrine facilities. There is need for utilizing the earmarked financial resources of the World Bank and Environmental Improvement of Urban Slum (EIUS) scheme in the right earnestness for improving the living conditions of slum inhabitants of Mumbai.

The Sulabh Sauchalaya Scheme of toilet facilities should be made popular, especially in the city of Mumbai on paying basis. However, in nearly all the metropolitan cities such a provision of sanitation should be provided through the local authority.

In a large number, the slum dwellers of Mumbai are the service personnels to the inhabitants of tall buildings. The concentration of economic development in Mumbai alone is mainly responsible for the population explosion resulting from the alarming growth of migrants. Further, due to the acute shortage of land and accommodation, migrant population of Mumbai are forced to live in *zopadpatties* and *chawls*.

The unauthorized construction and pavement dwellings have been growing rapidly in recent years. It needs to be pointed out that 'today slums and the more recent squatter settlements, which together embrace all types of low income housing, are not isolated and temporary phenomenon but a national issue linked with the growing rural-urban migration.'

When migrants reach the city, they invariably find themselves pushed towards the slum or squatter settlements. One of the reasons for this is that they eventually depend upon the kinship, caste and regional networks not only for the choice of destination but also for their adjustments to harsh conditions of urban living. These settlements, therefore, have an effective overtone of village environment reflected in their total physical, social, economic and cultural organizational set-up.

It is estimated that at least 40 per cent of Mumbai's population is distributed in tenement slums and hutment colonies and this level is not likely to be reduced by the year 2001, but it may, in fact, gain an alarming proportion.

A survey led to the following threefold classification of slums in Mumbai, namely: (a) *Chawls*—permanent multi-storeyed buildings built decades ago according to the standards prevailing then, but which are presently in a dilapidated condition. (b) *Patra Chawls*—semi-permanent structures, both authorized and unauthorized, often built with corrugated iron sheets or with some such hard material (*patra* means tin sheets).

(c) *Zopadatties*—squatter settlements consisting of hovels made from a variety of hard and soft materials, including wood, rags, tin sheets, mud and bricks (*zopad* means hutment).

A radical change in policy has to be adopted from incorporating the spatial and economic planning in its regional perspective for checking the large scale influx of migrants in the context of Mumbai.

The city of Mumbai is confronted with population explosion and lack of public utility services. B.K. Boman Behram and A.N. Contractor in their book *The Decline of Bombay* have emphatically highlighted that only 4.8 per cent of Mumbai's residents have their own homes. Thus, the remaining 95.2 per cent live in rented premises, in hutments or on the streets. About 70 per cent of Mumbai's citizens are deprived of privacy due to the inadequate facilities. There are only 13 per cent who have independent toilets; the rest have to share the common toilets—sharing one toilet between 60 to 100 persons. Eight per cent have no toilets whatsoever, having to squat in the open.

Interestingly Mumbai, being a political and economic centre, has attracted a large number of people from the mofussil and other towns not only from the State of Maharashtra, but also from other states in the country. Thus, there has arisen the acute shortage of housing which has been responsible for the growth of slums in Mumbai.

A Supreme Court judgement had exposed the tardiness of the Government of Maharashtra and the Municipal Corporation in clearing the slums in urban areas. By striking down an Act passed in 1975, the Court had admonished the Government for persisting with a law declared to be defective by the Bombay High Court and thus allowing the "slum lords" to encroach on public and private lands and extort high rents from tenants.

The Supreme Court had emphatically observed that while the object of the Act was "unquestionably laudable", the provisions were "discriminatory" and hence warranted to be set aside. The Act vested in the Executive the power for declaring any plot of land as under encroachment and proceed with a summary eviction of the tenants. Unfortunately, the Act did not lay down the necessary guidelines for clearly defining the limits of this extraordinary power and hence raised the possibility of its discriminatory exercise. The High Court declared the Act void precisely on this ground. Instead of amending it in the context of the judgement, the State Government and the local body rushed to the Supreme Court by enabling the State Government the "legislativ competence'' for undertaking this mammoth operation for which the political will was required.

Interestingly the slums of Mumbai can be planned if 'some of the urban land is reserved for locating the well-planned hutment colonies with all the basic amenities'.

TABL 2

Slum Population of Metropolitan Cities from 1981 to 2021

(in Millions)

Name of the Metropolitan City		*Population*				
		1981	*1991*	*2001**	*2011**	*2021**
1. Greater Bombay	U.A.	2.83	4.31	6.59	8.29	10.04
2. Calcutta	U.A.	3.03	3.59	4.26	5.12	6.04
3. Delhi	U.A.	1.80	2.63	3.85	5.05	6.19
4. Madras	U.A.	1.36	1.72	2.15	2.88	3.72
5. Hyderabad	U.A.	0.50	0.84	1.41	2.25	3.16
6. Bangalore	U.A.	0.31	0.43	0.60	1.20	1.93
7. Ahmedabad	U.A.	0.54	0.67	0.87	1.48	2.25
8. Pune	U.A.	0.27	0.41	0.60	1.20	1.97
9. Kanpur	U.A.	0.61	0.79	1.02	1.64	2.42
10. Nagpur	U.A.	0.42	0.53	0.68	1.26	2.01
11. Lucknow	U.A.	0.29	0.46	0.75	1.42	2.23
12. Surat	U.A.	0.23	0.39	0.65	1.30	2.09
13. Jaipur	U.A.	0.30	0.44	0.65	1.27	2.05
14. Kochi	U.A.	0.17	0.28	0.47	1.05	1.80
15. Vadodara	U.A.	0.12	0.18	0.26	0.40	0.53
16. Indore	U.A.	0.13	0.17	0.22	0.74	1.46
17. Coimbatore	U.A.	-	0.23**	0.28**	0.40	0.84
18. Patna	U.A.	0.58	0.70	0.84	1.41	2.15
19. Madurai	U.A.	-	0.22**	0.26**	0.42	0.91
20. Bhopal	M.C.	0.06	0.09	0.14	0.21	0.32
21. Visakhapatnam	U.A.	0.15	0.26	0.46	0.98	1.72
22. Ludhiana	M.C.	0.31	0.52	0.85	1.36	2.07
23. Varanasi	U.A.	0.26	0.34	0.43	0.59	1.01
		14.27	20.28	28.29	42.92	57.81

Note: * Estimated figure of 2001, 2011 and 2021

** 20% of Urban Population

Source: Town and Country Planning Organisation, Ministry of Urban Development, Government of India

Cited from National Buildings Organization, Handbook of Housing Statistics, Part-I, 1996, Ministy of Urban Development, Government of India.

The emphasis should be laid on rehabilitating the existing unplanned colonies to well-planned hutment colonies with all the basic amenities. Further, liberal credit facilities should be given to the cooperative slum dwellers if they come forward to improve their colonies or individual dwellings. There is an imperative need for planning the *chawls* of Mumbai with the provision of a congenial environment.

Slums of Chandigarh

The slums are a part of the system of capitalist development choosen by India. It is evident from their existence in the new planned cities where they were not supposed to exist. Chandigarh was founded in 1951 and has not been exempted from the existence of slum and squatter settlements.

Chandigarh, planned by Le Corbusier was designed to cater to a five lakh population. However, according to the original idea it was to be an administrative city and not an industrial city alone. It is an epitome of town planning achievement of India. Later, contrary to the original plan an additional area was developed.

When the work was undertaken in the city, out of a total of 6,067 existing structures, only 34 per cent were authorized. As a result of a screening process recommended by a special sub-committee, 32.6 per cent of the unauthorized dwellings were further classified as the approved unauthorized. However, such a process could hardly prevent the process of growth of slum shelters.

The growth of labour colonies and unauthorized structures have increased manifold. Beside the enormous slum colonies there are a large number of unauthorized units. People who live in such hutments are those who are in the low menial jobs and are unable to afford a better shelter in the city.

This is the picture one gets from the most planned new city in India, one that was framed as an architectural paradise. In the unauthorized slums of this beautiful city of Chandigarh the construction workers and the casual industrial workers are living. The workers in the service population, consisting of tailors, washermen, barbers and sweepers, so on, are only a shade better off as they have been provided with authorized dwellings. The areas inhabited by the slum dwellers are dirty and neglected and have the highest density per square kilometre.

Calcutta's Horrorful Slums

Calcutta is traditionally known as a city of slums. Here, the creation of slums on a massive scale started with the industrialization of the city in the 19th century which attracted a large number of people. In order to provide cheap labour to the industries, the slums were created legally under a peculiar three-tier system in which the landlords leased out their lands to some middlemen called *thika* tenants who constructed the huts and rented them out to the migrants. Such clusters of slums have been gradually spread out all over the city. Formerly, the *thika* tenants had no permanent right over the land and could be ousted any moment.

After independence due to a large scale migration of refugees into the city of Calcutta, the land prices have shot up tremendously. Demolition of *bustees* on a large scale started specially in the core of the city, thus calling for an immediate intervention by the Government, which came in the form of repeated amendments to the Thika Tenancy Act, giving more and more permament right over the land to *thika* tenants. However, the latest amendment to the Act passed by the Left Front Government, vests in the Government the ownership of such type of slum land clusters.

In Calcutta, the take over of ownership of slum lands by the Government was necessitated by the fact that with repeated amendments to the Thika Tenancy Act, landlords of the slums were least interested in providing facilities to the inhabitants.

In the meanwhile, a new type of slum in the form of squatter settlements had emerged on public lands such as on canal sides, railway land, bridge embankments and roads, parks and other open spaces as also on private lands.

Unlike the most other cities in India, Calcutta's slum population is mostly confined to the unhygienic *bustees*. For long there have been debates about the methods to be adopted for betterment of slum dwellers in the city of Calcutta. A fairly powerful movement of slum dwellers was responsible for such debates as to whether slums should be cleared or improved and ultimately the authorities be forced to opt for improvement.

After independence, an attempt was made to remove the slums by rehousing the slum dweller elsewhere in four-storied wall-ups. Subsequently, few hundred tenements had been built, but the scheme had to be abandoned as the location and type of construction of such tenements was not in conformity with the economic needs of the people to be moved into the specified area.

It was then felt that given the size and spread of slum growth, clearance was not a feasible proposition. The qualitative improvement of slums enabled an overall improvement in living conditions at an affordable cost. Further, this had led to the framing of the West Bengal Slum Areas, (Improvement and Clearance) Act of 1971, where the slums were recognized as part of the city housing stock. However, under a programme of improvement in later years, slums were provided with basic facilities like latrines, potable pipe water supply, drainage, paved roads and street lighting. The programme has benefitted, in the course of nearly two decades, more than 21 lakh of the 30 lakh of slum dwellers of Calcutta metropolitan district.

The land tenure and improvement of shelters may be envisaged as the second stage of this process which was initiated by transferring the ownership of the *bustee* land from the landlords to the government by the Calcutta Thika Tenancy Act of 1981. However, together with this the government is undertaking a number of measures for improving the quality of life in slums by financing the small-scale enterprises and introducing education, health and nutrition programmes, which may enable them in sustaining the benefits of the improvement programme.

Surprisingly, in Calcutta, the builders and promoters go on constructing multi-storied apartments without consideration for the environment management or of pressure on urban services. Poorer people belonging to the labouring and middle classes are forced to move away from the city to its suburbs.

There are few pockets of squatter settlements in Calcutta and they have overgrown in population size. The problem associated with proper shelter to the poor population remains a serious issue for the municipal authorities.

The slum and squatter settlements of Calcutta are confronted with the population explosion due to lack of rural development.

Slum Pollution

One of the serious challenging problems in the slum and squatter settlements has been human excreta and garbage pollution. Around the slum and squatter settlements of metropolitan cities, there is threat of an epidemic spread of human excreta. The low-deep handpumps installed in the slum and squatter settlements have been responsible for the widespread water borne diseases.

The garbage pollution would assume a serious threat by the 21st century due to the unmanageable growth.

Growth Legislation

According to the 138th Report on 'Legislative Protection for Slum and Pavement Dwellers' and earlier Supreme Court decision, it has been announced that the slum and pavement dwellers should be protected through the legislative measures, when eviction is undertaken by the local authorities, and the alternative site and accommodation should be provided.

There is need for a suitable legislation to be enacted for checking the encroachments on squatter settlements for preventing the distortion of the Cities' Master Plans and landuse provisions concerning the developmental activities.

In the national capital, Delhi there are various legislations to check encroachments and unauthorized constructions, namely. (1) Public Premises (Eviction of Unauthorized Occupants) Act, 1971 (which permits eviction of any unauthorized occupant from the public premises. (2) Delhi Lands (Restriction on Transfer) Act, 1972. (3) The Delhi Development Act, 1957; Section 30 restricts the unauthorized constructions and subsequently stops its development. (4) The Delhi Municipal Corporation Act, 1957 (as mentioned in 1894) restricts unauthorized constructions and subsequently stops its development (5) The Delhi Municipal Corporation Act, 1957 (as amended in 1894) restricts unauthorized constructions. The powers are vested with the competent authority to demolish, seal and prosecute those responsible. The law also provides for imprisonment and fine.

Section III of the Delhi Lands (Restriction on Transfer) Act, 1972 reads that no person shall purport to transfer for sale, mortgage, gift lease or otherwise any land situated in the capital, which has been acquired by the Central Government under the Land Acquisition Act, 1894 or under any other law providing for acquisition of land for any other purpose. There have been instances when *jhuggies* have been forcefully occupied and resold.

Slums have been multiplying in large number in the metropolitan and other large cities. Due to this phenomenon, large areas of metropolitan and other large cities have been occupied by unauthorized constructions and encroachments. In such a process, the land earmarked in Master Plan for a specific use is swallowed by the emergence of squatter settlements. Thus, the landuse planning of Cities' Master Plans have got distorted. The private developers and colonizers have taken the advantage of unauthorized areas and have promoted construction activities, thereby enhancing the process of real estate activities in the metropolitan and other large cities. The legislation to curb such activities is needed. The slum is defined as constituting the dilapidated buildings, lack of space with high density occupancy and deteriorating basic services like water supply, sewerage and drainage.

The Central Act titled as the Slum Areas (Improvement and Clearance) Act, 1956 (as modified upto July 1st, 1976) is largely applicable to slum areas of certain Union Territories for protection of tenants from eviction.

Surprisingly, 'the Slum Clearance and Improvement Act, 1956 does not concern itself with the legality of occupation. The Act refers to the inadequacy of shelter in terms of its structural quality, hygienic condition and availability of services. It does not concern itself with legality or illegality.'

The Slum Acts of different states are, namely (a) Andhra Pradesh Slum Improvement (Acquisition of Land) Act, 1956 is to safeguard and make provisions in slum areas of basic civic services like sewerage, water supply, road and drainage. In the State of Andhra Pradesh, in the context of slum areas, the Act is particularly concerned with the acquisition of lands for rehabilitation of urban poor. (b) The Madhya Pradesh Slum Improvement (Acquisition of Land) Act, 1956. It provides for improvement of civic services in slum areas and also emphasizes land acquisition schemes. (c) The Assam Slum Areas (Improvement and Clearance) Act, 1959 envisages the adequate sanitary facilities to the slum areas to protect public health and to provide a congenial living environment. (d) The Punjab Slum Areas (Improvement and Clearance) Act, 1961 provides protection to tenants from eviction in the slum areas. (e) The Uttar Pradesh Slum Areas (Improvement and Clearance) Act, 1962 provides the inhabitants of slum areas with a proper planning for rehabilitation of residents and safeguard from eviction of tenants. (f) The Tamil Nadu Slum Areas (Improvement and Clearance) Act, 1971 is concerned with providing hygienic conditions of proper public health, sanitation, water supply and drainage in slum areas. The Act provides a better accommodation for the slum dwellers. Subsequently, the improved living conditions are contemplated through land acquisition for developing and improving slum areas and also redeveloping the slum clearance areas and rehabilitating the inhabitants through proper basic civic services. The legislation is mainly concerned with the improvement and clearance of slums in the State of Tamil Nadu. (g) The Maharashtra Slum Areas (Improvement, Clearance and Redevelopment) Act, 1971 as modified in 1987 concerns with the adequate provisions of amenities in slum areas while envisaging improvement and clearance through rehabilitation programmes and provision of protection from eviction. (h) The West Bengal Slum Areas (Improvement and Clearance Act, 1972. The Gujarat Slum Areas (Improvement, Clearance and Redevelopment) Act, 1973 and the Mysore Slum Areas (Improvement and Clearance) Act, 1973 envisage the developmental civic services by emphasizing greater importance for the improvement and clearance of slum areas.

The major issue in tackling the slum problem arises from the legislation concerning the notified areas with reference to congested lanes, dilapidated houses and unsatisfactory public utility services, like open drainage, sanitation and water supply, etc.

The Central legislation is known as the Slum Areas (Improvement and Clearance) Act, 1956. It is concerned with the improvement and provision of basic civic services. The vital issue is the demolition of dilapidated buildings which are dangerous to the inhabitants.

In the slum areas of walled city of Delhi, namely, Daryaganj and Paharganj the larger area has been occupied for a commercial activity. With the result, the area has become highly congested with chaotic slum like conditions. The Act needs to perceive the implications of restricted commercial activities in the notified slum area. This has been overlooked by the Act.

In 1994, the Government had abandoned the slum clearance approach and the improvement scheme had gathered importance. Greater stress is given to improvement in Tamil Nadu and the slum settlements have been built on the already existing inhabitated area and earmarked for the built up accommodation. Thus, the Tamil Nadu Slum Clearance and Improvement Act has mainly been concerned with slum area improvement built up scheme. The identity card has enabled the inhabitants to seek, in an effective manner, the rehabilitation scheme benefits.

EIUS: Evaluation

The Government had discontinued its Slum Areas Clearance and Improvement Scheme, under which a one room set as alternative accommodation in lieu of the removed dwelling unit was an obligatory phenomenon. Instead, the Government has now decided to improve the environment in the slums without clearing them.

The Environmental Improvement of Urban Slum (EIUS) considers the provision of items, namely, the (i) paved pathways, (ii) street lighting, (iii) public latrines, (iv) water facilities, and (v) sewerage and sanitation facilities.

In the Sixth Plan 150.45 crore had been sanctioned for the EIUS. The Seventh Plan had made provisions for 269.45 crore for EIUS. There is need to assess the provision of public utility services with prescribed standards according to the size of population requirement, has not been undertaken in the context of statewise evaluation in relation to the expenditure incurred in the EIUS scheme.

The statewise reporting has been defective when one out of five items is completed, it is eventually taken for granted that EIUS has achieved the fulfilment of its target. Such an erroneous conclusion is an eyewash. In certain slum and squatter settlements, the electricity poles exist without a street lighting facility.

Surprisingly, some of the states are not following the guidelines of standards prescribed for the provision of services in relation to per capita size of population. Largely, the states are furnishing information for projecting and over-exaggerating the success of EIUS, whereas in reality, the services provided to the slum and squatter population are unsatisfactory from the point of view of the alarming magnitude of Central Government expenditure incurred in the name of urban poor welfare programmes. It seems that the agencies undertaking the EIUS scheme seems to be in a hurry for achieving the targets on paper and are least bothered for the actual results. The responsible state agencies of EIUS scheme are not maintaining the comprehensive list of squatter settlements, so as to compare the trends of failure and achievement. Such has been a piecemeal approach of planning to the habitation of the urban poor.

The EIUS is based on an evaluation of a defective formula of Planning Commission which is presently on the basis of total expenditure divided by the per capita norms which is equal to beneficiaries. This is an erroneous calculation. Without the physical verification with respect to the expenditure, the benefits to the slum dwellers is not feasible. There is an imperative need to check the financial leakages as the urban poor are not receiving the benefits in slum clusters in accordance with the enormous financial outlays.

The population coverage is not an appropriate method for assessing the EIUS scheme beneficiaries, but for the physical achievements of the proposed items. One of the vital factors in the EIUS scheme is the provision of drinking water and maintenance of latrine facilities. Though paved pathways and electricity are vital for the slum inhabitants, the provision of drinking water and latrine facilities have to be accorded a top priority in terms of developmental facilities. The EIUS schemes have not improved the quality of life of inhabitants in a big way, particularly with reference to the metropolitan and other large cities. It has been observed that in the large number of squatter settlements on a statewise basis the public latrines provided have not been maintained properly under the EIUS scheme. However, the proper planning for maintenance of public latrines has not been emphasized as a vital factor of environmental concern for improving the living condition of slum and squatter settlements.

It may be mentioned that in the EIUS scheme, second-hand pumps are provided, yet the provision of water outlet through a proper sanitation system has not been planned. Thus, the water stinks on the unmetalled pathways and causes unhygienic conditions and health hazards. The water borne diseases and the spread of epidemics are well-known in the context of slum squatter settlements of urban India.

A notable example of unsatisfactory implementation of EIUS scheme is of Ahmedabad. In the large squatter settlement clusters in Ahmedabad only few clusters have the independent bathroom and latrine facilities. Dustbin for each house has been provided, yet the collection mechanism has not been satisfactory. The households' garbage dumping creates environmental health hazards. The EIUS scheme in the city of Ahmedabad is a piecemeal affair as a negligible percentage of squatter settlement population has been covered by the services.

Political Basis

In the State of Bihar, the EIUS scheme has not been adopted rationally and in selected cities a large portion of the amount has been allocated on the basis of political influences. As such, the EIUS scheme in Patna has been mismanaged in relation to per capita population. Similar situations have also arisen in the states of Uttar Pradesh, Gujarat, West Bengal, Maharashtra, Rajasthan, etc. In the cities of Mumbai, Calcutta, Baroda and Kanpur too, the worsening situation exists with overcrowding of slum and squatter settlements, without the adequate services like drinking water and latrine facilities.

The *bustees* of Calcutta have grown on the vacant land. There is inadequate water supply and public latrine facilities. In fact, the unhygienic conditions of *bustees* have resulted in environmental health hazards. It seems that the EIUS scheme has not shown any significant achievement, especially in the context of the *bustees* of Calcutta.

The Dharavi slum of Mumbai presents a picture of a high density overcrowding with unhygienic and uncongenial living environment. The city of Mumbai has innumerable squatter settlement clusters spread in haphazard manner. As such, the EIUS scheme in Mumbai has not been able to record a significant achievement.

TABLE 3

Plan-wise Financial Outlays, Expenditure, Physical Targets and Achievements of Environmental Improvement of Urban Slum Scheme (EIUS)

Period	*Financial Outlay*			*Total Outlay (O)* *Total expenditure (E)*	*Physical Target*	*Physical Achievement*
	Under	*Central*	*Total*			
6th Plan	151.19	20.97	172.16	172.16 (O) 186.00 (E)	94.58	93.38
7th Plan	236.06	-	236.06	236.06 (O) 241.98 (E)	76.90	99.80
1990-91	65.29		65.29	65.29 (O) 65.99 (E)	15.40	19.36
1991-92	63.42	-	63.42	63.42 (O)	12.96	16.23
1992-	79.64		79.64	79.64(O) 81.79(E)	11.78	11.72
1993-94	62.84	-	62.84	62.84 (O) 62.84 (E)	13.18	13.01
1994-95	78.47	-	78.47	78.47 (O) 78.47 (E)	14.63	16.66
1995-96	108.33	-	108.33	108.33 (O) 108.33 (E)	15.89	17.41
1996-97	--	-	-	15.71	20.10	
Total	845.24	20.97	866.21	866.21 (O) 866.21 (E)	271.03	307.67

Note: The implementation of the scheme of EIUS has brought about marked improvement in the quality of life of the slum dwellers. The provision of services like community latrines, drinking water, street lights, pavements, baths and drains has led to healthier and satisfactory life.

1. Figure given in columns 2, 3, 4, 5 are in Rs Crores.
2. Figures given in column 5 are yearwise allocated outlays (O) and total expenditure (E).
3. Physical targets/achievements are persons in lakhs.
4. The per capita assistance permissible under the EIUS scheme since 1972 is given below:

1972 (3rd year of 4th Plan) Rs 120
1978 (3rd year of 5th plan) Rs 150
1.4 1984 (last year of 6th Plan) Rs 250
1.4. 1985 (1st year of the 7th Plan) Rs 300
1.4. 1991 (Annual Plan) Rs 525
1.4. 1995 (4th year of the 8th Plan) Rs 800

Source: Training Programme on Tackling Urban Slums Background Material held on 17-21 November, 1999 sponsored by Department of Personnel and Training, Ministry of Personnel, Public Grievances and Pensions organized by Town and Country Planning Organization, Ministry of Urban Development.

The baffling question arises that in spite of the enormous expenditure outlay of EIUS, the quality of life, the level of services in slum settlements have not shown an appropriate progress in a statewise perspective. There is vital need for improving the services in urban slums in a comprehensive manner. The Planning Commission's formula for evaluating EIUS is erroneous as it takes into consideration the total expenditure divided by the per capita norm been equal to beneficiaries. It should be corrected by assessing the investment outlay corresponding to the physical amenities as provided.

The cost of services per capita squatter settlements population was initially estimated at Rs 120 and in the Eight Plan perspective it was Rs 800. There is need for promoting a strict financial accountability in the context of the EIUS scheme in a statewise perspective. The achievement of physical target has to be verified on the basis of spot-based observations in relation to expenditure and number of physical facilities provided. The EIUS scheme has to be directed of planning the utility services in relation to the per capita need of slum and squatter settlement population in a statewise perspective.

The voluntary or compulsory contributions should be promoted from the inhabitants of squatter settlements for mobilizing the financial resources in an effective manner.

The governmental report review had revealed the shortcomings of EIUS scheme with the following observations:

The local bodies do not have sufficient funds and manpower for maintaining the improved slums. Subsequently, the financial funds have not been released in time by the state governments concerned to the executing agencies resulting in delayed implementation of the scheme. Some of the states have not yet identified the slums in all towns and cities by conducting survey and so on.

One of the important aspects of the scheme is the maintenance of the assets created under the scheme in the past. At present, there is no agency in the states entrusted with the job of looking after the maintenance of the assets created in the urban slums. In fact, the responsibility for maintaining these assets should specifically rest with the concerned local bodies.

Surprisingly, there has been tremendous delay in the notification of the slum areas by the concerned State Governments and Union Territories. However, the plans for the execution of the schemes have taken a long time for approval from the concerned State authorities.

The problem hindering the EIUS are because it involves the multifarious developmental authorities. The taps are stolen, the handpumps installed are of inferior quality, and so on. Further, the garbage in the slum pockets is often not immediately removed and thus it leads to the spread of innumerable diseases.

Compendium of Indian Slum Report prepared by the Town and Country Planning Organization, Ministry of Urban Development (Government of India had elaborated the important retarding factors of the EIUS during the early three years. These were, namely (i) absence of long-term strategy of slum improvement in the states; (ii) lack of adequate administrative and technical expertise at state and local levels; (iii) inadequate budgetary resources of the local bodies; (iv) absence of city-wise data on slums and projects; (v) local problems in taking up slum improvement on private slums; (vi) problem of maintaining the improved slums; (vii) problem of coordination among concerned agencies dealing with water supply, electricity, sewerage, etc.; (viii) the slum improvement programme was regarded as a temporary solution and assumed that the beneficiaries would not remain permanently on the side; (ix) lack of efforts made by the state to link improvement schemes with security of tenure and assistance in house construction; and (x) no evidence of slum dwellers involvement in the EIUS programme. The scheme was being implemented mainly as public works programme.

At present, a Centrally sponsored scheme for extending special assistance to states for slum development, the National Slum Development Programme (NSDP) is being operated. This programme for upgradation of urban slums envisages provision of physical amenities, community infrastructure including community primary health care, etc. The scheme also envisages shelter upgradation by construction of new houses (including EWS), as may be required. Not less than 10 per cent of the allocation to states under this assistance is to be utilized for construction and/or upgradation of houses for the urban poor. This scheme recognized the situation as one of 'taking services to the people' and not 'taking the people to where new services can be created'. Ensuring tenancy rights to land through 'pattas' would enable collection of development charges or maintenance charges from the slum dwellers and they will be involved in the development process to keep the environs in a hygienic and sanitary state. It also gives motivation to them to upgrade their existing shelters in course of time.

Interestingly, the voluntary organizations can play a significant role in the slum welfare schemes. Government should allow the participation of industrialists with adequate tax relief through voluntary organizations for promoting, in an effective manner, the provisions of public utility services, mainly water and latrine facilities. As such, the EIUS scheme should be mainly assessed with reference to the actual physical achievements. The manipulation in the functioning of the EIUS scheme has got to be strictly checked. On the whole, a significant progress in the EIUS scheme in collaboration with the public participation, has not been achieved.

According to the National Housing Policy Document, Ministry of Urban Development (Government of India), it has been revealed that to arrest the growth of slums in urban areas, the Central and State governments should take steps to (i) avoid forcible eviction of slum dwellers; (ii) encourage in situ upgradation, slum renovation and progressive housing development with occupancy rights wherever feasible, and to undertake selective relocation with community involvement only for clearance of priority sites in public interest; (iii) expand provision of water supply, sanitation and other basic services in slum and other settlements occupied by the poor; (iv) ensure proper maintenance of amenities through community involvement and decentralized institutional arrangements; (v) integrate the provision of physical amenities with basic services, including material and child welfare services and health care structured on community participation and involvement of voluntary agencies and management by local bodies; (vi) promote incremental construction and upgradation by poorer households through access to land and services, through technical support, outlets for low-cost technology and materials, opportunities for skill upgradation and access to housing finance on flexible terms; and provide night shelters and sanitary facilities to the footpath dwellers and the homeless.

The Task Force of the Planning Commission, 1983 on Housing and Urban Development, in its report titled 'Shelter for Urban Poor and Slum Improvement', had rightly observed the following shortcomings of the EIUS, namely: (a) no systematic evaluation of the scheme has been done to determine the extent to which it has achieved its basic goals; (b) the scheme does not provide for flexibility in determining the priorities for amenities needed or variation in expenditure due to varying locational attributes or nature of slums; (c) the system of monitoring the progress needs to be improved; (d) the method of determining the physical achievement or the number of beneficiaries is defective and leads to erroneous assessment of import or coverage of the scheme; (e) the per capita ceiling cost needs to be revised upwards in a substantial manner; (f) the scheme does not provide security of tenure to the beneficiaries and, therefore, it does not encourage self help in improving their environmental conditions. Environmental improvement programmes are, therefore, regarded as temporary solutions; (g) most of the projects under the scheme are poor in the absence of proper survey and socio-economic data concerning the slum dwellers to be covered; (h) there is no evidence of involvement of the target group in the scheme which is mainly being implemented as a public works programme; (i) there is lack of adequate administrative arrangements at the state local level. Frequently, there are problems of coordination with the concerned agencies, and so on; like water supply, electricity; and (j) even though it is the responsibility of the government to provide environmental services, they do not have financial participation in the scheme.

While discussing slums and squatter upgrading programmes and resettlement, attention is invariably drawn to the four large metropolitan cities of Delhi, Calcutta, Mumbai and Chennai because infrastructure, services and facilities are largely inadequate for catering to these agglomerations, and in the process the urban poor are the worst affected.

In Calcutta agglomeration, thrust has been on increasing the scope of the core area sanitation programmes in and around all identified pockets. In Mumbai the programmes are likewise oriented and supplemented with repairs to the structures. In Chennai, an attempt is being made towards integrated slum upgrading and community development and also towards comprehensive site and services, as against the serviced open plot concept elsewhere.

In Hyderabad, the Community Development Programmes are the main thrust of slum upgradation, and in Ahmedabad incentives are oriented towards encouraging in situ redevelopment through tenements and sanitizing squatter settlements. However, the city of Kanpur, with its thin division between core area of slums and non-slums, has concerned itself with upgrading as many pockets as possible. Bangalore, on the other hand, with a smaller proportion of slums than other metropolitan areas is a late starter in efforts on behalf of the urban poor, and is therefore engaged at present in only core area sanitation. Pune, with the extensive slum pockets on private land has embarked on partial upgrading in such areas and effective improvement programmes in slums on public land.

In other smaller cities, environmental improvement is being attempted to the extent that limited resources allow, but comprehensive programmes for this target group has not yet been apparent. The provision of shelters and related infrastructure in urban India continue being on Housing and Urban Development Corporation (HUDCO) financial pattern which are all above the capacity of the marginal circuit. However, such programme at best would probably reduce the pricing out of the lower income groups, but primarily they operate for the benefit of those in the upper urban circuit.

Nevertheless, the current efforts indicate a greater concern for the urban poor than ever before, not only at the level of the Central and state governments, but also at the level of the local authorities. Thus, though the marginal circuit (comprising the population below the poverty line) in the urban areas has not yet been recognized as a separate entity in census data, concerted efforts on their behalf are now being attempted.

The Central Slum Area (Improvement and Clearance) Act, 1956 offered the first positive response to the problems of slums and squatters in the country. This has lead to the slum clearance scheme to be replaced by the environmental improvement programme. Since 1970, various states have enacted separate legislations to have areas declared as slums for the purposes of clearance and upgrading through state level Slum Boards to supplement the local government action.

Until recently, the funds allocated under the slum clearance and environmental schemes were being diverted to other state level priority sectors. This trend has been stopped and in most cases the limited Central allocations are being substantially supplemented by state governments and local bodies, so as to maximize the population coverage. In fact it has been realized that it is politically expedient to recognize the urban poor as a main target group in cities and towns, and accordingly cater to their needs and welfare through integrated programmes. It is also being noticed that where initially the main metropolitan areas were beneficiaries of central and state level funds, the tendency now is to ensure that such programmes are spread over as many corporations and municipal areas as possible, even if these result in token allocations to the smaller municipal areas. Such a coverage helps in mobilizing opinion, resources and self-help in the settlements.

There has also been a shift in strategy from slum clearance and tenement building to that of slum and squatter upgrading (family in core areas) and serviced open plot development with prospects of comprehensive sites and services, which has emerged as planning proposal. Most important of all, recognition is being given to the fact that in dealing with these target groups the sole consideration until recently, is being supplemented by socio-economic inputs designed to make the built-environment suitable to homogeneous communities. Surveys indicate that the urban poor are responding to these efforts, especially as such efforts gave hope of leading to safe tenures, the most important motivating force for the poor to better their environment. It has resulted in self-help, community participation and settled urban neighbourhoods.

Cognizance is also being given to the role of voluntary agencies in helping the urban poor and to the efforts at better dialogue between official and voluntary agencies. This conforms to the entire urban community and it has generally been accepted that the urban poor are part of a complex of socio-economic and political processes that have led to rapid urbanization and development. The malaise is that despite best efforts the resources necessary for comprehensive solutions are never enough and with rapid growth of urbanization the number of persons below the poverty line continually increases.

Different states are dealing with the Slum Improvement and Clearance legislation prevailing in the country. The Task Forced on Housing and Urban Development, Government of India, had recommended a full scale review of legislation related to slums and housing developments within the country and specifically to address itself to strengthen the legislation for facilitating improvement programmes in squatter settlements, upgradation of slums in built-up areas, speedier acquisition of private lands under slums, grants of tenure to residents of improved slums. Realizing the importance of secured tenureship for house improvement as well as to encourage household savings, the Task Force in its report had emphasized the importance of security of tensure for shelter for the poor.

Regional Perspective

The haphazard growth of urban slum and squatter settlements has been the outcome of aggravating rural unemployment situation. Due to the wide income gap, huge rural migration is directed towards the metropolitan and large cities. The squatter settlement dwellers are the service persönnels in the occupational categories of washermen, cobblers, peon, conductors, drivers, factory workers, *ayahs*, vegetable sellers, hawkers, domestic servants, and so on.

The rural migrants have played a significant role in the urban economy. However, the process of decentralization of urban economic activities and integrated development of small and medium towns should be emphasized. Therefore, the balanced regional development has to be recognized by ensuirng the rural and urban continuum of spatial and economic development. There should be an emphasis on counter-magnets equivalent of metropolitan cities for attracting migrants and checking them at the source of origin. Then only the migrants, flow into the urban settlements will be minimized and thus the number of squatter settlements would be checked to a considerable extent.

REFERENCES

1. Bhargave, Gopal: Slum and Squatter Settlements of Urban India, Real Estate, June, 1989.
2. ____________Urban Slums : Planning and Policy Perspective, The *Financial Express,* January 2, 1992.
3. __________ Yet Another Problem, *The Hindustan Times, Sunday Magazine*, December 26, 1993.
4. ____________ Delhi's Squatter Settlements, *Evening News, The Hindustan Times*, August 17, 1993.
5. _________ Rehabilitation Programme should be well Planned, Real Estate, June, 1989.
6. Bhargava, G., and Batra, B.K: Make Space for Immigrants in Plans, The Economic Times, May 3, 1992.
7. Bhattacharya, K.P.: Housing in India—Observations on the Government Intervention Policies, Edited by Gil Shidlo, Published by Routledge, London, 1990.
8. Birdi, H.D.: Slum Law and Urbanization, Vidhi Publishing, New Delhi, 1995.
9. Editorial. Move on Slums, Civic Affairs, Volume 32, No. 7, February, 1985.
10. Joshi, Prabha: Slums Improvement in Greater Bombay, seminar papers, Centre of Urban Studies, Indian Institute of Public Administration, New Delhi, Madras, 1979.
11. Mehta, Meera: Housing in Delhi Squatter Settlements Increase Development Alternatives, *Newsletter*, Volume 4, Number 4, May, 1994.
12. Meshram, D.S. and Bansal R.P.: Town and Country Planning Organization, Legislation, Some Basic Issues, *Journal of the Institute of Town Planners, India*, Volume 11, Number 4, (154) June, 1993.
13. Nangia, Sudesh: Slums of Urban India: Planning and Policy Actions, The Civic Affairs, December, 1987.
14. Panicker, Rita: The Urban Poor Can Stand on Their Own, Social Welfare, Volume XXIX, Number 3, June, 1982.
15. Riberio, E.F.N.: Poor on Review of the Provision of Infrastructure in Slum and Squatter Settlements in Urban India.
16. ____________ Planning for the Urban Poor : Basic Needs and Priorities, Social Action, Volume 32, April-June, 1992.

17. Suresh, V.: Strategies and Solutions for Squatter Settlements, Shelter, Volume 1, No. 3, July-September, 1998.

18. Shety, Madhu: Bombay Slum Under World Remains a Challenge, *Patriot*, 15th January, 1985.

19. *The Economic Times* (November 14, 1993), The Challenge on Urban Slums.

20. Varashar, Pradeep, Slums in Delhi, *Delhi Vikas Varta*, Volume 5, No. 2, April-June, 1992.

CHAPTER 4

URBAN ENVIRONMENTAL CHALLENGES ACTION PLAN

Awareness and consciousness is the need of the hour concerning the environmental pollution with reference to the Indian urban settlements. The large urban centres like Ahmedabad, Bangalore, Calcutta, Chennai, Delhi, Mumbai, Pune, Kanpur, Lucknow, Jaipur and Hyderabad, so on, have been victimized by the acute threat of environmental pollution of air, water, noise, garbage, slum and squatter settlements. The greatest source of pollution is man and he has plundered the forest, swallowed the agricultural and open land for excessive urbanization, which has eventually become responsible for an uncongenial environment. With the haphazard growth of urbanization there has risen the excessive growth of industries and also the rising motor vehicle emission. This has been largely concentrated in the metropolitan and other large cities. As such, the problem of pollution is challenging and alarming in urban areas as spill over of population, economic and industrial activities have not been undertaken in a balanced regional perspective.

The cause of attraction of migrants to the metropolitan cities is mainly due to the fact that they are able to provide innumerable skilled and unskilled job opportunities in the formal and informal sectors.

Consequently, with alarming population growth concentration in few big urban centres, the environmental problems of industrialization, traffic and transportation bottlenecks, slum and squatter settlements and acute shortage of housing, medical and educational facilities has arisen. The emerging trend of motor vehicle pollution has threatened the health of urban inhabitants. Such a trend will present a challenging task, particularly in the 21st century and will cause an environmental disaster in the urban areas.

Vehicular Pollution

One of the serious tasks of city planning has been to check motor vehicle emission. The road capacity of urban areas has been unsatisfactory and has caused congestion which has been responsible for the rising trend of accidents.

In the last decades, the urban population in India has nearly doubled from 109.5 million in 1971 to 217.0 million in 1991 and it is expected to reach 325 million by 2001. With the increasing pace of urbanization along with a conglomeration of industries and commercial activities in the urban areas, the transport demand has also risen in an alarming proportion. However, due to an inadequate public transport system, the use of personal vehicles has grown in a big way. About one-fifth of the vehicular population in India is concentrated in the major metropolitan cities.

The major pollutants emitted by vehicles are carbon monoxide (CO), hydrocarbons (HC), oxides of nitrogen (NO) and particulate matter (PM). Vehicles using petroleum-based fuel also emit polynuclear hydrocarbons and aldehydes in traces. A varying amount of sulphur dioxide SO_2 is also emitted depending upon the sulphur content in the fuel. In addition, the exhaust gases from petrol-driven vehicles contain lead compounds because of the addition of tetraethyl lead in motor spirit. The exhaust pipe is the major source of air pollution from the automobiles which accounts for 65-70 per cent of pollution, while about 20 per cent pollution occur through blow-up the crankcase breather and the remaining through evaporative emissions from the fuel tank breather, carburettor and spillage losses. The heavy duty diesel-powered vehicles contribute more of NO and PM emissions while light-duty gasoline-powered vehicles and motor cycles are the major sources of CO and HC emissions.

It is revealed that the metropolitan city, Delhi has contributed over 7,00,000 tonnes of CO while approximately 5,00,000 tonnes of CO has been contributed by Mumbai. Motor vehicles in India contribute about 0.52 per cent of the world road transport related CO_2 emissions. In India, motor vehicles have contributed about 10 per cent of total fossil fuel related CO_2 emission as compared to the world average of 15 per cent. A study by the Central Pollution Control Board (CPCB) in Delhi, on the ambient noise levels in the metropolitan cities, has indicated that the noise levels exceed the standard and that the vehicles are the main source of noise pollution.

In such a scenario it is necessary to focus attention on pollutants causing local and regional health disorders as well as global impacts. A study by the Central Road Research Institute (CRRI), on the effect of environmental pollution due to road traffic on the health of Delhi traffic policemen, showed the excessive intake of carbon dioxide in their breath;

a majority of them complained of eye irritation, respiratory problems, discomfort, annoyance and other problems due to vehicular and noise pollution.

HOW THE POISONS IN THE AIR AFFECT YOU

Lead OO

A toxic metal that is present in normal petrol and in the air as fine particles can affect the central nervous system, cause renal damage and hypertension. Children are three times more at risk than adults.

Suspended Particular Matter OOO

Particles of dust and carbon, coated with toxic gases, all emanating from factory emissions and vehicle exhaust. They coat the lungs cause respiratory infections, persistent cough and throat irritation. Aggravate asthma.

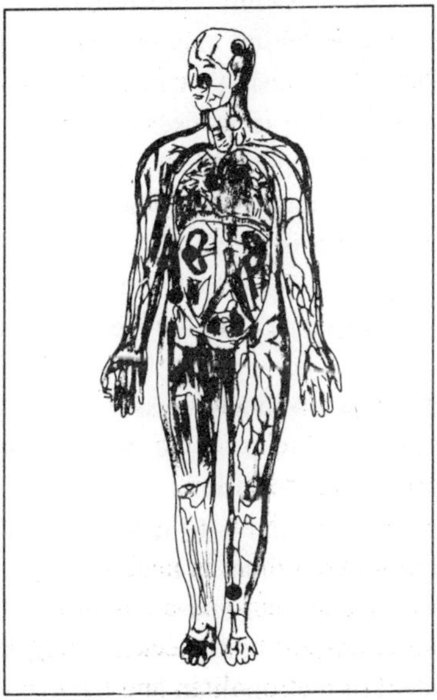

Carbon Monoxide O

Colourless and odourless, it comes from petrol vehicles mostly two and three wheelers. Reduces the ability of blood to carry oxygen. Exacerbates heart disorders.

Areas Affected

- O Lungs
- O Respiratory Tract
- O Nose/Eyes
- O Brain
- O Kidney
- O Entire body

Polycyclicoo Aromatic Hydrocarbons (PAHS) OO

Unburnt fuel from diesel engines. Cause drowsiness, eye-irritation, cough and are suspected to be cancer-causing. There is no such thing as a safety level for PAHS.

Sulphur Dioxide O

Colourless gas that is a part of diesel exhaust and factory emissions. Affects upper respiratory tract, causes bronchial problems, nose blockage and a hacking cough.

Benzene OO

Cannot be seen. It's a part of unleaded petrol and is emitted from catalytic converters. A known carcinogen, it has been linked to lung cancer and leukaemia and is said to damage the central nervous system. No safe limit there just should is not be any benezene around.

Oxides of Nitrogen O

Formed duting fuel combustion in motor vehicles and power stations. Convert to nitrogen dioxide, which leads to bronchial infections, colds, headaches and eye irritation. A recent spurt in fibrosis cases in Mumbai has been traced to these pollutants.

Source: Samar, Halarnkar and Subhadra Menon 'Gasping for Life' *India Today*, December 15, 1996.

In the city of Delhi, the instance bronchitis is 12 per cent higher than all India average. Due to the alarming motor vehicle emission, Delhi inhabitants are confronted with irritation of eyes, throat, insomnia, nervous breakdown and suffocation breathlessness. The respiratory diseases have spread in an alarming proportion in the Indian urban settlements. Further more, the effects of motor vehicles emission have led to abdominal cramps and loss of appetite. In future, due to the rising number of motor vehicles the health hazards of urban inhabitants will threaten their survival.

With the enormous pollutants emission, Delhi has become the fourth largest polluted city of the world. In Delhi, 50 per cent of pollution emitted by the motor vehicles. Thus, the inhabitants of Delhi are breathing the dangerous chemicals which are poisonous and there is rising trend of diseases of like lung cancer, asthma, tuberculosis, bronchitis and other respiratory ailments. The alarming magnitude of air pollutants in Delhi is also damaging kidney and causing mental disorder among the children. The national capital Delhi too is witnessing the lethal pollutants in an alarming proportion. It is estimated that Delhi's atmospheric pollution level is going to rise nine times higher than the prescribed limits.

In Delhi, wearing of gas mask will become a vital necessity in near future due to the enormous motor vehicle emission. It seems the gas mask will become compulsory in nearly all the metropolitan cities by the 21st century.

Surprisingly, in India too much stress has been given to the large-scale production of motor vehicles. In the Western countries, importance has been given to public transportation and the effort is to go back to the cycle culture. If Indian cities have to get out of the serious threat of environmental pollution, then there is need to check the rising trend of vehicles, movement. A one-man-and-a-car in an alarming number is causing the traffic and transport bottlenecks, pollution threats and health hazard is in the context of metropolitan and large cities. However, there is need for stressing the importance of an efficient public transport network for reducing the motor vehicle emissions.

The emphasis has to be given the battery to run motor vehicles by the government for checking the high atmospheric pollution level in the metropolitan cities. The efforts of innovation, research and development in this direction has to be recognized. The experiment to run the solar battery cars should be given top priority, so as to create conditions for reducing the motor vehicles emission.

Specific attention should be given to the lead free petrol. The control and regulation of vehicle pollution in the metropolitan cities must assume a vital policy issue, keeping in view the health aspects of the urban inhabitants.

Health Hazards of Automobiles Emission

Automotive emissions may be a risk factor for the development of atherosclerosis and cononary heart disease. Carbon monoxide is the most likely substance in automobile emissions to cause atherogenesis (thickening of blood vessels).

Eye irritation is the most frequent complaint evoked by emission exposure. Since the neurobehavioural toxicity of many compounds present in automative emission is unknown, these should be studied systematically.

Carcinogens are the compounds capable of producing cancer. Petrol is a complex mixture of hydrocarbons and additives. Benzene is the source of most concern because of its proved carcinogenicity in human beings. Diesel engine exhausts can cause chromosomal (genetic material) damage.

The lead content in petrol may cause behavioural changes in children affecting their capability for finer movements of hands and even lead to brain damage, high blood pressure and kidney failure.

The method of bringing vehicular pollution under control may be subdivided into four categories namely: (1) The control of control devices or techniques in vehicles; administrative procedure to ensure pollution reduction; (2) environmental and health surveillance programme to evaluate the effectiveness of emission regulation; and application of urban planning to ensure the widest possible disperson of pollution emitted by cars.

To keep pace with the increasing pollution by vehicles, adequate attention should be given to the administrative procedures and the provision of funds to carry out control programmes. There is need for strengthening the environmental health services, particularly in respect of laboratory facilities, field technical services and planning, educational and administrative aspects of the problem.

In the Western countries there are strict and prescribed detailed emission standards for vehicles and are effectively enforced. These standards are being progressively regulated.

Periodical checks of all motor vehicles indicate the pollution control strategy is followed in a regulated manner. Petrol in the Western countries is lead free and the engines are devised accordingly. In India, except for a few vehicles we do not even have an officially accepted integrated vehicle emission control strategy. This is one of the serious loopholes in the Indian environmental policy.

The bigger cities in India are particularly susceptible to large-scale vehicular pollution. Nearly 50 per cent of all the cars in our country are reused in metropolitan cities like Mumbai, Calcutta, Delhi, Chennai and Bangalore. They also account for 20 per cent of two and three wheeler vehicles and 15 per cent of diesel vehicles.

It has been estimated that at present petrol vehicles contribute about 80 per cent of carbon monoxide and diesel vehicles contribute about 90 per cent of oxides of nitrogen in the major Indian metropolitan cities. Two and three wheelers are the principal source of hydrocarbon emission, accounting in Delhi and Bangalore for upto 65 per cent of the total vehicular pollution.

Specific steps are required by the Government to promote lead-free petrol. Stress should be laid on manufacture of motor vehicles with engines which can absorb the lead-free petrol. A strict regulation through legislation should be followed for periodical emission check of all motor vehicles.

Control Strategies

For prevention and control of vehicular pollution, it is necessary to have multi-pronged approach. This should, inter-alia be addressed to the following tasks: (1) Upgradation of fuel quality and use of cleaner fuel. (2) Reduction of lead content in motor-spirit. (3) Enforcement of emission standards for vehicles on the road and at the manufacturing stage. (4) Public transport facilities. (5) Improvement of roads and traffic systems. (6) Zoning of areas for regulation of traffic movement. (7) Restriction on indiscriminate growth of urban centres, industrial and commercial activities.

The pollution load from vehicular exhaust depends on the characteristics of fuel and efficiency of combustion. The main pollutants from gasoline include lead, carbon monoxide, hydrocarbon and sulphur dioxide, the quantum of which varies with the quality of fuel. A high aromatic content results in increased emissions of hydrocarbons while a high sulphur content increases the sulphur dioxide emission. Similarly, the exhaust from diesel driven vehicles carries a significant amount of unburnt hydrocarbons, oxides of nitrogen, carbon monoxide and sulphur dioxide. To meet the growing demand for diesel, the technique of increasing the boiling range for extraction of heavier fractions is often used. It results in an increase of sulphur, asphaltic content and fuel which in turn causes vehicular exhaust containing significant amount of particulates, smoke and sulphur dioxide. On the other hand, through proper refining it is possible to have fuel with a lower sulphur content.

Sulphur content in various types of fuels used in India are as follows:

Fuel	*Sulphur content (per cent)*
Kerosene	0.25
Fuel oil	3.5-4.5
Gasoline	0.25
Diesel-HSD	1.0
Diesel-LDO	1.8

The quality of fuel used in India is one of the worsts in the world. It is, therefore, essential to upgrade the quality of fuel through reduction of sulphur, tetraethyl lead and aromatics and an increase in the cetane number. Hydrosulphurization units for reduction of the sulphur content and catalytic reformer units for lead free petrol are required to be installed in the refineries. An increase in the cetane number by 3 to 5 units will result in fuel economy and improvement in vehicular exhaust quality. This is possible through reduction of aromatics in the refining process. Lowering of aromatics will also help in reducing emission of volatile organic compounds (VOC) during combustion

Keeping these considerations in view, the Central Pollution Control Board (CPCB) has recommended the following specifications for diesel and petrol.

Diesel	0.5%
Sulphur	
Cetane Number	45
Petrol	0.15gm/1
TEL	
Sulphur	0.15%
Aromatics	25% by volume (maximum)
Benzene	11% by volume (maximum)

Due to techno-economic reasons, the refineries are not in a position to introduce modifications in the process technology and install catalytic reformer units as needed for production of lead free petrol. Hence, it has been proposed that the refineries should do so in a phased manner so as to reduce the lead-content to 0.15 g/litre by 1995 and subsequent phasing out of lead to 0.03 g/litre by 1997. It is also proposed that till such time the refineries, which are producing petrol with a high lead content, comply with the desired specifications, it should be ensured that metropolitan cities with high density of vehicular traffic are provided with petrol with a relatively low content of lead. To reduce the consumption of leaded petrol, it is proposed that the transport authorities encourage the use of compressed natural gas (CNG).

For vehicles on road and for new vehicles, emission standards have been prescribed. As yet, a cost-effective design for a catalytic converter or such other control devices which could be used for leaded petrol is not commercially available. It is still in the research and development stage. However, with requisite maintenance which includes carburettor adjustment for regulating the air-fuel mixture, it is possible to comply with the standards. With this in view, a procedure has been established for periodic testing of emissions and imposition of penalties for non-compliance of standards. Public awareness campaigns have also been launched for encouraging proper driving habits and vehicle maintenance to meet the standards.

Various other measures that are required for containing vehicular pollution control include the following: (1) proper location of inter-state bus terminals and freight terminals to avoid the use of urban roads by such traffic; (2) measures to make road carriageways available only for moving traffic through restrictions on encroachment of roads and footpaths, parking on carriageways and streamlining of traffic signal systems; (3) priority to energy conservation in transportation network.

The pollution problems posed by vehicular traffic in urban areas have already reached alarming proportions. In order to prevent further deterioration, it is necessary to take an integrated approach. Apart from conventional curative measures, we may have to find innovative ways for urban transport which should be economic, efficient and environmentally acceptable. For a long-term solution; we also need to look at policy measures for regulating the haphazard growth of 'urban areas'.

Some of the easier solutions are pooling the cars compulsorily, not using your vehicle for one day a week, proper maintenance and tuning to check excessive emission and strict enforcement of fine and punishment on those whose vehicles emit pollution.

Industrial Pollution

The Air Pollution Act abides to the regulations of industrial discharges, yet the air pollution has become a menace in metropolitan cities. With the haphazard growth of polluted industries, surprisingly the legislation is silent on controlling the menace of air pollution since the polluters have not been taken to task. There is need to have a complete information of pollutants assessment at sources in the urban settlements.

The poisonous industrial plants should not be located in the habitat urban areas, so as to avoid the Bhopal gas type of tragedy. It is emphatically pointed out that in the Bhopal gas tragedy leakage of several tonnes of methyl-isocyanate from the Union Carbide has gained for itself a notorious distinction of being the worst industrial disaster in the human history. Infact, many of the survivors who had been seriously affected by the disaster are still suffering from a variety of physical and psychosomatic disorders.

Presently, the concerned urban development authorities should not sanction the permission of obnoxious and explosive type of industries in populated urban habitats. Thus, there is need for completely banning the industries which are threat to the human survival in urban areas.

It is realized that by the decentralization of economic and commercial activities in small and medium town settlements, the traffic and transportation movement can be diversified. This would ease the environmental pollution from the metropolitan cities in a big way.

Noise Pollution

One of the challenging threats of urban environment is the noise pollution. In the Indian metropolitan cities like Ahmedabad, Mumbai, Calcutta, Delhi, Chennai, Kanpur, Pune, so on, noise pollution decibel level has gone beyond the specified standard limit and is responsible for rising incidence of deafness among the inhabitants. According to the findings of the Institute of Road Traffic Education (IRTE), Delhi is the noisiest city in India with 83 decibels (against the accepted normal level of 50 decibles at the maximum) during the day and 77 decibels at night. Significantly, Calcutta has corresponding figures of 82 and 75 decibels respectively for day and night.

Within residential areas of Delhi, industries are operating day and night and they cause serious noise pollution threat to the inhabitants. The residents of Delhi have complained to the municipal corporation about the industries noise nuisance in the residential areas, yet no action has been taken. The municipal corporation and municipalities in urban settlements should ban the functioning of industries in the residential areas which has become a great source of noise pollution.

Indiscriminate use of horn by the vehicles and widespread use of loudspeakers in the Indian social and religious ceremonies have caused health hazards to the urban inhabitants. It may cause deafness, nervous breakdown, mental disorder, heart troubles and high blood pressure, headaches, dizziness, inefficiency and insomnia.

In the Western countries, the noise level is specifically controlled in selected zones like hospitals and educational institutions, whereas such a regulation is not strictly abided to in our country. As such, in the developed countries like the United States of America, the United Kingdom and Canada etc., there is strict enforcement of noise pollution legislations which regulate the noise menace in the urban settlements.

At present, in India there is no comprehensive noise pollution act. To control noise pollution through law, certain scattered references in various states including the Indian Penal Code, 1980, Motor Vehicles Act, 1939, Aircraft Act, 1944, Railway Act, 1890 and Factories Act, 1948 etc., are available. However, the provisions of these Acts are sketchy and insufficient for checking the menace of sound pollution.

In the context of Indian society, the use of loudspeakers has become a nuisance and no suitable action has been devised for checking the noise pollution by the concerned authority. There is need to promote a suitable legislation to not allow the use of loudspeakers for religious and social functions in public places. The loudspeakers may be used for Jagratta (religious and social functions) in the community halls which exist in nearly all the localities of urban areas.

Police and the civic authorities should try to control the noise menace by checking late night use of loudspeakers at religious and social functions. However, for such a situation strict enforcement through municipal laws is needed for checking the menace of noise pollution in the urban areas. The public awareness through the mass media should be emphasized in metropolitan and other large cities.

Water Pollution: Implications

Indian river, sea and coastal areas have become highly polluted due to the discharge of industrial wastes, particularly lead, mercury, sewage and half burnt dead bodies into these water bodies. As such, the holy Ganga, Yamuna (Delhi) and Gomti (Lucknow) have become highly polluted. Surprisingly, the river 'Yamuna is the most polluted river in the country and domestic sewage has largely contributed to this. Experts have estimated that about 90 per cent of the pollution is caused by domestic sewage and the rest by industrial effluents'. In Delhi alone about 1,400 million litres of sewage waste is dumped into the Yamuna everyday rendering it unfit for use, except for irrigation.

The National Commission on Urbanization in its final report pointed out that by the year 2001, the city of Delhi will generate about 4,000 million litres of sewage a day out of a total water supply of about 5,000 million litres a day.

As per *The Hindu* survey 1992, on environment in the city of Chennai out of a population of 3.8 million, nearly a million do not have sanitary facilities. This includes not only slum dwellers and squatters who have not been covered by any sewerage scheme but also many of those living in pucca buildings. Apart from this, only 85 per cent of the population is served by full fledged sewers. Most of the sewers are too old for coping up with the alarming pressure. As a result they get clogged almost daily leading to flooding of the streets.

The inadequacy of the system and poor maintenance of treatment plants and lack of electricity supply, constantly plague the project which aimed for constructing 262 schemes to clean up the river. Meanwhile, 120 industries along its bank discharge their effluents unhindered.

Rivers throughout the country are polluted with toxic effluents. In a paper 'Impact of Urban Environmental Pollution on Human Health' by K.A. Reddy and K. Kalpalatha points out that 'the Kalu river which flows through Mumbai industrial suburbs of Amarnath and Ulhasnagar receives effluents from over 150 industrial units. The toxic wastes include heavy metals, chlorides, dyes and organic acids. There are dangerously high levels of mercury and lead in the water near the village of Ambivali and the villages are slowly being poisoned as the heavy metals enter the food chain through the cattle browing on river bank vegetation.'

The fishes in Indian rivers and seas have become poisonous due to the intake of industrial waste of lead, mercury and chemicals. The fish eaters too have became victims of stomach disorders and skin ailments. The worst industrial polluters are paper mill's pulp straw board units, leather tanneries, sugar mills, petroleum refineries, fertilizer plants and textile mills. The 'effluents containing compounds of mercury, copper, iron ore, nitrogen, coal, bauxite, mica and other chemicals are regularly discharged into rivers by the industrial units situated in the vicinity of these rivers.' The water borne diseases that spread in metropolitan and other large cities are mainly cholera, diarrhoea, dysentery, jaundice, typhoid, and so on.

The Water Pollution Prevention and Control Act, 1974 has not enforced a strict action against those industries which discharge their poisonous industrial wastes like lead and mercury into rivers and seas. At present, the penalty imposed for industries which discharge their wastes into rivers and seas by the municipal corporations and municipalities is a meagre amount. Therefore, there are large scale offenders. The urban local bodies through proper legislation should strictly administer the industrial waste treatment before it is discharged. However, efforts have to be made for providing an adequate tax relief to industrialists for the installation of industrial effluent treatment plants, as their closure would become a serious detrimental factor for the national economy.

It is worthwhile to point out that 'barely 7 per cent of the 3000 odd towns and cities in the country treat their domestic sewage. The rest just dump them either into the river or directly into the sea. Industries too are major culprits. Out of the 132 industrial plants that pump water into the Ganga, hardly 12 have waste treatment plants'. In the Western countries, the sewage is not dumped in river or sea but is treated in the plant processing system for the manufacture of manure.

It is realized that enormous financial amount will be required for treating sewage in a statewise perspective. However, the municipal corporation and municipalities are confronted with a serious challenge of treating the sewage. Efforts should be made by them for installing sewage treatment plants.

Garbage Pollution

One of the serious challenges in urban areas is that the landfills are getting exhausted and in the 21st century this problem will become a serious health hazard.

Garbage pollution has become problematic in urban settlements. Metropolitan and other large cities have recorded an enormous volume of garbage which has become unmanageable. In small towns, garbage is dumped in the lanes and byelanes and stinks for days together as the municipal authority is not only slow but ineffective. There is need for exploring electricity from garbage. Garbage is a vital potential source for generating electricity and it should be explored in its optimality through the application of an appropriate technological power generating plant. However, efforts should be made for converting the urban garbage into fertilizer through a proper treatment process. It is emphatically pointed out that 'instead of the traditional pit compositing, experiment is being carried out in Mumbai where the garbage heap will be left alone after spray composition which can then be sold as organic fertilizer'.

In the Indian urban settlements, the total output of refuse is transported to disposal site. The disposal system is mainly landfill. The problems of solid waste disposal get further compounded by the inadequate transport system, lack of vehicle maintenance support and inhospitable traffic conditions. Thus, one of the serious challenges before the municipal corporation and municipalities has been the solid waste management through the mechanically operated trucks and also to ensure the organizational functions of the sewage treatment every day. Therefore the collection and disposal also contribute to the poor sanitary conditions in the city.

According to an estimation it is learnt that in Delhi 2,400 tonnes of solid waste is generated daily. Most of it is dumped in landfill sites which are developed along the river bank or in low lying areas. Despite technological advances, the city authorities are worried about solid waste disposal as there are not enough landfill sites for dumping it. Over 90 per cent of the city's solid waste is being dumped in landfills at present.

It has been reported that the solid waste is not cleared completely and it stinks in the metropolitan cities. Also it is dumped in the agricultural fields of rural settlements and thereby has resulted into a serious problem of environmental degradation.

In urban areas the problem of sanitation has become an uphill task for the urban development authorities.

In a paper, 'Population and Environment Scenario of the 21st Century' Dilip K Biswas has pointed out that there is lack of potable drinking water which continues to be a serious problem for a large portion of population. It is estimated that only one-third of the urban population is provided with sanitation facilities. Even in metropolitan centres like

Mumbai, Calcutta and Chennai all the people do not have an access to adequate drinking water supply and sanitation facilities. Thus in the 21st century the municipalities will have to be managed effectively for the provision of drinking water, treatment of sewage and industrial waste. If this is not done then water of the rivers will be highly polluted and will lead to a serious threat to urban inhabitants, survival due to acute outburst of water borne diseases.

The Ganga river along the vast stretches of 600 kilometres has continued to remain highly polluted as the Action Plan for cleaning it runs into obstacles. 'The plan identified 27 cities like Haridwar, Kannauj, Kanpur, Allahabad, Varanasi and Patna that dump million of tons of untreated sewage into the river. Apart from making the river water unfit for drinking, it also resulted into the death of plenty of acquatic life. Consequently, in the squatter settlements the human excreta is one of the serious health hazards, an epidemic threat in the metropolitan cities. Poverty has been the greatest challenge of environmental degradation in the urban settlements.

The Delhi Municipal Act of 1957 specifies that 'those found defecating or easing themselves in public places could be penalised. As per Section 397 of the Delhi Municipal Corporation (DMC) Act has imposed a fine of Rs 50 for the offenders. And Section 398 of the DMC Act empowers the Municipal Commissioner to impose a fine of Rs 500, with an additional fine of Rs 25 per day, if the misuse and nuisance persisted'. These sets of laws prohibiting and penalising such acts, may threaten the very existence of a substantial poor people in the national capital Delhi. There are more than 1,080 slum clusters all over the city of Delhi. The largest concentrations are in east, north-east and outer Delhi. More than 22 lakh people are living in the *jhuggies* and slum clusters and most of them use the open public land as lavatories due to absence of public lavatories. The defecation offence under the Act is unrealistic and inhuman.

The municipal corporation of urban settlements should try to ensure an appropriate drinking water and maintenance of latrinc facilities by providing a congenial environment for the inhabitants of slum and squatter settlements. It is emphatically spelt out that due to the alarming growth of slum and squatter settlements in the metropolitan and other large cities, the unhygienic conditions should be tackled effectively by the municipal corporation.

Open Space Dilemma

One of the serious challenging problems in Delhi has been concentrated developments of tall buildings in the centralized area of Connaught Place. With result, the area has witnessed traffic and transport bottlenecks, acute parking space shortage and dire safety hazards.

It is sad that the open spaces and agricultural fields are disappearing from the Indian metropolitan and other large cities. However, due to excessive urbanization and housing, the agricultural land and open areas have been swallowed in an alarming proportion. As a result the open spaces would gradually disappear by the 21st century. The municipal laws should preserve the open spaces, playfields, parks and agricultural fields of metropolitan and other large cities.

Environmental Cases of Urban Areas

The notable environmental cases are the 'Ratlam Case (AIR: 1980: SC 1622), in which the judge invoked the Directive Principles to direct the Ratlam Municipality to check pollution; the Doon Valley Case (AIR 1985: SC 652) in which Article 21, the right to life, was invoked by the judge to check the degradation of the Mussoorie Hills and to give an appropriate compensation to those affected; the Slum Dwellers Case (AIR 1986: SC 180) in which the right to life was interpreted as a right to livelihood, and the State was directed to rehabilitate the displaced slum dwellers. The right to life and an appropriate compensation for the environmental damage has also come up in relation to the Tehri and Narmada Dam Projects and the pollution and damage caused by the Shriram Fertilizers in New Delhi. There is a landmark achievement in environmental jurisprudence in India, because for the first time it explicitly makes the offence of environmental damage by pollution a matter of strict liability.

It is learnt that the 'Municipal Acts provide for a two way approach towards enforcement: (1) The defaulters can be prosecuted leading to fines etc., or on conviction; and (2) the Municipal Authority is in many cases authorized to take steps to provide necessary facilities and remove causes of pollution and recover the cost from the person concerned. The second course is not adopted because of the difficulties in execution and large probability of non-recovery of such expenditure. In some cases, powers are vested with the local authorities in respect of enforcing sewer connections and removal of diaries. As regard the legal processes, prosecutions are not launched promptly and even when proceedings are taken up, the decisions are hardly deterrent—while the cause of pollution are allowed to continue'.

Legislation is not enough and 'it must evolve as a response to the sensitive body of public opinion moulded through the movements and struggles launched by those at the receiving end and in the environmentally degraded locations. However, in the ultimate analysis, it is environmental consciousness of the masses resulting from their perception of the adverse effects of its degradation, in terms of their loss of health and livelihood and of the irreversible damage to their production resources, that will determine their political initiative and capacity to organize themselves into mass organizations to enforce the enactment of a comprehensive and radical environmental policy.'

The serious threat of environmental pollution cannot be necessarily met through legislation by imposition of penalty and imprisonment alone. The Environmental Protection Act, 1986 has imposed fines and imprisonment for water and air polluters. Even the Municipal Act has imposed fine penalty. Above all, the people's awareness and cooperation is an imperative necessity in a democratic set up for combating the environmental challenges both in rural and urban regions.

REFERENCES

1. Bhargava, Gopal: Environmental Challenges and Ecological Disaster: Global Perspective, Mittal Publisher, New Delhi.
2. Bhargava, Gopal: Pollution and its Control, published by Mittal Publisher, New Delhi, 1992.
3. Biswas, Dilip and Dutta, S.A.: Vehicular Pollution Combating the Smog and Noise in Cities, *The Hindu*, Survey of the Environment, 1994.
4. Puri, M.M.: Hazards of Automobile Emissions, *Link,* February 17, 1991.
5. Saigal, P.S.: Environmental Concern, edited by Dr. S.C. Bhatia.
6. *The Financial Express*, May 10, 1994, Check the Hazardous Pollution.

CHAPTER 5

URBAN INFORMAL SECTOR: CASE STUDIES

In Indian metropolitan and other large cities, the informal sector has played an important role in accelerating the tempo of economic and industrial activities. Whereas the physical facilities, in terms of infrastructural facilities, is not provided as per capita population requirement. A large bulk of informal activities are mainly concentrated in cities like Ahmedabad, Mumbai, Bangalore, Calcutta, Delhi, Chennai, Kanpur, and so on. It will multiply by the 21st century and thus the urban informal sector would grow in a haphazard manner.

The organized sector has embodied the industrial and business functions with enormous financial overhead cost and restrained the employment opportunities. However, it is well managed in terms of power infrastructure, financial institutions and raw material facilities.

The informal sector is an inevitable phenomenon in the context of urban settlements. However, informal activity of hawkers is a doorstep service and does play an important role in meeting the large scale consumer requirements. The industrial informal sector is involved in mass production of consumer goods for poor and middle income groups.

The informal activity is highly competitive and involves the bargaining prospects in urban areas. This is not true for the organized sector which is governed by the Factory Act. However, such a situation does not exist in the context of industrial informal sector and the related business informal activities.

One of the classic examples of informal industrial unit and business activities do provide the self-employment opportunities. Independent hawkers are classified as informal activities catering to the self-employed occupation. Though the informal sector has not been approved by the government, yet it is functioning with vigour and vitality in promoting the economic activities of metropolitan and other large cities.

The informal sector's households are confronted with serious housing problems in the metropolitan and other large cities as they are forced to live in the slum and squatter settlements. Specific action is required for planning the informal housing sector with the adoption of suitable innovative techniques in the building technology know-how.

The occupational categories of informal sector have been classified as domestic servants, construction workers, cobblers, carpenters and so on. However, the industrial informal sector workers are mainly unskilled in its occupational classification. The formal sector has been well organized and consists largely of skilled workers. Furthermore, hawkers specified in the informal sector are less qualified but they do have an adequate source of earning prospects in the metropolitan and other large cities as compared to the skilled workers in the organized sector.

An industrial oganization would fall under the informal sector if it employs less than ten workers as spelt out by the International Labour Organization (ILO). In fact, a survey of the industrial informal sector in Anand Parbat, New Delhi had revealed that many small scale units had entered less than ten workers in their employment register, but actually they employed more in number. However, such a practice is followed to avoid the implications and regulations of the Factory Act. Thus, the ILO definition of informal sector should be modified.

Informal Sector : Characteristics

The informal sector is mainly characterized by labour intensiveness conforming to the small-scale enterprises, with low income for workers. It embraces a vast range of activities involving production of both goods and services. Due to the limited capital and management, persons operating it have relatively limited skills and management experience. In the informal sector, the financial utilization is carefully done with the use of second-hand machineries and by practising similar other economies. However, the sophisticated technology is seldom accessible to it and extensive use is made of indigenously developed or adapted technology. Furthermore, the market unregulated therefore, competition is keen and the absence of tariff and quota protection precludes earning the monopoly profits. The official statistics contain an insignificant amount of information about this sector leading to far too little knowledge about it, both in terms of its size and the persons falling within the prescribed limit. Thus, due to this reason it has also been referred to as the 'unenumerated' or the 'unorganized' sector.

Prevalent Attitudes

The typical attitude adopted towards the informal sector by the urban authorities of misunderstanding, leading to its being viewed as undesirable, ugly, unhealthy, a nuisance and highly problematic. Thus, the official procedure adopted for dealing with it are either of hostility resulting in the infliction of frequent harassment, eviction, imposition of fines etc., or virtually totally ignoring it. The licensing laws and regulations are framed for its application and sometimes these are flouted and are virtually abandoned. The excessive movement of migration population is usually due to illiteracy of the persons operating within the informal sector and also because of the often discretionary or corrupt and tedious processes through which licences are obtained.

As a consequence of such a phenomenon, many of the economic agents in this sector operate illegally, though often pursuing the similar economic activities in the formal sector. The illegality has been generally not due to the nature of the economic activity but due to official limitation of access to the legitimate activity. Thus, the consequence is always twofold; the risk and uncertainty of earning a livelihood in this low-income sector are magnified and the regulations ensure the high quality of services and commodities for the wealthy few at the expense of the impoverished many.

Urbanization and the Informal Sector

Sheer magnitude of urban population growth in India is beyond the manageable limit. Two factors influencing such a growth have been the natural increase of population and the stream of rural migrants flooding into the cities. Whereas, a certain proportion of the immigrants consist of educated and skilled persons, a vast majority represent the illiterate and traditionally oppressed unskilled agricultural labours coming to the cities in search of better income opportunities and, a chance to escape the fate assigned to them in the traditional rural hierarchy. Problems faced by this latter stream of immigrants in the cities are of a particular nature, involving a shift from a largely subsistence level to a money economy and the need to get absorbed both occupationally and economically in the context of an urban fabric. It is largely these people who conform to economic and industrial activities of urban informal sector.

Unless an understanding of the perception of priorities of these migrants is assimilated by the urban authorities and an alternative situation provided, no satisfactory solution is likely to emerge. As such, the regulations and laws pertaining to the urban migrants are alien to them and owing to their high degree of illiteracy, they often remain unaware of their new responsibilities. Thus, the often hostile and ruthless treatment meted out to them by authorities only adds to their growing problems.

The demographic upward trend is expected to increase the urban population to about 340 million by the turn of the century. Assuming that 50 per cent of the increase in urban population would be contributed by rural to urban migration, about 90 million jobs have to be created in non-agricultural sector to absorb the increased labour force in the near future.

TABLE 1

Workforce in Urban Formal and Informal Sector

(in millions)

Year	*Total work-force in India*	*Total*	*Workforce in Urban India*			
			Organized Sector	*% in Total*	*Un-organized Sector*	*% in Total*
1	2	3	4	5	6	7
1971	226.87	57.86 (25.30)	18.83	32.54	39.03	67.46
1973	236.06	60.18 (25.49)	20.30	33.73	39.88	66.27
1978	260.90	75.14 (28.80)	23.80	31.67	51.34	68.33
1981*	270.24	78.41 (28.82)	25.93	33.07	52.48	66.93
2001*	325.00		35.00		65.00	
Annual Growth Rate	1.8	3.00	3.2		3.0	

Note: Figures in parantheses denote the percentage share in total of work force (Column 3).

* Figures are derived through simple linear extrapolation equation based on change between 1961 given in the Plan document.

** It is projected that in 2001 the total workforce will become an alarming proportion mainly in urban areas. In the organized and unorganized sectors the composition of workforce in urban India will be 35 million and 65 million in 2001 respectively. It is notable that the workforce in unorganized urban informal sector will show an upward trend of growth.

Source: Draft Sixth Five Year Plan, 1978-83, Planning Commission, New Delhi, cited from Rajendra P. Mamgain, Pattern of Employment and Income in Urban Informal Sector (Background paper) presented at the seminar on Informal Sector organized by the Institute of Allied Manpower Research, New Delhi (February 11-12, 1988).

Mumbai's Situation

In the city of Mumbai, hawking has increased over the last decade. According to Section 230 (1) of the Bombay Provincial Municipal Corporation Act, 1949, no person shall, except with the written permission of the Commissioner, place or deposit upon a street or in a public place, any stall, chair, bench or other things, so as to form an obstruction or an encroachment.

The Mumbai Police Act also empowers the police under Section 102 to prosecute hawkers. The illegal status granted to the hawkers exposes them to official, economic and social exploitation. Subsequently, the suppliers often employ exploitative credit relationship with them as they do not have any effective access to institutional credit to establish their business.

Ahmedabad's Growth

A study on hawkers by Dr. Meera Mehta and Dr. Dinesh Mehta reveals that in the city of Ahmedabad only 3000 out of the 21,000 hawkers have been granted licences by the Ahmedabad Municipal Corporation. However, the remaining 18,000 are prone to harassment by civic and police officials.

The main problem of the hawker community is the allegations levelled against them by the establishment and the public that they obstruct the traffic movements and create congestion. But in reality most of the problems are related to vehicular and pedestrian traffic which are arising out of factors other than hawkers. The hawkers are simply responding to the specific movement and patterns which exist.

In the city of Ahmedabad, the informal sector activities have shown a better performance and continue to have a good potential for income and employment generation, and there is a linkage with the formal sector. The finance has not been a problem for informal sector enterprises in the city.

Legal Issues

The Ahmedabad Municipal Corporation Act has spelt out that 'the Municipal Commissioner permits the use of municipal streets to the hawkers, subject to the specific terms and conditions and annual renewal of licence'. Therefore, subsequently the total licence fee recovered from the hawkers usually varies from 5-6 lakh rupees per annum.

The High Court of Gujarat had directed the Ahmedabad Municipal Corporation for issuing licences to the hawkers with certain conditions. It seemed to be a worthwhile administrative measure of action. It is broadly spelt out as:

1. The licence permits the licensee to move in the area where hawking is permitted. This licence does not permit the licensee to remain stationary on any part of the footpath, pavement or road. Even though he may remain stationary for about 30

minutes to sell goods at a particular place, he shall do so in a single file and keep as near to the kerb as possible. He shall keep his lorry at least 30 metres away from any bus stand or the end of the corners of roads. However, failure to comply with such a condition shall result in cancellation of the licence.

2. A licenced hand lorry as per the design of Municipal Corporation shall not be more than 1.10 metres in breadth, 1.5 metres in length and the height including the stocking of goods shall not be more than 1.40 metres from the ground level. This does not include the roof over the lorry. Stacking over 1.40 metres from the ground level shall not be permitted. No fixtures and trimmings will be allowed outside the said length and breadth of the lorry.
3. The licensee shall not cause any nuisance or obstruction to traffic on any street or footpath.
4. No licensee shall hawk on any public street or places prohibited by the municipal commissioner or in the context of non-hawking zone.
5. While passing through the non-hawking zone, the licensees are required to cover the articles, so that they may not be visible from outside. Thus, the failure to do so will be considered a breach of the conditions and the hawking licence shall be liable to be cancelled.
6. The licensee shall not sell any articles within 50,000 metres of a market either municipal or private.
7. The licensee shall not ring any bell or use any mechanical contrivance to attract attention.
8. The licensee shall observe utmost clearliness in regard to his articles.
9. Under any circumstances the licensee is not transferable whatsoever and cannot be used by any person other than the one in whose favour it is issued.
10. The licence shall always be carried by the licensee and produced subsequently to any municipal officer authorized in this behalf or a police officer whenever demanded.
11. The licence fee is non-refundable.
12. A tin plate showing the licence number and year, supplied by the municipal corporation every official year with the grant of licence shall be affixed to the hand lorry, till it is replaced by a new tin plate supplied for the next official year.

13. The licensee shall produce his two passport size photographs along with the application. The hawkers will not be allowed movement on roads less than 12 metres in width which are in the residential areas, except the hawkers dealing with vegetables, fruits, kerosene and other essential commodities as may be prescribed by the municipal commissioner from time to time.

Calcutta Crisis

In Calcutta a large bulk of working population is classified as informal sector, namely hawker and hand-driven rickshaw pullers, factory and construction workers. The industrial informal sector workers are confined in the residential and peripheral areas.

The informal housing sectors of Calcutta is known as the *bustees* clusters of inhabitants and its working population is largely engaged in informal occupational activities. The inhabitants of *bustees* have close contacts with their rural relations and money is regularly sent to them. Usually, in *bustees* the groups of village acquaintances have clustered together. Such a situation has led to alarming growth of workers in the informal sector.

Industrial Informal Growth: Anand Parbat, Delhi: Case Study

A large complex of informal industrial cluster is located at Anand Parbat (Karol Bagh Zone), Delhi. A controversy has arisen as the Delhi Administration, particularly the Commissioner of Industries and the Municipal Corporation of Delhi, (MCD) have not recognized the Government Gazette Notification Document Master Plan for Delhi, 2001 Perspective recommendations that Anand Parbat be set aside for the light industrial development.

The DDA's official viewpoint is that though the Master Plan for Delhi had suggested the Anand Parbat for light industries, the redevelopment plan for the area needs to be the concern of the MCD. Thus, the industrial informal settlement of Anand Parbat, Delhi has been subjected to a dilemma of confusion and contradiction in terms of planning and redevelopment proposal. The report Informal Sector in a Metropolis : Case Study of Delhi, Industrial Informal Cluster, Anand Parbat prepared by the Town and Country Planning Organization, Government of India had recommended the regularization of Anand Parbat area. Surprisingly, such a proposal is yet to be recognized by the Delhi Government. The case study of an informal settlement with reference to the industrial cluster located at Anand Parbat, Delhi was conducted in form of survey for assessing the types, interdependent functions of industrial units, the working capital and turnover. The objective was to ascertain as to whether the area can be regularized or not.

The Anand Parbat Industrial area belongs to the Ramjas Trust and comprises 125 acres with more than 5,000 small-scale industrial units employing over 50,000 workers in day and night shifts. The area in the Delhi's first Master Plan was earmarked as a green belt area. Its unique characteristic is that it is functioning through the optimal operational efficiency within the small enterprise undertakings.

The industrial informal sector of Anand Parbat commands the sale-ability of consumer goods throughout the city of Delhi and northern India. As such, the raw material is easily available in the area and adds to the economic advantage.

It is interesting to note that the area depicts the small-scale industrial units with the involvement of both skilled and unskilled workers. The percentage distribution of workers in different units is approximately 60 per cent as skilled and 40 per cent as unskilled with respect to the broad classification of occupational structures in the Anand Parbat industrial informal framework. The unique characteristic of the area is that it has a large absorption capacity for unskilled workers in different small-scale interdependent industrial units.

The wages of skilled and unskilled workers are approximately between Rs 854 to Rs 1000 and Rs 600 to Rs 700 respectively. Another unique characteristic of Anand Parbat industrial area is that training is given within the units itself. This enables the workers to get a specialized work skill. Further, it promotes efficiency and accelerates productivity. However, there are no formal training centres in the industrial complex. The workers are directly employed through contacts of employment notices on the area board.

The workers already employed in the units are able to seek employment for their relatives of rural origin. Therefore, the industrial informal settlement of Anand Parbat has been a source of attraction for the rural migrants. However, a majority of workers are able to frequently visit their home settlements.

Largely, the workers, both skilled and unskilled change their jobs for securing higher wages. Thus, the permanency in one job is not true in the Anand Parbat industrial informal cluster of industrial settlement. However, the constraint of loan advances, which the workers are compelled to take from their employees, is a delaying factor in looking for new assignments.

To a large-scale the workers prefer to stay at their work place. A large number of workers live at Trinagar, Sarai Rohila and Anand Parbat residential complexes. Thus, the workers do not suffer fatigue from travelling up and down to their work place. Due to the negligible work place distance, the workers of Anand Parbat informal sector are able to thereby promote the optimal scale of labour productivity.

The industrial activity of Anand Parbat is notable in terms of manufacture of (i) motor and scooter rubber parts, (ii) air conditioners and coolers, (iii) electric wires, cables and press, (iv) electric box for generating the current distribution system, (v) electrical ancillaries (switches), (vi) steel utensils, (vii) steel and wooden furniture, (viii) machine tools, (ix) clutch plates, (x) mixers and grinders, (xi) scientific glass for laboratory purposes and (xii) wire knitting and forgings and castings.

The area is also manufacturing (i) labels used for cloth tailoring purpose, (ii) metal boxes, (iii) cardboard boxes, (iv) chemicals, (v) powerlooms etc. Besides the predominance of manufacturing activities at the industrial informal settlement of Anand Parbat, the following economic activities have assumed importance, namely (i) tin plating, (ii) electroplating and nickel polishing. Subsequently, the repair of machines has a specialized economic function. The characteristic of jobs at the Anand Parbat industrial complex has been mainly identified in its operational efficiency as (i) lathes machines, (ii) welding and (iii) moulding.

One of the special characteristics of industrial informal cluster of Anand Parbat is that there is no single industrial unit which is self-sufficient in terms of production activities. Therefore, each unit is dependable on a specialized manufacturing unit for various processes like (i) moulding of iron sheet of a round shape design, (ii) polishing the round frame, (iii) glass manufacturing, (iv) bulb manufacturing and finally, (v) the assembly.

The wholesale dealers of consumer goods are the bulk purchasers from the Anand Parbat industrial settlement. The cost economy of an industrial informal settlement. The cost economy of an industrial informal sector is predominantly based upon optimal operational efficiency. The small industrial units of Anand Parbat have three important growth factors, namely (i) direct links with the suppliers' market, (ii) skilled and unskilled advantages and (iii) locational factors.

The Anand Parbat informal industrial sector is producing goods and services worth more than 54 crores per annum. The pertinent question that arises is as to why the Anand Parbat industrial settlement has not been regularized as it is a great money spinner.

The industrial prospects for promoting an accelerated pace of production and employment have been curtailed due to the non-availability of power requirements in the Anand Parbat area. There is an imperative need that the Delhi Electric Supply Undertaking (DESU) should provide the required electricity to the area. Presently, DESU supplies 12 megawatt of power to the Anand Parbat industrial area, whereas the requirement is 17 megawatts.

The Anand Parbat industrial informal settlement also depicts a picture of environmental chaos. Regularization will generate a great source of revenue in terms of taxation. It will also create the possibility of mushrooming of financial institutions. Thus, for promoting an accelerated pace of industrial activities, the need has risen for regularizing the Anand Parbat industrial area and simultaneously providing the socio-economic and infrastructural facilities.

The prevailing scenario revealed by Town and Country Planning Organization, in its report on Anand Parbat Industrial Area (APIA) had been incorporated in the draft proposal of Revised Master Plan after being contemplated and recommended by the Industrial Advisory Board. It was reconsidered by the High Power Committee, constituted to review the Master Plan for Delhi, 1962 and finally the Master Plan for Delhi-2001 perspective was promulgated on August 1, 1990. Industrial Area Redevelopment Scheme had recommended for preparing the redevelopment scheme for three industrial areas including APIA as Light Industrial Area. The chapter concerning the "Areas of Industrial Activities" indicated that industrial activity shall be conducted at the following locations in the prescribed use zone as indicated in the landuse plan i.e., for Light Industries: Anand Parbat alongwith other locations and Chapter "Modernization and City's Personality" indicated the landuse plan, its sub-clause (v) elaborated that the landuse modifications were already approved. The sub-title in the Light Industries use zones/ use premises, the Industries were mentioned in Group ABCDE of Annexure-III of the Master Plan and had been permitted under the classification of Light Industrial Areas.

It has now become conspicuous that the APIA is earmarked as Light Industrial Area and its landuse is for light industries that are functioning in the area. Furthermore, by virtue of the Master Plan, they are permitted to function at Anand Parbat from their existing site.

The administration has taken an indifferent stand, sticking onto the notion that facilities will be provided only after preparation of Redevelopment Plan by DDA. The objective of Master Plan for the preparation of Urban Renewal Plan is to upgrade the scheme taking into consideration the existing physical and socio-economic conditions, which are evident in the guidelines under heading "Other Urban Renewal Areas" that the redevelopment scheme for different use zones generally shall adopt regulations prescribed in the development code. However, the authority may adopt suitable regulations where it is not feasible or it is not advisable to adopt the general regulations as prescribed. It is neither asserted in the Industrial Policy to put an embargo on the existing industries nor recommended in the Master Plan to withdraw their facilities, which were earlier provided to them by the administration. Secondly, the APIA is already a developed area with almost all infrastructural facilities such as industrial light power connections, telephones, police station, dispensary, post office, nationalized banks, water connection facilities, etc. However, if few services which are to be provided in accordance with redevelopment plan in the complex, then that can be provided in due course by the concerned agencies.

The Central Government is rigid on its stand to provide the inevitable facilities only after the preparation of Redevelopment Plan by the DDA. Though on February 18, 1990 the decisions taken by Chief Secretary, Delhi were related to Ramjas Foundation but were wrongly implemented on the existing industries working at present site since a long duration of period.

The ifs and buts and the polyarchy has not only stagnated the growth of hardworking entrepreneurs by denying them the basic industrial necessities such as SSI Regularization of Electric Connections, Municipal Corporation Licences etc., but has threatened their survival due to the alarming increase in electricity charges. Most of the units are constrained to pay Rs 7.37 per unit as compared to Rs. 2.20 per unit or Rs. 2.20 per unit to the DESU. However, when the decision was taken to deny these facilities as interpret ed by authorities, the landuse of the area was for green belt, but according to Government Notification, the present landuse is for Light Industries. More so any order issued by an individual can be superseded by the Notification issued by State/Central Government. However, there has been neglect of the provisions of facilities at APIA. Presently, the small entrepreneurs of APIA have expected from the Government of NCT of Delhi not only their survival but the survival of an enormous workforce depending on APIA. (As cyclostyle paper of Mr. S.K. Tandon on APIA).

Decentralized Policy

At present, the alarming flow of migrants to metropolitan cities has given rise to working force in the category of informal sector. There is need to adopt a decentralized approach of planning to promote balanced process of development in a regional perspective. This would lead to spillover of population and economic activities in creating spatial harmony in human settlements.

An effective measure of planned action has to be adopted for developing a growth-centre around villages. At the same time, the counter-magnates of urban centres have to be selected with adequate infrastructural, socio-economic and financial institutional facilities to sustain the industrial process of development in a big way.

The informal sector and its activities could be controlled in the congested metropolitan cities since the working force is devoid of adequate roof over the head. The informal housing sector has threatened the availability of basic amenities as the urban inhabitants are becoming conditioned to an unhygienic living condition.

Informal Sector and Regional Planning

Amongst the common theories that have been put forward to cope with the phenomenon of large-scale migration to cities are: (1) it should be discouraged to whatever extent possible by harassment at the urban end or even by consciously not improving their conditions, whether living or working, in the feat that betterment and the provision of greater amenities will trigger off still greater inflows and (2) the solution lies not in doing anything at the urban end but in the development of rural areas themselves. However, a study of the push and pull factors affecting migration reveals a preponderance of the push of economic backwardness, poverty, exploitation and unemployment or underemployment and subsequently the pull of better income opportunities in the cities. Other than in the case of better educated category of migrants, the existence of better educational, health or recreational amenities are not significant attractions in themselves.

In a democratic set up, pertinent question which arises is whether people can be forced to restrain themselves from seeking their economic betterment. Even in a country like China where an attempt was made to forcefully prevent migration to cities, the experiment was not wholly successful. In a liberal form of Government as in India, the efforts of preventing migration are doomed to fail from the start. Any realistic policy framework or a strategy for the situation first of all demands a thorough understanding as to why migration is being concentrated in few urban centres. Further, such a trend is largely due to the regional imbalances and economic disparities accompanied by stark differences in rural and urban areas, is beyond dispute. However, this in itself cannot be enough. An integrated policy framework for the national development must incorporate a strategy for a balanced process of regional development.

At present, cultural land reforms aimed at giving ownership of land to landless workers, irrespective of economic viability of the size of the land holding are in direct conflict with the national requirement for maximum productivity of agricultural land. If a strategy is worked out aiming at labour intensive rather than labour extensive (as at present) agricultural production, the number of the agricultural labour force is likely to be released for non-agricultural occupations which will also need to be absorbed in urban areas. So even while taking the view that rural development is essential for removing the socio-economic disparities between urban and rural areas, it does not relieve the urban authorities from the burden of planning effectively for the productive assmilation of an ever increasing flow of rural migrants in the context of urban centres.

The appalling condition of the masses in some of our older cities has beome a well-known phenomenon. Their problems are considered almost insurmountable, but it is generally believed that this is largely due to the inheritance of enormous backlogs of non-planning of new towns. It offers an invaluable opportunity for devising comprehensive urban systems capable of absorbing the whole cross section of urban population owing to the benefit of being able to make future projections. Have our new towns succeeded from this point of view? Virtually each one of them has been planned since independence and is plagued by the same problems of the growth of unauthorized settlements, very similar in nature to those found in older cities. Bhubaneshwar, Chandigarh, Durgapur, Gandhinagar, although barely a few years old, have their unauthorized components. The methods adopted for dealing with the situation in most cases is identical, thereby relying on the use of force and the framing of stringent legislation for controlling such development, varying only in the degree of severity of enforcement.

The development policy has to consider as to what extent the informal sector is capable of providing productive employment to both the unemployed and underemployed. In low-income agricultural economy having pressure on agricultural holdings, it is not just employment, but the industrial employment that can bring about a structural change in the economy. The question is how this can be accomplished. It is unlikely that employment in the formal sector could expand any faster than it is doing at present, the absorptive capacity of urban informal sector, which provides a wide variety of service opportunities of self-employment as buffer zone, could be recognized and developed. Simple recognition of the fact that the informal sector is linked to the formal sector through inter-relationships and interdependence which affects the national economy is not sufficient. It is pertinent that the nature of determinates of these linkages needs to be promoted. The positive growth possibilities of the informal sector is largely dependable on the nature and types of linkages that are operating within its economic system framework.

The informal sector represents a very heterogeneous group in terms of employment structure. The coexistence of sub-sectors within the sector (i.e. small establishments, independent workers, and casual workers working within households and informal workers within formal industries, trade and commerce establishments), vitiates the internal 'homogeneity' of the informal sector. To define the framework of policy for dealing with this sector has to recognize its vast heterogeneity. Since the informal sector holds all kinds of surplus labour including new entrants to the labour force, the incidence of poverty and low-income is higher in this sector. The government therefore, should not overlook the growing needs of skill development, technology, transfer and marketing of products of this sector. This requires suitable policy measures for supporting and upgrading the informal sector. But growth and development of this sector should not lead to the formalization. Such a situation has been responsible for disappearance of important character of the informal sector.

REFERENCES

1. Bhargava, Gopal: Role of Government in Informal Sector, *Manpower Journal*, Volume XXIX, No. 3, October-December, 1993.
2. Government of India: Interim Report of the National Commission on Urbanization, January, 1987.
3. Papola, T.S.: Urban Informal Sector in a Developing Economy, Vikas Publishing House, New Delhi.
4. Sarin, Madhu: Paper: The Informal Sector, Regional Planning and National Research Project financed by grant from Overseas Development Administration, Britain.
5. Tandon, S.K.: Anand Parbat Industrial Area (Cyclostyled Paper).
6. The Ahmedabad Municipal Corporation Development, Ahmedabad; Document.

7. Town and Country Planning Organization, Government of India; Informal Sector in Metropolis: Case Study of Delhi Industrial Informal Cluster—Anand Parbat.

8. Urban Affairs Quarterly Journal *Nagarlok,* Centre for Urban Studies, Indian Institute of Public Administration, Volume XII, No. 1, 1980. Urban Informal Sector: Concept, Policy, Issues and Measures.

9. Wishwakarma, R.K.: Informal-Formal Sector Linkages: Its Implications for Development Policy, *Manpower Journal,* Volume XXIX, No. 3, October-December, 1993.

CHAPTER 6
URBAN LAND CEILING ACT, 1976 AMENDMENTS AND REPERCUSSIONS

The objective of Urban Land (Ceiling and Regulation) Act, 1976 (ULCRA) was directed to provide for the imposition of a ceiling on vacant land in urban agglomerations, for the acquisition of such land in excess of the ceiling limits, to regulate the construction of building on such land and for matters connected therewith, with a view to prevent the concentration of urban land in the hands of a few persons and with a view to bring about an equitable distribution of land in urban agglomerations to subserve the common good.

The ULCRA was passed in Parliament on February 17, 1976. In the annals of Indian Parliamentary history, this was the only enactment which was pushed through in less than seven hours during the Emergency. The Act was the product of an 'Emergency mindset' and the manifestation of the much talked about 20 Point Programme announced by the then Prime Minister, Mrs. Indira Gandhi. The following states had adopted the Act, namely, Andhra Pradesh, Gujarat, Haryana, Himachal Pradesh, Maharashtra, Orissa, Punjab, Tripura, Uttar Pradesh and West Bengal and all the Union Territories. Subsequently, the Act was also enforced in the states of Assam, Bihar, Madhya Pradesh, Manipur, Rajasthan and Meghalaya.

The dismal performance of ULCRA is well known. As per the interim report published by the National Commission on Urbanization (NCU) in 1987, of the estimated 1,66,192 ha. of vacant land, only 14,589 ha. (8.78 per cent) was acquired and only 3,852 ha. (2.32 per cent) brought under physical possession and 621 ha. (0.37 per cent) was used for housing construction. The performance of the major cities in matter of actual taking over of the vacant land has been extremely poor. According to data compiled by the Ministry of Urban Development in 1996 of the total 2,20,675 ha. excess vacant land identified only 15,321 ha. (6.7 per cent) could be acquired physically and only 5,327 ha. (2.4 per cent) brought under various housing schemes.

According to the NCU report, in Hyderabad much of the vacant land was on the periphery and was either used for agriculture or was lying waste. Almost nothing had been acquired within the built-up areas of the city.

In Calcutta, where there was a government with a commitment to land reforms, only 34.67 ha. were actually taken into possession. With regard to allotment for housing, Delhi had allotted nothing. Chennai had allotted only 10 ha., Ahmedabad 2.79 ha. and Calcutta 4.22 ha. It was only in Hyderabad that 28,343 ha. of land was allotted for housing.

In Mumbai 21,000 landlords filed returns accounting to an area of about 25,000 ha. Of this the government has completed scrutiny only in respect of 12,000 cases amounting to around 600 ha. of surplus land. Tardy progress is attributed to the lack of cooperation from the landowners who were to submit various details of their holdings. Many went to court challenging the orders of the competent authorities. As of now about 300 cases are pending in courts. Exemptions were given in respect of most of the declared surplus land ostensibly to built houses for EWS. But according to one report about 52,000 flats were constructed on the exempted land. Finally, after all the fuss government acquisition in Mumbai is not more than 213 ha., 7 per cent of the declared surplus land.

Exemption provision was one which wrecked havoc with the performance of the Act. Sweeping powers have been vested with governments to exempt any land prospectively or retrospectively from the provision of the Act. According to the review by the NCU 43,863.50 ha. of land which accounted for about 26 per cent of the total declared surplus was exempted for EWS housing and 40,419 ha. was exempted on other grounds. The commission categorically stated that in the matter of acquisition of surplus land, the Act was ineffective.

While unduly restricting the supply of land for meeting various needs, the provisions of the Act have led to corruption and unnecessary harassment of the people hold small pockets of land in the 64 notified urban agglomerations.

The ULCRA has become ineffective as the land distribution on the basis of social justice is denied. The presumptions of the Act have lost the validity in reality. In an interesting document 'Urban Ceiling Law Anomalies' K.C. Mehta makes observation that the ULCRA provides for a ceiling on vacant land in urban areas, the acquisition of buildings constructed on such land and matters connected therewith. However, it was meant to bring an equitable distribution in urban areas to subserve the common good for checking the land speculation and profiteering activities. The Supreme Court had struck down the restrictions imposed by Section 27(1) in its judgements in Maharao Saheb Singhji versus Union of India, AIR 1981 S.C. 324.

Despite the Supreme Court's judgement and several amendments in rules and regulations by the government, the ULCRA has been enforced in vain.

The Act (vide Sections 3 and 4) provides that no person should hold vacant land in excess of prescribed ceiling limit mentioned in the section for different categories. However, in practice, the enforcement of the connected provision of the section is impractical as the corporation acts of different states have not been considered. The floor area ratio has to be worked out. Two-thirds or alternatively one-half of the total area under construction has to be left vacant under the corporation acts.

Moreover, these corporation acts provide for calculating the floor area ratio based on the road width.

If one goes further, one finds that it is quite impossible to enforce the provisions of the ULCRA concerning the vacant land under industrial units as well as for buildings used for commercial purposes. Further, obtaining a 'no objection certificate' from the urban land ceiling authority is a time consuming process, and industrialists and businessmen get harassed.

As such, the term "dwelling units" has a vague concept as specified in Section 2(e), which treats a dwelling unit in relation to a building or a portion of a building used solely for the residential purpose. But people, as well as the urban land ceiling authorities, have started considering the out-house attached to the main building as dwelling units. However, these are not considered ordinarily as separate residences.

Thus, the ceiling limit benefit has been given to each and every dwelling unit defeating the government's intention. For these reasons, the Act seems to have failed. The government must review and amend suitably the provisions of the Act, so as to make it simple and practical, to boost housing and industrial developments in a statewise perspective.

The Act has been termed as a draconian law. The implementation of the Act in the States/Union Territories has been dismal, mainly due to the following reasons: (1) Vesting too much of discretionary power in the state governments for granting exemptions: (2) highly expropriatory nature of the Act; (3) the Act, as it stands, does not provide for a mechanism to force the entry of the vacant urban land into the land market through appropriate fiscal measures.

The report of the NCU has rightly pointed out that the ULCRA has provided no relief to urban householders and flat-seekers, and it has also created many unexpected hardships. It has hamstrung new construction and invited encumbrances on land in the shape of hutment colonies. Instead of taking over the excess land and distributing it among the eligible sections of society, the government has so far hardly acquired any substantial urban vacant land. However, even where such acquisition has taken place, it is being conditioned to the long pending cumbersome litigation procedure.

ULCRA has largely put a check on purchase and accumulation of vacant land by big landholders, though clandestine purchases have taken place on small scale.

There has been inherent weaknesses in the conceptual and legal framework of the Act which came in the way of acquiring land under it. Thus, the land actually taken into possession has been insignificant.

There has been administrative apathy, legal loopholes, delays and lack of political commitment in the implementation of the Act. It could have made much better impact had it been possible to focus attention on major landholders with vigorous efforts.

ULCRA has failed to acquire and generate sufficient vacant land for housing economically weaker sections. What has been done is inhibit access of public agencies to urban land thereby adversely affecting the delivery of affordable shelter. In addition, it has frozen large chunks of land in the urban areas, pushing up the prices considerably and thereby further reducing the accessibility of land to the urban poor.

The housing development is mainly governed by profit. However, without an incentive, the owner of excess urban land would not get involved in cumbersome procedures for building tenements for the weaker section of society. As a result, the excess land has not been developed on the basis of ULCRA's presumption. Though the Act has certain inherent anomalies and vagueness, such as the defining of the limits of urban agglomeration by parapherial belt ranging from one to eight kilometre distance irrespective of the complexity and size of the towns or its immediate need for land, the acquisition of strips of land or marginal excess or places of high urban aesthetic values with wide discretionary powers of the competent authority, the hardships to rural cultivators and inadequate compensation for investment already made in them. Likewise the inadvertant delays has been caused to industries and commercial houses in getting exemption under Sections 19 and 20 and building permits for building on holdings.

Unrealistic Presumptions

The presumption of the ULCRA that the owner of urban excess vacant land will construct houses for the weaker section is indeed an impractical proposition. The higher income group would not like to build houses to satisfy the unrealistic condition of ULCRA. So the excess of vacant land will not be of any use to the weaker sections of society.

Recently, the states monopolistic house building agencies have been in position to command a high price in auctions. It can be emphatically said that with the enforcement of ULCRA, the land value has multiplied. This is mainly true for cities like Ahmedabad, Bangalore, Mumbai, Calcutta, Delhi, Chennai, Luknow, Kanpur and Pune etc. Surprisingly, the urban development authorities have not been able to arrest the alarming rising trend of urban land values in the context of metropolitan and other large cities.

The ULCRA presumes, the coexistence of mixed land-use planning in a residential complex, an agglomeration between the rich and poorer sections. However, such intermixing has not become an acceptable phenomenon in the context of neighbourhood living. This has led to hinderances in the housing development programmes.

The declaration of excess urban vacant land in states was filed before the competent authority (CA) when the Act was enforced. Surprisingly, the CA has not been able to dispose of the filed declarations. With the result, the freezing of land has boosted the land market rate in an alarming proportion. Housing activities, particularly in metropolitan and other large cities have been hard-hit due to the acute land scarcity. ULCRA has restricted the buying and selling of excess urban land.

A large number of statements had been filed in Delhi about the non-possession of excess urban vacant land. As such, the owners claim that either the land is agricultural or unfit for construction or is covered by municipal bye-laws. The CA of Delhi under Section 10 of ULCRA had sent notifications and the parties had taken stay orders. Therefore, the acquisition of land has been negligible in Delhi.

The CA under section 21, exempts surplus land if tenements are built for weaker sections. However, the CA's discrimination procedure for exemption of such land has been responsible for rampant corruption and has weakened the implementation of ULCRA. Delays and cumbersome administrative bottlenecks have distorted CA's functioning.

The imposition of ULCRA has been confined to those whose excess land holding has been fixed on an individual plot basis. However, the lengthy procedural formalities have caused a slow process of land development.

The complete restriction on buying and selling as enforced under ULCRA has also virtually jeopardised the mass scale housing construction. For example, the monopolistic control of the DDA and other urban development authorities has restricted the housing developmental activities. Land value has shown an increasing trend in Delhi and other cities, where the controls are confined to single housing and land development agency.

It is learnt that the ULCRA has led to speculation in land prices and has been unprecedented, a poor man's dream of a flat deluded, the middle-class' access to housing made more difficult and nothing intended by the legislation has materialized.

The enforcement of ULCRA has led to the outburst of severe criticism of the Act by the public as also by the professionals. Nobody has gained anything from the Act, not because the provisions were impractical, but the will for implementation did not appear to be there among both the elected members and the bureaucrats. The government officials and politicians have new interpretations of the Act either to secure some sectarian advantages or deny benefits to the entitled groups.

In past, during the period of twenty years hardly any acquisition has taken place, which is surprising since the Act makes acquisition proceedings rather simple. Instead of taking over the excess land and distributing it among eligible sections of society, the government has so far hardly acquired any land. Even whether such acquisition has taken place, there is a litigation to put a stay over the whole matter.

The report of NCU has categorically pointed out that in the matter of acquisition of surplus land, the Act has been ineffective.

It is observed that for purpose of determining the ceiling limits, four categories of urban agglomerations have been formed. The ceiling on vacant land for agglomerations in category 'A' consisting of Delhi, Mumbai, Calcutta and Chennai is 500 square metres. For category 'B' agglomerations covering Ahmedabad, Bangalore, Hyderabad, Kanpur and Pune, the limit is 1,000 square metres. In respect of categories 'C' and 'D' covering the towns listed in schedule-I of the Act, the ceilings are 1,500 square metres and 2,000 square metres respectively. Thus, there is no uniformity in the imposition of ceiling limits in the urban areas.

The government has been empowered to acquire excess vacant land at the maximum rate of Rs 10 per square metre in categories 'A' and 'B' and at the maximum rate of Rs 5 per square metre for categories 'C' and 'D'. The Act has also regulated the transfer and use of urban properties. The provision of compensation is unrealistic and has hampered the housing activity in the metropolitan and other large cities. For inducing the development of excess urban land and for boosting the housing development in urban settlements, the rate of compensation, the amount as stated in the Act was required to be enhanced.

The Urban Land Ceiling Act has Led to Rampant Corruption

Source : The Pioneer, June 28, 1997.

Rampant Corruption

The enforcement of ULCRA has encouraged the practice of rampant corruption. However, the red-tapism has flourished since the competent authority has the discretionary powers of exemption limits of excess vacant land in Sections 20 and 21. Largely in the states progress of ULCRA has not been able to improve the tempo of house building developmental activities. Cumbersome procedure of urban land management has remained ineffective for the promotion of quick process of land developmental and housing construction activities in an alarming proportion. Thus the Act has failed.

Discretionary Powers

It is worthwhile to learn that there are two sections of ULCRA which virtually nullify all its provisions, that is, Sections 20 and 21, read with the instructions issued by the Central Government from time to time. Section 21 virtually makes it mandatory for exemption to be given to anyone who wants to build dwelling units not exceeding 80 square metres each in plinth area. Because the process is not automatic and requires the sanction of the competent authority, harassment becomes possible and almost an inevitable phenomenon. However, the existence of this section does mean any owner of land in excess of the ceiling limit has merely to prepare a scheme for constructing such dwelling units and then the land would have to be given in exemption. In other words, whilst such a provision of law may or may not encourage construction of small dwelling units, it certainly has prevented the transfer of vacant land to public ownership. Odd parcels of land or land which is actually used for agriculture and held by people with little political clout is acquired. Such land do not contribute significantly to the public purpose.

In a seminar on 'Housing and Urban Development' February 5, 1996, the background paper of Federation of Indian Chambers of Commerce and Industry (FICCI) had elaborated an important legislation which has had considerable adverse impact on building activities in the country in recent years. ULCRA forms part of the Ninth Schedule of the Constitution of India. The administrative set up too gives prominence to the negative side of the legislation. The implementation has been unsatisfactory. The number of authorities required to be approached for clearance are large in number. These approval are, by their very nature, cumbersome and dilatory. As such, the Act has also not made any significant impact on the mopping up of excess vacant land, but it has led to freezing effect on the urban land, by pushing its price in an alarming proportion.

The Government of India has been considering the amendment of ULCRA. One of the proposed amendments of the Act has been the introduction of Shelter Fund (SF) with a view of increasing the housing stock for the weaker sections of society and also providing infrastructure. A person, who develops his land in excess of ceiling within a period of 5 years as per the Master Plan provisions for construction of houses for weaker sections in accordance with the scheme approved by the government, was to be granted exemption for developing his land. Besides, land for institutions/commercial purposes can also be developed as per Master Plan provisions on payment of aforesaid contribution to the SF.

The government must reconsider the matter and decrease percentage of levy of SF and conversion charges so that it is made into an economically viable proposition.

It has been seen that to come out of the ULCRA administrative clarification it will take number of years. However, so far thousand of cases are pending with the competent authorities making the implementation of the Act an impossible accomplishment for a common man. A single window system, for all the permissions at one authority within 60 days from the date of application, is required to be implemented to provide an alarming magnitude of releases resulting into the formation of excessive number of dwelling units stock.

The report of the NCU observes that there is need for the amendment of ULCRA. The suggestions are: (a) Sections 20 and 21 of the Act, which allow the discretionary exemptions should be deleted; (b) all exemptions should be brought within the ambit of Section 19 by expanding its scope, if necessary. In other words, what is exempted is mandatory and what is not exempted cannot be exempted by any authority; (c) all lands which are vacant and surplus, must be developed during the five year period of the moratorium of transfer to the state, a state undertaking a statutory corporation or authority dealing with the housing and urban development or a cooperative organization concerning the housing developments.

Revival

In a draft memorandum on ULCRA, 1976, FICCI had observed that out of 3,92,093 applications filed in relation to the surplus land, only 2,17,738 cases have been finalized. At least 2,11,670 hectares of land was declared surplus, but the extent of land taken over was a meagre 9,752 hectares. Thus, the surplus land that was expected to be released did not come through its enforcement for built-up tenements.

Section 2(g) has given a negative definition of vacant land. A more exhaustive definition is called for changes are also required in Section 2(g). It is suggested that the Section should be amended, that if there is a plot of land which cannot be sub-divided, such land should be deemed vacant.

As per Section 21 of ULCRA, a person can declare that he wants to utilize the excess vacant land for the construction of dwelling units for weaker sections. The greatest folly of ULCRA, 1976 is that the weaker section has not been defined. Apart from the weaker sections, there is no reason why the Act should not cover workers and employees.

Governmental Proposals for ULCRA Amendments

The inter-departmental committee set up by the Union Government to suggest amendments for ULCRA has rejected countrywide demands to repeal the legislation. It has however proposed a series of amendments for shifting the emphasis from acquisition to guided development of vacant land.

Most significantly, the amendments propose that exemptions from acquisition of excess vacant land under the Act be made almost automatic, subject to certain levies and other conditions.

In its final report, the committee headed by Mr N.P. Singh, the Union Urban Development Secretary, had noted that the ULCRA had failed to achieve its objectives. As is evident from the fact that only seven per cent of the identified excess land had been acquired.

In a separate note circulated to state governments by the Union Urban Development Department, it has been stated that while the committee considered the question of repealing the Act, 'the general consensus was against doing so, as it was felt that the social objectives proposed to be achieved through the Act are still relevant.

Some states have been asked to pass resolutions proposing amendments. The committee has proposed that the Act's coverage be limited to urban agglomerations with population above 10 lakh as per the 1991 census.

In a major redefinition of urban agglomerations category A cities have been redrawn as those with population above 50 lakh, category B, ranging between 20-50 lakh and category C, ranging from 10-20 lakh. However, the state governments should be empowered to extend the Act to town with population above five lakh. These towns will be classified as category D.

While the ceiling for urban land holdings for category A and B has been maintained at 500 sq.m. and 1,000 sq.m., the ceiling for category C and D has been hiked to 2,000 sq.m. and 4,000 sq.m. from 1,500 sq.m. and 2,000 sq.m. respectively. In case of companies engaged in industrial production, the ceiling will be twice the applicable figure.

The current Act empowers states to grant exemptions on grounds of 'undue hardship' or 'in the public interest'.

Under the proposed amendment, urban vacant excess land holder has been given the option to retain part or whole of his land provided he fulfils certain conditions. For instance, he can hold whole of his excess land if he pays 20 per cent of the market value of the land to the Shelter and Urban Development Fund.

As an alternative, the landholder can surrender 20 per cent of excess land free of cost to the state government. The committee has proposed, such surrendered land should be pooled to create a Land Bank for the urban poor.

The proposals have suggested that the Shelter and Urban Development Fund be set up for each city for financing low-income housing and urban infrastructure.

The committee has proposed hike in the compensation for excess vacant land from Rs 10 per sq.m. for category A and B to Rs 250 and Rs 125 per sq.m. respectively. For C and D category from Rs 5 per sq.m. to Rs 50 for C and Rs 25 for D per sq.m.

The report has suggested creation of a separate machinery in the form of commissioners of urban land ceiling for each state or city to carry out surveys and inspections of land, maintain records and supervise the functioning of the competent authorities.

The panel has proposed revamping of the adjudication machinery to reduce delays in the finalization of excess vacant land. The number of appellate authorities have been reduced to one, while the second appeal to a high court on an order of Urban Land Tribunal has been done away with.

The committee has recommended the title of the Act be changed to Urban Land (Ceiling and Reforms) Act.

Remodifications

The ULCRA amendment proposals by the Union Government has not revolutionized the changes to promote easy availability of excess vacant land. The questions arises as to whether the shelter and urban development fund would provide, in each city, the appropriate financing of low-income housing and infrastructure. The authority has not been visualized to regulate and control the administrative execution in meeting the mass scale housing for urban poor.

The amendment proposal considers that while the ceiling for urban land holdings at 500 sq.m. to 1000 sq.m., the ceiling for category C and D has been hiked to 2,000 sq.m. and 4,000 sq.m. from 1,500 sq.m. and 2,000 sq.m. respectively. This is a serious error for determining the urban land ceiling limits. In fact, the cities of C and D categories comprising the small and medium towns are rising in population size and eventually land scarcity has risen. Through the proposed amendment of Union Government, the increasing ceiling limits in cities of categories C and D are unjustifiable and irrational. Infact, the urban ceiling limits should not vary within cities categories but must have uniformity.

The hike of compensation has not been substantial as in Class A, it is proposed from Rs 10 to Rs 250 per sq.m. and in Class B city Rs 125, Rs 50 for Class C city and Rs 25 for category D as per sq.m. Presently, the compensation of market rate of Category A is more than Rs 2000 per sq.m. for Category B Rs 1000 per sq.m. for C Rs 500 sq.m. and D Rs 250 sq.m. The proposed compensation rate by the government is extremely low and it would not attract a significant response from the urban vacant excess land owners to provide voluntarily the land availability for acquisition.

If every holder of excess vacant land pays 20 per cent of the market value of the land to the Shelter and Urban Development Fund, then it can be retained. Obviously nobody would give vacant excess land in acquisition and would pay the 20 per cent of market rate and retain it. Thus, the ULCRA amendment proposal would be defeated.

The amendment proposals by the government has not evoked the Sections 20 and 21 of ULCRA concerning the discretionary powers of exemption by the competent authority. Due to this provision, the rampant corruption prevails in competent authority. ULCRA has not been effective due to discretionary powers of exemptions.

It is perplexing as to whether the excess vacant land assembly and development would be in a continuous bulk number for its disposal for built-up properties for developers, builders and housing building cooperative societies. It is possible that marginal urban excess land cannot be derived as it is scattered in entire urban areas. Such a situation would lead to the non-implementation of vacant urban excess land.

Notable States' Suggestions

The large number of states are confronted with the innumerable administrative and legal difficulties in the enforcement of ULCRA. The pertinent question which strikes all states, big urban centres is concerning the enhancement of compensation amount of excess urban vacant land. Secondly, the issue is misuse of agricultural land and extension with the urban ULCRA in the peripheral area of urban agglomeration.

Viewpoint of the Orissa government is that 'many land owners have not filed the return within the prescribed date. They avoid to receive notice and to file return under Section 8(2) of the Act. The Act does not provide that draft statement can be prepared under Section 8. As a result, law abiding people suffer while the law evaders get scot free'.

The Government of Uttar Pradesh has been confronted with the administrative difficulties in the implementation ULCRA, specifically with reference that (i) 'the relief available to urban land holders of agriculture land under Section 20(i) (b) of the Act is being misused. The exempted land is subdivided growth and (ii) the provision in Section 26(2) of the Act which was intended to remove undue hardships to prospective sellers of Urban, Land has been misused on mass scale'.

The Karnataka Government has emphatically declared that 'there is no provision in the ULCRA for the extension of the peripheral area/ urban agglomeration area, when the city develops far beyond the municipal limits and the developed area considered while enacting the Act, including the peripheral area. Hence, suitable provision may be considered to be provided in ULCRA for the extension of peripheral area/agglomeration area in a situation like that of Bangalore where the developed area has spread much beyond what was considered in the Act.

The Gujarat Chamber of Commerce and Industry concerning ULCRA has observed the 'cumbersome provisions and tardy implementation have resulted in inordinate administrative delays in getting requisite permission and sanction from respective authorities. The Act has proved to be one of the most complicated legislations in the statute book. Besides opening up litigation, it has been the root cause of corruption and other malpractices, and has resulted in considerable reduction in building activities in urban agglomerations. Inevitably this has encouraged unauthorized constructions and proliferation of slums and has led to large scale underhand dealings.

One pertinent question arise whether the ULCRA should be scrapped. Indeed, it was once struck down as unconstitutional by the Andhra High Court, but it later passed the acid test of the Supreme Court which, in a case decided in 1980, held it to be valid, save for Section 27(1) which sought to impose restrictions on the transfer of land with buildings on it in an urban area. Ironically, to most people, the Act seemed to be epitomised by Section 27(1), now defunct, which equally affected an ordinary citizen thinking of buying or selling a tiny house or flat in an urban area and a giant industrial enterprise seeking a multi-crore loan by mortgaging its assets.

Several issues have been thrown up in regard to the provisions of amendments of ULCRA. In a paper 'An approach to Urban Land Policy', Louis Menezes has highlighted the difficulties of ULCRA, which raises the following questions: (a) Has the Act achieved its objectives or is it too early to pass a judgement on its operation, which was hampered by prolonged litigation in the initial years? (b) As several practical difficulties have been experienced in the implementation of the Act, should it continue in the present form or should it be amended and, if so, in what manner. In particular, the Act has restricted housing activities, expecially for the middle and low-income groups, and has been responsible for the escalation of land prices and rents.

The law has discouraged the concentration of urban land in a few hands, but the illegal holdings cannot be ruled out. As such, the process of implementation of ULCRA has been unsuccessful. The other objectives of preventing speculation and mopping up unearned increases in land value have not yet been achieved.

Repealing the Act*

1. ULCRA, 1976 was passed when the Emergency was in operation with a laudable social objective in mind. The said Act was passed

*The Urban Land (Ceiling and Regulation Repeal, Bill 1998 as announced by Ram Jethmalani, the Union Minister of Urban Affaris and Employment, Government of India, June 4, 1998.

pursuant to resolutions passed by the state legislatures under clause (1) of Article 252. Unfortunately public opinion is unanimous that the Act has failed to achieve what was expected of it. It has on the contrary, pushed up land prices, practically brought the housing industry to a stop and has provided copious opportunities for corruption. There is widspread clamour for removing this most potent clog on housing.

2. Parliament has no power to repeal or amend the Act unless resolutions are passed by two or more state legislatures as required under clause (2) of Article 252.
3. The Urban Land (Ceiling and Regulation) Repeal Act, 1999 was notified in the Gazette on March 22, 1999 in replacement of the Ordinance on the same subject. The Repeal Act has already come into force in the states of Haryana, Punjab, Uttar Pradesh, Gujarat and Karnataka and in all the Union Territories. The states governments of Andhra Pradesh, Assam, Bihar, Madhya Pradesh, Maharashtra, Orissa, Rajasthan and West Bengal have not adopted the Repeal Act. The Central Government has issued guidelines to all the state governments. These guidelines emphasize the need for imposition of vacant land tax, on the land likely to be made available after the repeal of the Act and provision for LIG category houses, while sanctioning housing projects.
4. The proposed repeal, along with some other incentives and simplification of administrative procedures, is expected to revive the stagnant housing industry and provide affordable living accommodation for those who are in a state of undeserved want and are entitled to public assistance. The repeal will not, however, affect land on which building activity has already commenced. For that limited purpose, exemptions granted under Section 20 of the Act will continue to be operative. Amounts paid out by the state government will become refundable.
5. The Repeal will facilitate construction of dwelling units both in the public and private sector and help in achievement of targets contemplated under national agenda for governance. The repeal will facilitate land assembly and a flexible regime for administering urban land to suit the varying local conditions based on state level legislation/requirements.

Appendix-I

The Urban Land (Ceiling and Regulation) Repeal Bill, 1998*

A BILL

to repeal the ULCRA, 1976

Whereas it is considered necessary to repeal the ULCRA, 1976:

And whereas Parliament has no power to make laws for the states with respect to the aforesaid matter except as provided in Articles 249 and 250 of the Constitution;

In pursuance of Clause (2) of Article 252 of the Constitution resolutions have been passed by the legislatures of the states of Haryana and Punjab to the effect that the aforesaid Act should be repealed in those states by the Parliament by laws.

It is enacted by Parliament in the Forty-Ninth Year of the Republic of India as follows:

Short Titles, application and Commencement

1. This Act may be called the Urban Land (Ceiling the Regulation) Repeal Act, 1998.
2. It applies in the first instance to the whole of the states of Haryana and Punjab and to all the Union Territories. It shall apply to such other state which adopts this Act by resolution passed under Clause (2) of Article 252 of the Constitution.
3. It shall come into force in the states of Haryana and Punjab and in all the Union Territories at once and in any other state which adopts this Act, on the date of such adoption, and the reference to repeal of the ULCRA, 1976 shall, in relation to any state or Union Territory, mean the date on which this Act comes into force in such state or Union Territory.

Repeal of Act 33 of 1976.

1. The Urban Land (Ceiling and Regulation) Act, 1976 (hereafter referred to as the Principal Act) is hereby repealed.

Saving

2. The repeal of the principal Act shall not affect-
   (a) the vesting of any vacant land under sub-section (3) of Section 10 with respect to which the competent authority has-

The Bill as introduced in the Lok Sabha, June 11, 1998. Bill No. 56 of 1998.

(i) by notice in writing under sub-section (5) of that section ordered any person to surrender or deliver possession of such land to the state government or to any person duly authorized by the state government in this behalf; or

(ii) taken possession of such vacant land under sub-section (6) of that section. The use of such land for the purposes of 21 principal Act has commenced:

Provided where such use for the purposes of the Principal Act has not commenced, the state government shall restore such land to the person from whom it was taken over and the amount paid shall be liable to be refunded.

Provided further that where such land was subject to any encumbrance before vesting absolutely in the state government under sub-section (3) of that section, such land shall be restored with all the encumbrances from which it was freed under that sub-section as if no declaration had been made under that sub-section.

The Principal Act makes the following observations that the ULCRA provides for a ceiling on vacant land in urban areas, the acquisition of buildings constructed on such land and matters connected therewith. However, it was meant to bring an equitable distribution in urban areas to subserve the common good for checking the land speculation and profiteering activities. The Supreme Court had struck down the restrictions imposed by Section 27(1) in its judgements in *Maharao Saheb Singhji versus Union of India*, AIR 1981 S.C. 324.

Despite the Supreme Court judgement and amendments in rules and regulations several times by the Government, the ULCRA has been enforced in vain.

The Act (vide Sections 3 and 4) provides that no person should hold vacant land in excess of prescribed ceiling limit mentioned in the section for different categories. However, in practice, the enforcement of the connected provision of the section is impractical as the Corporation Acts of different states have not been considered. The FAR has to be worked out. Two-thirds or alternatively one-half of the total area under construction has to be left vacant under the corporation acts.

Provided also that no such land shall be restored unless the amount paid has been refunded to the state government.

From the government standpoint the repealing of the ULCRA will result in multiple benefits to the urban poor. The state governments will have three options. (i) To adopt the repeal; (ii) to adopt the repeal and enact a law suited to their needs and (iii) not adopt the repeal and allow the Principal Act to continue in force. States thus have a freedon of choice.

The other benefits will includes easing of land prices due to increase in the supply of land leading to fall in real estate prices, thereby making it possible for the economically weaker sections of the society to have access to housing. The Ministry of Urban Affairs and Employment was likely to issue suitable guidelines to the states for ensuring this possibility.

These guidelines will include suggestions such as stiff vacant land tax, provision for a shelter fund and reservation for the economically weaker sections, low-income group people within the town planning framework and building rules.

Besides, there will be speedy growth in sectors like housing, industry, transport and other urban infrastructures due to better availability of land. About two lakh hectares of land will be available in 64 cities all over the country for housing and urban infrastructure development following the ordinance.

Investment will be attracted for housing and other sectors. Land assembly, development and disposal of excess land for various purposes, particularly for housing will be facilitated.

Impact of Repeal

Speaking at the discussion on the Bill, Mr Ram Jethmalani, the then Union Minister of Urban Affairs and Employment had claimed that the government was determined to free vast urban lands from the clutches of corrupt bureaucrats and real estate magnets for the benefits of the poor. He also asserted that the government was committed to end the sorry state of affairs which enabled the rich to grab the land in the cities. He further described the ULCRA as a corruptly used statute in the country. According to one version about two lakh ha. of land is expected to be released if all the states decide to repeal the Act. Chennai Urban Agglomeration has about 370 ha. of identified surplus lands under the Scrapped Act. About 300 ha. of this are in parcels of more than 30 grounds (6000 sq.m). This is likely to give a boost to housing projects. The Draft

National Housing and Habitat Policy would facilitate construction of 20 lakh additional units annually to benefit the poor and the deprived. The protagonists contended that the repeal would send the death knell for corrupt practices, scrap the impediments to land supply and free it from the obsessive government control.

However, the perception of the housing activists was what different. They believed it was a retrograde step and would hurt the interest of the urban poor for which the Act was intended. According to them, the public ownership of urban lands is insignificant in almost all cities and through this move, the governments would further pauperize themselves to the detriment of slum dwellers and other low-income residents. They further felt that the bureaucrats, politicians, petty officials and builders were to be blamed for the poor performance, and repeal was not the answer. They apprehended that the repeal would result in increase in land value in the long run.

Even assuming that large extent of urban land would be released in the wake of the repeal, it is extremely unlikely that those lands would be available for the poor. For example, Godrej, the private limited company would get hundred of acres of prime land in Mumbai, which had been involved through litigation.

The genesis of the repeal of the ULCRA could be traced to the decision taken by the Union Cabinet under the Prime Minister, Inder Kumar Gujral to that effect on November 13, 1977. The contention of the Government was that the decision would set the stage for a sharp fall in land prices across the country and a faster growth in construction activities in 64 cities to which ULCRA applied. With that decision, Prime Minister, Inder Kumar Gujral practically nullified an Act which he, as Housing Minister, had brought into being over 20 years ago. Finally, the last nail was driven on the coffin of the ULCRA when the Lok Sabha passed the Bill to repeal it, by a voice vote, with the entire opposition staging a walkout, bemoaning it 'antipoor', on March 8, 1999.

Amendment to the Bill

The repeal of the ULCRA, 1976 has given greater emphasis to laissez-faire. The larger chunk of land available with the owners and private developers would deprive the availability of land for social welfare. The repeal of the Act will ensure greater private land availability for a profit motive. It has not been able to determine land in urban areas for social welfare purpose.

It is important that the ULCRA repeal must be substituted with a radical transformation in socialisation the urban land and according pricing for urban poor and middle income group has to be assessed on a countrywide basis.

REFERENCES

1. Bhargava, Gopal: Socio-Economic and Legal Implications of Urban Land (Ceiling and Regulation) Act, 1976, Abhinav Publisher (P) Ltd., 1983.
2. __________: Urban Land Ceiling Act has Failed, Viewpoint, Patriot, December 3, 1985.
3. __________: Need to Amend Urban Land Ceiling Act, *Evening News, The Hindustan Times*, August 3, 1996.
4. Editorial: Urban Planning and Development, *Journal of Institute of Town Planners*, India, No. 90, 1976.
5. Federation of Indian Chamber of Commerce and Industry, Background Paper: Seminar on Housing and Urban Development, February 5, 1996.
6. Government of India, Ministry of Urban Development: Agenda Notes: Conference of Ministers of Local Self Government and Urban Development of States and Union Territories, held on 17-18 January, 2000 at New Delhi.
7. Government of India, Ministry of Health: See Report of the Committee on Urban Land Policy.
8. Jagmohan: Challenges of Our Cities, Vikas Publishing (P) Ltd., New Delhi.
9. Krishnan, Jairam: Urban Ceiling Law Proves Counter Productive, *The Economic Times*, September 6, 1985.
10. Lok Sabha Bill No. 56 of 1998 Introduced in Lok Sabha June 11, 1998: The Urban Land (Ceiling and Regulation) Repeal Bill, 1998.
11. Meeting of Committee on Housing and Public Works—Madras Item No. 1, Agenda Draft Memorandum on the Urban Land (Ceiling and Regulation) Act, 1976 organized by Federation of Indian Chambers of Commerce and Industry, February 16, 1992.
12. Menezes, Louis: An Approach to Urban Land Policy, Social Act, 1982.
13. *National Herald*, January 13, 1999. Ordinance Promulgated to Repeal ULCRA.
14. Report of National Commission on Urbanization, Interim Report, January, 1987.
15. Subramanian, K.P.: Urban Land (Ceiling and Regulation) Act, (ULCRA): Lessons Learnt, *Nagarlok* Volume XXXI, Number-2, April-June, 1999.
16. Shukla, T.N., Gupta, D.K. and Mehta, K.C.: Urban Land (Ceiling and Regulation) Act, 1976 (With Rules and Forms as Amended Upto-date, Kamal House, Calcutta, 1983.
17. *The Economic Times*, June 5, 1997. New Urban Land Ceiling Act to reclassify towns, to cover only cities with population of over 10 lakh. Thrust on Development of Vacant Land not Acquisition.
18. Town Planning Department, Government of Karnataka, Town Planning Department, Government of Uttar Pradesh and Town Planning Department, Government of Orissa.

CHAPTER 7

MASTER PLAN APPROACH FOR URBAN DEVELOPMENT STRATEGY FOR REGULATORY CONTROLS

In India, the increasing pace of urbanization is a well-known phenomenon. It must be guided in such a way that it generates mutually complimentary spatial and economic development. According to the United Nations estimates, the population of India in 2025 will be about 1,442 million. The current rate of urbanization of 25.7 per cent is expected to double during the period. However, with such a rate of urbanization, the urban population of India will touch 721 million mark which will be about two-and-a-half times the projected total population of all countries in Europe in the year 2025. To plan and manage such a magnitude of urbanization in India in the next century will be an uphill task.

The Master Plan has traditionally been used as a tool to guide the process of urban development. However, in many cases, the desired results have not been achieved. It is probably because the implementation process was slow, restrictive and indirect, where the positive results were not seen immediately. As such, this has generated a general apathy among people, politicians and administrators who are generally interested in quick and visible results. Therefore, the Master Plans has become a target for severe criticism.

The Master Plan is divided into Zonal Plan and Sub-Zonal plans. It clearly indicates the landuse of each and every plot. While preparing the Master Plan, due consideration is given to the FAR of each sub-zone, so that the development should occur in a systematic order according to the building bye-laws. The zoning regulations, building bye-laws and other rules and regulations should not be too rigid and should rather be simple and objective, so as to become a vital catalyst for the development of an urban settlement.

For each and every city the Master Plan is a vital necessity. In the United States of America, each small town has an architect and town planner for the development of the city and he has a full power for the implementation of Master Plan. However, in USA, the politicians have no power to overrule the planning decisions and implementation of Master Plan.

Conceptual Framework

Within the conceptual framework, the Master Plan or the comprehensive plan also the development plan or the general plan is (a) guide to orderly city development to promote health, safety, welfare and convenience of the people of a community; (b) organizes or coordinates the complex relationships between the urban land and many civic amenities; (c) charts a course for growth and change; (d) expresses the aims and objectives of a community delineating the form and character it seeks to achieve; (e) reflects the policies by which goals, may be reached; (f) is responsive to appropriate change, and to maintain its essential utility is subject to continual review; (g) directs the physical development of a community and its environs in relation to its social and economic well-being. For the fulfilment of rightful common goal, according to a 'Master Plan' based on careful and comprehensive surveys and studies of present conditions and prospects of future growth of a city and embodying thereby the scientific techniques and creative experience.

In brief this is an exercise of state's inherent authority to have recourse to such measures as may serve the basic common moral and material needs. The Planning to this end is as old as the Government itself is—the very essence of an orderly and civilized society.

The Master Plan therefore, must be:

(a) a balanced and attractive design, best suited to present and probable future needs;

(b) in scale with the population and economic prospects of the community and

(c) in scale with its financial resources present and prospective.

The fulfilment of these conditions calls for the application of scientific as well as artistic efforts, in order to provide an attractive city plan pleasing balance and a detail formulation attuned to the economic and social activities of the community.

It is appropriate to define Master Plan as a process. However, it is envisaged as a pattern for the physical development of the city, a pattern for guiding the citizens in locating their investments and measuring the prospects for success. As such, the Master Plan concerns a design for the physical, social, economic and political framework of the city. It welds the sociological, economic, geographic properties of the city into a structure.

As we approach the end of the 20th century, there are signs of urban explosion in our cities, environmental degradation, financial crunch and widespread poverty. Urban development in this context is indeed a big challenge and a gigantic task. If urban planning cannot keep pace with the requirements of growing population, the living conditions are going to deteriorate further in cities. To maintain the levels of living condition, it is essential to ascertain the new lands are added with a provision of necessary facilities and services. The size and speed of urban development must match the magnitude and rate of growth of population. Since, finance is a major constraint financially viable development alternatives have to be devised. The urban development of cities must be controlled through Master Plans.

In the Third Five Year Plan (1961-66), recognition was given to the fact that urbanization was an important aspect of the process of economic and social development, closely connected with many problems such as migration, better water supply, sanitation, transport, power, pattern of economic development, location and dispersal of industries, civic administration, fiscal policies and the planning of landuse. It was the Third Plan which specifically provided for undertaking the preparation of Master Plans for practically all the major cities and their surrounding areas including industrial centres and also some of the rapidly growing regions. The Central Government made provisions for hundred per cent financial assistance for these exercises, provided the states were able to establish a satisfactory legal base and to continue the work thereafter.

Besides guiding the action of the Government and public agencies the Master Plans were also meant to control the use of privately owned property. They had to be necessarily backed by restrictive legislations enabling the exercise of police power. In fact, in the early seventies it was felt that 'Master Plans were ready but implementation was marginal because of lack of appropriate legal tools, administrative machinery, and financial budgeting'. Therefore, beginning with the Maharashtra Regional and Town Planning Act, already enacted in 1966, several states enacted town and regional planning acts. By the late seventies, most states did have legislation and the Master Plans could then be notified under such laws.

Notifying a plan is only a beginning. The plan has to be thereafter administered for decades. All Master Plan legislations enable subsequent modifications to the plans. Many modifications are a natural requirement in the public interest. Policy guidelines notified alongwith landuse maps can help the governments in handling such situations and in providing a basis for planned administration in general.

Another factor hindering the Master Plan is the multifarious authorities which do not cooperate in an integrated manner in the developmental process of cities. Even though the Master Plan may have made prescriptions to resolve various multifarious problems, the development authority has invariably lacked in resources, power and mandate, and institutional capacities to implement the prescription.

On the whole, the Master Plans have been subjected to the uncertainty that arises from the long-term projections, haphazard urban developments, unpredictable private investments in developmental projects. Further the rigidity that emerges from the occupied governmental land and the Master Plan proposals get distorted in terms of landuses and developmental requirements.

The Master Plan is not flexible to absorb the policy implications affecting the developmental programmes, which seems to be an inevitable phenomenon in a developing country like India. Due to this fact, there has been a widening gap between planning and development leading to distortions in the plan itself. Therefore, there is need for emphasizing the role of planning and development as integrated package for attempting the reforms.

According to the latest available estimates prepared by the Town and Country Planning Organization of the Government of India, Master Plans for some 1000 towns have been prepared, of which nearly half are sanctioned and considered to be in operation through the various Acts. It is interesting that about 150 developmental authorities have been created in various cities with the responsibilities of preparation, enforcement and implementation of the Master Plans.

MASTER PLAN FOR URBAN DEVELOPMENT

Source: The Economic Times, October 8, 1995

Delhi Master Plan: Salient Features

As per Delhi Development Act 1957, Sections 7(2) and 7(3), the essential contents of the Master Plan are as given below:

The Master Plan shall—

(a) define the various zones into which Delhi may be divided for the purpose of development and indicate the manner in which the land in each zone is proposed to be used (whether by carrying out development or otherwise) and the stages by which any such development shall be carried out; and

(b) serve as a basic pattern of framework within which the zonal development plans of various zones may be prepared.

The Master plan for Delhi, enforced in 1962, consisted of two sections (i) landuse plan and (ii) zoning and sub-divisions regulations. The major concepts/control/recommendations of the plan are:

(a) Characteristics of the plan—The landuse plan for urban Delhi has conceived to find solutions to the complex inter-related problems, namely social, economic and governmental. It may logically be termed as a comprehensive plan. The landuse plan in general (by the nature of the legislation under which it has been prepared) carries legal sanction and has a certain amount of rigidity; though it can be amended according to the law from time to time.

(b) Major policy decisions (i) Delhi will continue as major governmental centre being the capital city. What is required is a balanced economic base for the city as it will also continue to be a major financial, business, commercial and distributive centre. (ii) There shall be large scale acquisition, development and disposal of land as a policy for planned development.

(c) Planning synthesis (principles)—(i) For balanced development there should be decentralization of employment centres. (ii) To create conditions for healthy social living, a hierarchy of city structure is to be built from bottom onwards. (iii) While guiding developments of new areas along desirable lines, the areas having a healthy organic pattern must be conserved from encroachments and undesirable and conflicting landuses.

(d) Sectoral recommendations have been given to provide for space and parking standards, land allocation etc., for different sectors/ landuses.

(e) Zoning and sub-division regulations: The plan states that in order to promote public health, safety and the general moral and social welfare of the community, it is necessary to apply reasonable limitations on the use of land and buildings. This is to ensure that most economic and healthy developments of the city takes place in accordance with the landuse plan. For the purpose of regulations, the NCT of Delhi has been divided into 29 zones. For non-conforming uses, established prior to the enforcement of the Master Plan, a time schedule has been given for shifting of the non-conforming uses to the appropriate use zones. In different use zones a list of (i) uses permitted, (ii) uses permissible if allowed by competent authority after special appeal and, (iii) uses prohibited has been given.

The plan provided for maximum ground coverage and maximum permissible FAR in group housing, farm houses, government offices, district centres, community centres, local shopping centres, wholesale, warehousing and storage, industries and manufacturing and institutional use zone and so on.

(f) The plan provides a policy note on industries; the main recommendations being not to allow heavy and large scale industries in the capital city.

Prior to 1962, there was no comprehensive planning or plan implementation experience available in the country. The Master Plan was implemented during 1961–81, which provided such experience. Based on this experience and also fresh planning studies conducted during 1980-81, the Master Plan is comprehensively revised. After incorporating suggestions from general public, professionals and others concerned the revised Master Plan with Perspective 2001 is enforced from August 1, 1990. The main contents of the plan are:

(i) The Master Plan Development (MPD)-62 emphasizes that Delhi should be planned in the context of its region and there should be decentralization of employment.

(ii) The MPD-2001 is based on the following basic concepts: (a) Delhi to be planned as an integral part of the region. (b) Ecological balance to be maintained by conserving the ridge and the river Yamuna. (c) Central city area which is full of mixed use to be treated as special area for the purpose of planning and zoning regulations. (d) Urban heritage of the historic city to be conserved. (e) The city centre to be decentralized by developing metropolitan passenger terminal and major freight complexes and commercial complexes like Sub-Central Business District and District Centres. (f) Mass transport to be multimodal with emphasis on rail-based system for mass transit. (g) The urban development to be low rise high density. (h) City structure to be hierarchical in form.

(iii) The section on development policies have provisions for: (a) population and employment projections, (b) regional and sub-regional frame, (c) urban extension, (d) channelization of the Yamuna, (e) shelter, (f) New Delhi bungalow area, (g) urban renewal of old city areas, (h) industries, (i) trade and commerce, (j) government offices, (k) transportation, (l) infrastructure,

(m) environment, (n) energy, (o) special areas and (p) rural areas.

(iv) The landuse plan 2001 is based on: (i) the policies enunciated, (ii) higher intensity landuses along ring road, (iii) requirement of physical and social infrastructure, (iv) restructuring required for interrelationship of urban activities.

(a) The development code is given to promote the quality of life by organizing the most appropriate development of land in accordance with the development policies and landuse proposals. It is a systematic code to decide activity (use) in two levels—(i) conversion of use zone into use premises and (ii) permitting use activities on use premises. The development code identifies the use of premises permitted in different use zone, use activities in use premises and sub-division regulations for residential and industrial areas. The development code provides for a system of setbacks, parking standards and maximum grounds coverage, FAR and maximum height permissible.

(b) Special area regulations: special regulations for the old city areas, that is Walled City, Karol Bagh and other old areas. The development code also gives regulations for mixed use to be allowed in residential areas.

(c) MPD-2001 provides for regular monitoring of the city and plan performance.

Delhi's Master Plan had the following objectives, namely:

(i) Balanced distribution of population in Delhi and selected ring towns.

(ii) Development of city through planning divisions of equitable distribution of resources and facilities.

(iii) Improvement of living and working conditions in the existing built-up areas.

(iv) Provision of developed land to individuals and cooperatives.

(v) Provisions of tenements to *basti* dwellers.

(vi) Reservation of land for first migrants to the city to

counter squatting and integrating this population with city developmental process.

(vii) To accelerate the rate of supply of land and provide mass scale housing for the low income population.

All this was to be achieved through a unique large scale land acquisition, development and disposal policy aimed at socialization of land. The objectives of the policy were:

(i) To ensure availability of land in adequate quantity at the right time, right price and at right place.

(ii) To prevent concentration of land ownership in few hands to safeguard the interests of urban poor and the urban privileged.

(iii) To control urban land values and to eliminate speculative profits.

Experience of Implementation

The results of the implementation of Master Plan are mixed. In spite of reasonably good achievements in land development for various uses, construction of more than two lakh dwelling units for all income groups, large-scale growth of squatter settlements, unauthorized colonization, large-scale misuse of residential properties, are the indications of inadequacies in the Master Plan. The limited supply of developed land and the lavish standards were responsible for widening the gap in supply and demand for housing for low-income group and urban poor. This had manifested in large-scale growth of squatter settlements and unauthorized colonization. One of the massive resettlement programmes in the country was carried out in Delhi during the Emergency, when two lakhs families were resettled on 21 sq.m. plot. The DDA till December 1990, had developed an allotted 19,735 hectares of land for various use.

TABLE 1

(Hectares)

Residential Scheme	—	7484 Ha.
Slum and J.J. Resettlement	—	2346 Ha.
Horticulture	—	2954 Ha.
Industrial	—	1034 Ha.
Commercial, Institutional	—	3957 Ha.
Government, Semi-Government		
Cooperative Societies	—	1945 Ha.

Source: Delhi by Delhi Development Authority

This shows, out of 19190 Ha. of residential land to be developed and allotted by the end of Master Plan period 1981, DDA could develop and allot 11775 Ha. (61per cent) of land till December 1990 (Nine years after the expiry of First Master Plan). This is an indication of slow rate of land supply for residential purposes.

The huge backlog of registered applicants with DDA for plots and flats since last decade is a pointer towards the rethinking that is required in the approach. As per the estimates the housing need is to the tune of 80,000 dwellings per annum. The Master Plan for Delhi, 2001, envisages acquisition of another 18000–24000 Ha. of land to accommodate 3 to 4 million population.

The factors which call for change in the approach/alternative are:

(i) Slow pace of developed land supply.
(ii) Large-scale growth of squatters and unauthorized colonization.
(iii) Increasing cost of land acquisition, development.
(iv) Increasing cost of construction and low affordability.
(v) Lack of adequate finances.
(vi) Static nature of Master Plan which causes numerous procedural delays.
(vii) Lack of adaptability to changing socio-economic and political situations.
(viii) Master Plan tends to be too prescriptive rather than acting as a guide for the growth of city.
(ix) The non-applicability of development controls suggests their inadequacy for its realistic applications.
(x) National Housing Policy—difficult to operate through the mechanism of present day Master Plan.
(xi) Inflexible and too much restrictive nature of building bye-laws leads to more corruption rather than simplifying the needs of urban poor and low-income families.
(xii) Recognizing the efforts of informal sector of housing.
(xiii) General resource crunch.

TABLE 2

Status of Master Plans/Development Plans in India: (Statewise)

Sl. No.	*States*	*Plans approved by State Government*	*Draft Plans prepared*	*Plans under preparation*	*Total*
1.	Andhra Pradesh	93	–	12	105
2.	Assam	13	12	–	25
3.	Arunachal Pradesh	1	6	14	21
4.	Bihar	7	17	–	24
5.	NCT, Delhi	1	–	–	1
6.	Goa	14	–	2	16
7.	Gujarat	106	–	–	106
8.	Himachal Pradesh	6	1	8	15
9.	Haryana	36	–	17	53
10.	Jammu and Kashmir	1	5	4	10
11.	Karnataka	27	–	–	27
12.	Kerala	15	6	21	42
13.	Madhya Pradesh	19	5	–	24
14.	Maharashtra	224	4	14	242
15.	Manipur	1	9	–	10
16.	Mizoram	3	1	11	15
17.	Meghalaya	3	–	2	5
18.	Nagaland	9	–	–	9
19.	Orissa	40	24	27	91
20.	Punjab	77	–	–	77
21.	Rajasthan	35	8	19	62
22.	Tamil Nadu	79	29	6	114
23.	Tripura	8	–	4	12
24.	Uttar Pradesh	50	27	–	77
25.	West Bengal	7	–	–	7
	Union Territories				
	1. Chandigarh	1	–	–	1
	2. Dadar and Nagar Haveli	1	–	–	1
	3. Daman and Diu	1	–	–	1
	4. Andaman and Nicobar Islands	–	1	–	1
	5. Pondicherry	1	3	–	4
		879	158	161	1198

Source: Town and Country Planning Organization (1995) Master Plan Approach in India and other Countries. Cited Spatio-Economic Development Record, Volume 2, Number 2, March-April 1995.

Master Plan: Approach

The First Master Plan of Mumbai was prepared under the Bombay Town Planning Act, 1915 and it had laid down the initial legal framework. Further, the plan was implemented in a regulated planner manner. Today, there are many other innumerable master plans in the country but only few of them are able to promote a significant socio-economic and spatial development. Presently, the number of urban settlements in the country is 4,689 and it is expected to be around 5,200 by 2001. Only about 1,100 settlements so far have Master Plans and by 2001 some 4,100 urban centres will need the development plans. In spite of the preparation of a number of Master Plans, there is no single Master Plan which can be said to have hundred per cent implementation. In the case of Kanpur, the Master Plan was not implemented for 20 years and therefore, the projections and public utility requirements have become outdated.

The implementation problem of Master Plan is an important defect. For example, the Master Plans prepared by the Town and Country Planning Department exhibit a set pattern of proposals with display of major circulation; broad proposals of residential, commercial, industrial, office and open areas, community facilities together with zoning regulations, etc. Master Plans for urban areas of different sizes reflect proposals outlining the simple disposition of broad landuse pattern, together with very limited attention to feasible means of implementation anticipating the reaction of market forces and to assess the cost of various governmental agencies and economic effect on different income groups. Very often the various implementing agencies like developmental authority, municipal bodies, housing board, Public Work Department etc., are instrumental in changing/amending the Master Plan proposals to pursue their piecemeal developmental efforts.

The institutional set-up for implementation is weak. Misinterpretation of these plans has aroused question amongst a large section of people. Once the plan is approved after hearing it is subject to guiding the urban growth and exercising control on development of towns. However, rather than being a mere framework of reference for guiding the future development, it should be followed by zonal development plan which has rarely been given a priority. Reasons may be shortage of technical staff for detailed physical surveys, aerial surveys, etc. The implementation of Master Plan without detailing poses serious problems for the authority concerned and thus results in mockery of planning process itself. The standards and regulations formulated long ago or in the line of developed countries with minor changes are done by an ad hoc arrangement. Such standards very often do not match with requirements and affordability of the bulk of population. Naturally, the cost of implementation becomes high with little chance of recovery of the investment. The escalating prices of land infrastructure development have drastically crippled the local authorities to undertake feasible urban development scheme.

Owing to the static nature of Master Plans, urban land problems and the lack of effective landuse control polices the plan remains primarily an academic exercise, though having some direct influences on landuse.

Proposal Action

In the light of increasingly obvious shortcomings of the conventional approach of survey, analysis and the preparation of final plans, an attitudinal change is required towards planning. The change in planning methodology should be in the awareness of limited resources, complex population problems and economic criterions. Most important thing is that resource amount should be declared before hand to overcome the problem of overprovision beyond the capacity of majority of people as well as the local civic body. The process should be in any case dynamic and responsive to the acute problems of urban growth.

Public participation should be invited at the time of plan preparation from very beginning and co-opt the suggestions, if possible, after the judgement to have minimum opposition from affected people.

Different implementation organizations should be co-opted as members of the planning body to form a team, avoid duplicity of work and to give the planners an opportunity to dictate various schemes rather than present practice of co-opting the proposals of various departments.

A sound land policy/legislation is required to make the schemes viable. For example, in case of preservation/conservation most of the plans say so. Hence buildings are to be preserved or an area should be conserved either for environmental preservation or for heritage conservation. In a democratic set-up and under the provision of present Land Acquisition Act the Government cannot dictate a private body to preserve/conserve. A detail thinking is required to overcome this shortcoming of land policy otherwise it will be difficult to have futuristic long-term planning.

The Master Plan is able to evaluate the existing level of facilities in terms of socio-economic and physical factors. However, the shortcomings of the Master Plan are with reference to the population projections. For example, in Burdwan (West Bengal), The Master Plan had projected a population of 2 lakh, but it has been recorded as 7 lakh. Thus, with the projection of population going wrong, the Master Plan provision for public utility services and infrastructural facilities gets distorted. However, one of the vital issues while preparing the Master Plan is to assess in a comprehensive manner the factors which need to be considered while projecting population in a long-term perspective.

The main reason behind the failure of the Master Plan is firstly, the land required for development is not acquired in a specified period and secondly, whatever land is acquired is not developed. In the Master Plan, what is suggested is not practised and sometimes it is changed by the Government itself and taken for more profitable landuses. As such, the land acquired in a city should immediately be developed in that particular area. The pertinent issue is that when a large scale of land is acquired the fencing should be done around it by the concerned authority. Without fencing of the acquired land the unauthorized colonies and constructions have emerged in nearly all the metropolitan and other large cities. The specific landuse designated in the Master Plan becomes encroached and distorted in the context of the city developmental perspective. It is a fact that the encroached, unauthorized slum colonies cannot be demolished and alternatives sites are provided again and again.

The Land Acquisition Act should be reformulated for ensuring an effective process of implementation of Master Plan. However, there is need for examining the possibility of summary trials in matters of land acquisition in a short time period. Due to the delay, planning and development of the city has been hampered.

The vital issues and proposals of the Master Plan are green areas and open spaces. The swallowing of agricultural land, open spaces and green areas for housing developments has created serious ecological imbalances in the urban areas. The preservation of urban landscapes and ecological balance through the legislative measures should be emphasized in the Master Plan framework.

The Master Plan for Delhi: 2001 perspective had recommended 'that Ridge should be afforested by introducing indigenous trees with minimum or artificial landscape'. But there has been massive encroachment in the Ridge area. It is learnt that the forest area has been brought under use, both by people and the government bodies. These include the Central Reserve Police Force (CRPF), the PWD and the DESU which has set up 16 transmission towers in the northern Ridge.

The various authorities have interfered with the Master Plan proposals which get distorted with reference to planning and development. Thus, the vital issue is the speedy implementation of the Master Plan for which the administrative, legal and planning mechanism has to be spelt out in a comprehensive manner.

Policy Perspectives

One of the major issues to be emphasized is the administrative and legal framework in terms of landuses as specified in the proposals of the Master Plan.

The limitations of appropriate technology in implementation of the Master Plan proposals are with reference to the construction of high rise buildings, earthquake zones, flood areas, tornado areas, cyclonic areas, snow bound areas. These aspects need to be dealt in a comprehensive manner in the Master Plan framework. However, critical evaluation is required while a review is undertaken. Specifically, the Master Plan needs to be considered in relation to the implementation authority.

The Master Plan is considered as a purely governmental scheme. Public has no role in its making or in its implementation. Master Plan is a document which has been forcefully thrust on majority of the urban population. People's participation should be encouraged for planning, implementation and review, maintenance and the management of Master Plan.

Resource crunch has become a major issue which delays the implementation of Master Plan proposals. The suitable resource mobilization has got to be duly envisaged. There is need for considering the aspect of the sustained financial mobilization. This would ensure an effective process of implementation concerning the proposals of the Master Plan.

The existing city administrative system, having multifarious authorities looking after various departments, not well is coordinated for providing the adequate infrastructural and socio-economic facilities. Such a situation has left the Master Plan proposal unimplemented. The consideration for integrating the multifarious departmental authorities in a single window operation for the timely implementation of the Master Plan is suggested and should be accorded priority.

The time period of Master Plan is usually envisaged for a period of 20 years. However, it is a very small period as preparation of Master Plan takes five to ten years and its actual implementation commences after lapse of a longer period of time. For example, the Delhi Master Plan for 2001 has taken a long period of preparation. There is need for emphasizing the importance of the Master Plan time perspective period. As for a short time span of Master Plan the projections go wrong. There is a need to explore as to whether the Master Plan for cities the time period should be 30 years to 40 years or more with a periodic review of every five years.

It is visualized that the urban development authority like DDA should be concerned with the preparation of the Master Plan and not merely with its enforcement. The implementation of Master Plan should be done by a separate agency comprising the technical members of the Municipal Corporation of Delhi (MCD), New Delhi Municipal Committee (NDMC), Delhi Urban Arts Commission (DUAC), DESU etc. It is recognized that planning functions should not be too closely influenced by the development functions in order to avoid the needless compromises that are made in developmental work adversely affecting the long-term perspective.

It is surprising that many urban development authorities, land and building departments, etc., are not even aware as to how much land belonged to the authorities and where such land is located. Thus, it is evident that presently the land records of the different urban development authorities are not properly maintained. With the result, encroachments on public land and unauthorized constructions have come up in the metropolitan cities in a big way. Further, vigilance is absent and the concerned authorities have shown an indifferent attitude. Subsequently, the Master Plan proposals of landuse are distorted.

Largely the Master Plan of cities have ignored the provisions of adequate land for the service personnel. Consequently, on the vacant land or occupied constructed land, the unauthorized *jhuggi jhompri* clusters have emerged in metropolitan and other large cities in an alarming proportion and resulted in gigantic problems. The issues of urban land management and provision of land for the service personnel in the Master Plan needs to be duly recognized.

The informal sector which has so far been ignored in the Master Plan preparation must be made an integral part of the city planning process, so as to cater to the needs of the sector which constitutes about 65 per cent of the total employment in certain mega cities. The suitable locations should be earmarked in the development schemes for informal, residential, commercial and other activities. Due consideration has to be given to their development and management as an informal activity.

It is worthwhile to point out that the Master Plan for Delhi: 2000. Perspective has declared Anand Parbat industrial area for flattened factories. Yet, different authorities have not provided the required services. There is need to recognize a particular area for a specified land use in the Master Plan and provides developmental activities. The Master Plan should become an authoritative document with legal sanctions and accordingly developmental programmes should be followed.

Though the Constitution 74th Amendment Act gives more powers to the Urban Local Bodies for the development of their own areas, the basic infrastructure required for the preparation and implementation of Master Plan will take a long time. Therefore, a stop gap arrangement for regulating the appropriate process of urban development is required.

It is generally observed that Master Plan for the cities is confined to the boundary limits. The first Master Plan, 1962 had emphatically spelt out that Delhi should be planned in a regional perspective of the NCR. With the formulation of an inter-state NCR plan it becomes necessary to recognize the regional Master Plan of cities with a unified technical administrative coordinated agency. This would be able to ensure a balanced spatial and economic development of the area. The Spatial Regional plans should be prepared for all regions/districts for providing an orderly development of rural and urban settlements with continuum and providing thereby the alternative location of investments.

Yet another vital issue which needs to the considered is the monitoring of Master Plan proposals. It has been seen that this is the weakest part in the implementation of the Master Plan. There is a poor feedback and inefficient monitoring of development proposals of the Master Plan.

The main component of Master Plan are as follows:

(a) Master Plan should be an integral part of the overall development management;

(b) the Master Plan should define only the broad landuse pattern and major transport inputs;

(c) it should provide a framework for development control in conjunction with the land policy instruments;

(d) a two-staged development permission procedure, particularly for large-scale developments should be followed. The public participation during the first stage of outline development permission should be facilitated. This would require more informed review of development permissions and would require the trained manpower for this activity;

(e) computerized information systems, particularly related to land in terms of landuse and land prices should be developed in support of development management system;
(f) implementation of Master Plan, particularly its investment requirements, should become an explicit component of budgetary processes and capital investment programme.

The weakness of the Master Plan is that it is mainly confined to towns and cities. Subsequently, the map outlines of the proposals are generally not detailed out in terms of zonal development and layout plans for achieving the success of the implementable plans. As such, invariably the Master Plans for cities have not been conceived in terms of regional and national plans and policies. Therefore, the Master Plans are not oriented in terms of spatially integrated development programmes.

In Master Plan the authorities involved lack commitment for implementation. Specific action is required to be spelt out for speedy implementation of the Master Plan.

1. The land acquisition and development should be done simultaneously. Further, the compensation of the land required should be given at the market rate for speedy landuse developments as specified in the Master Plan.
2. The excess of land acquired for the Master Plan should have a strict vigilance as encroachment of squatting on public land has risen in a big way. Thus, such a phenomenon has distorted the planned developments of the Master Plan.
3. Master Plan should provide adequate land for the service personnel and for informal activities.
4. Master Plan of cities and towns should consider the presentation of open spaces, parks and playfields, so as to maintain an ecological harmony. City within the city in the context of Delhi has led to the overgrowth of population and consequently the demand for public utility services. National Capital Regional Plan has been formulated to reduce the population of Delhi. A greater stress is required for preserving the green belt of a city. However, the fundamentals of Master Plan principles of greenery seems to be forgotten.
5. For the speedy development of Master Plan the administrative, legal and planning set up has to be spelt out in a comprehensive manner.
6. Metropolitan and large cities which are already congested should not have the second Master Plan. What is required in the Master

Plan for infrastructure facilities like medical, water, electricity, transport, education and so on.

7. The Master Plan for the adjoining areas should confer within the Regional Perspective Plan. For example, to have separate Master Plans for Ghaziabad, Gurgaon and Delhi will be contradictory to the National Capital Regional Plan objectives.
8. The Master Plan of metropolitan and large cities should not allow the excessive growth of industrialization, trade and commerce and office establishments. For example, the wholesale trade of Delhi and offices like agricultural, Cement Corporation of India and Coast Guard Organization are not required in the National Capital Delhi as these have no ministerial linkages. These aspects have been overlooked in the Delhi: Master Plan Perspective, 2001.

The workshop 'Master Plan Approach: Its Efficacy and Alternatives' held at New Delhi was organized by the Town and Country Planning Organization, Ministry of Urban Development, Government of India. The following are its recommendations.

To develop realistic and effective urban development plans steps need to be taken to evolve: (a) spatial development plan—depicting broad landuse zones and major spatial proposals, (b) resource mobilization plan, (c) institutional mechanism to implement the development plan, (d) a set of comprehensive and simplified development management, promotion rules, regulations, laws which can be easily understood by the public, and (e) a mechanism to involve the participation of the public—especially the poor, socially disadvantaged groups, women, non-government and community-based organizations—in the planning process in case of all cities/metropolitan areas. For the smaller towns, outline development plans interim general plans with shorter time periods may be prepared. The growth potential and special functions performed by the urban areas such as marketing, industrial, tourism, pilgrim centres, etc. need to be explicitly recognized. The planning exercises should aim at guiding the activities of public agencies as well as the private sectors, including the growing informal sector while keeping the larger interests of the society in view. The Ministry of Urban Development and the state governments should take immediate action to develop model guidelines in this regard by constituting expert committees to provide appropriate advice to the concerned agencies.

The plan formulation exercises must be completed within a specified time period and the time schedule for plan preparation, public notification/

hearing and approval must be statutorily prescribed in the relevant Acts. Considering the importance of metropolitan cities, approval of the major changes in their development plans should be done at the highest level and within prescribed time periods.

In view of the severe strains on infrastructure and services in cities due to rapid urban growth and concentration, the preparation and implementation of development plans need to take into account the availability (existing and potential) of the environmental resources in the region. Landuse, development management, building byelaws and other regulations should take into account the availability of water, quality of air, traffic density and carrying capacity of roads, rail and other transportation networks, capacity of water distribution, drainage and sewerage systems, power supply, open spaces, and so on.

The periodic review and revision of plans are essential components of the planning process. Mid-term reviews of the plans should be undertaken at regular intervals to impart flexibility to the planning process. Necessary statutory provisions need to be made in the relevant town planning/Urban Development Municipal Acts in this regard.

Keeping in view the provisions of the Constitution (74th) Amendment Act, a strong push to the preparation of integrated development plans for urban areas integrating physical and socio-economic planning and taking into account the urban, rural, spatial and functional linkages, environmental protection and financial and non-financial resources available for implementation of plans is called for. These plans should be prepared utilizing the latest techniques and tools like Remote Sensing Aerial Photography, Geographical Information Systems (GIS) and other computer applications for preparing the base maps. In this regard, the Planning Commission should give utmost priority to regional and urban planning, including urban mapping. Since the Third Five Year Plan, priority accorded to these activities in terms of budgetary support has not kept pace with the growing complexities of urban problems and the demands of cities and towns. Both the Central and State Plan should make the adequate budget provisions in their annual and Five Year Plans in this regard.

The state governments should take the expeditious steps to constitute the District Planning and Metropolitan Planning Committees, with full regard to the need for involvement of adequate number of experts in the fields of physical and socio-economic planning. They should initiate suitable policies and programmes including a package of financial reforms, so as to ensure the availability of necessary resources to implement the plans as prepared.

The District and Metropolitan Development Plans should take into account cost-efficient and environmentally sound technologies and innovative implementation practices such as public-private partnership and private sector initiatives, while recognizing the role of the government as a facilitator.

The application of the concepts of land swaps, land pooling, town planning schemes, accommodation reservation, transfer of development rights, etc. which are innovative plan implementation techniques should be explored. The town planning, urban development authority, municipal, revenue and other laws may be amended to accommodate innovative practices while keeping the provisions of the 74th Amendment and the principles of economic reforms in view.

Base maps of towns/cities, which are required for a variety of purposes, need no longer be regarded as secret documents. Greater transparency will be in the interest of better public awareness, especially in the context of planning for development having been decentralized through the Constitution 74th Amendment, 1992.

Both the Central and State Governments should initiate steps to develop appropriate management information systems and data base which will assist the planners in developing realistic plans and programmes. They may organize public awareness programmes on regional and urban planning aspects and periodic training of planners and municipal functionaries.

REFERENCES

1. Bhargava, Gopal: Putting the Master Plan to Practise, Observer of Business and Politics, July 19, 1996.
2. Gambir, J.C., Narayan, Prakash: Planning for Development (including redevelopment) of Cities—Review of the Master Plan Concept, paper presented at the National Workshop on Master Plan Approach: Its Efficacy and Alternatives.
3. Goyal, A.K. and Shorey, S.P: Master Plan Approach Hyderabad Experience Spatio-Economic Development Record, Volume 2, No. 2, March-April, 1995.
4. Gupta, R.C.: Management of Urban Development: Issues and Imperatives, paper presented at 43rd Annual Town and Country Planning Seminar February 3, 1995.
5. Joseph, D.T. and Pathak, V.K., Flexible Planning and Innovative Development Management, Spatio-Economic Development Record, Volume 2, No. 2, March-April, 1995.
6. Kaul, Sheila: Need for Adaptation of Mixed Landuse Planning Approach, (inaugural address at the National Workshop on Master Plan Approach: Its Efficacy and Alternatives, 24-25 February, 1995, organized by the Ministry of Urban Development.
7. Kulshrestha, S.K.: Editorial Development Plans. Spatio-Economic Development Record, Volume 2, No. 2, March-April, 1995.

8. Risbud, Vijay D.: Alternative Approaches to Master Plan presented in the Settlement Planning Concepts and Systems Technical papers of 40th Annual Town Seminar, Pune 15-17, January, 1992.
9. Saha, Swati: Practice of Master Planning Approach in West Bengal: A Critical Study, paper presented in 40th Annual Town and Country Planning Seminar, 15-17 January, 1992.
10. Spatio-Economic Development Record. Volume 2, No. 2, March-April, 1995: Special Compilation National Workshop on Master Plan Approach—Its Efficacy and Alternatives.
11. Town and Country Planning Organization, Ministry of Urban Affairs and Employment: Workshop on Master Plan Approach—Its Efficacy and Alternatives, 1995.

CHAPTER 8

RURAL DEVELOPMENT AND GROWTH CENTRE PLANNING CASE STUDIES AND POLICY ISSUES

About 62.8 crore people, comprising three-fourths of country's population, are living in six lakh villages of varying sizes. Although proportion or rural population to the total population is steadily declining in our country, in absolute terms it is continuously increasing. Since the beginning of the century, the proportion of rural population to the total population had declined since 1901 to 1991, Gandhiji had rightly said that "India lives in villages, only when villages advance, India will advance."

Today, there is need to cater to the spatial and economic development in the rural areas in a comprehensive manner, as more than 7 per cent of India's population lives in villages. The process of migration from villages in an alarming proportion to big urban settlements indicates the lack of economic and employment opportunities in the rural settlements. The rural areas produce foodgrains for the urban population, materials for urban centres of industrial establishments and supplies for their manufacturing and commercial organizations. This importance of rural areas has to be recognized in the 21st century while planning development of rural settlements.

India is an agricultural country. The physical composition of its rural settlements are confined to sub-division and fragmentation. The farm cultivation in the context of rural settlements constitutes uneconomic size of holdings. The legal proceedings of land disputes have become time consuming which has hampered the agricultural productivity. This would lead to a serious challenge for the rural development in the 21st century.

The primary objective of the freedom movement under Gandhiji's leadership was to achieve tangible economic opportunities for the majority of the rural poor who barely managed to subsist in a system of fragmented holdings. Therefore, it is needless to say that the poor have been left with only inferior quality land for cultivation.

The agricultural landless workers are likely to multiply in an alarming number in the 21st century. As such, the acute crisis of rural poverty, unemployment and indebtedness has become a challenging confrontation in the rural settlements. In spite of the best efforts of the Five Year Plans in terms of huge investment outlay, the Integrated Rural Development Programme (IRDP) and other schemes have not been able to perform a significant progress in the process of structural transformation of rural economic base. Thus, there is an enormous influx of migration from rural areas towards the metropolitan and large cities.

In the absence of any meaningful development for the marginal farmers, agricultural labourers and the village artisans, it is a continuous struggle for survival. However, there is a vital need that their economic status be improved through appropriate landuse technologies which are labour intensive, cultivation of high yielding crop varieties, agro-forestry, subsidiary occupations such as animal husbandry and manufacturing of components for various industries.

The Report of the World Bank on 'Rural Development—Sector Policy' has made suggestions that a strategy for rural development has to recognize three vital factors. Firstly, the rate of transfer of people out of low productivity agriculture or related activities into more rewarding pursuits has been slow, in the context of relative size of the modern sector in most developing countries. Secondly, the mass of people in the rural areas of developing countries are confronted with the varying degrees of poverty. Their position is likely to get worse if population expands at an unprecedented rate, while limitations continue to be imposed on available resources, technology, institutions and organizations. Thirdly, rural areas have labour, land and at least some capital which, if mobilized in an effective manner, will remove poverty and ensure the improvement of the quality of life. Such a situation implies fuller development of the existing resources, including the construction of infrastructure such as roads and irrigation works, the introduction of new production technology and subsequently, creation of new types of institutions and organizations. The rural development is intended to reduce poverty in the Ninth Plan Perspective, enabling the enhancement of production distribution of the marketing products.

Emerging Issues

The rural problems have been confined mainly to the inadequate availability of infrastructural facilities like (i) power, (ii) road, (iii) transport and water supply. The absence of power has been he main cause of rural backwardness in terms of economic development. This responsible for a great setback in the implementation programmes of Five Year Plans.

In a paper, 'Methodology for Rural Areas' S. Paul has rightly pointed out that India at this juncture needs rural methodology and not the sophisticated technology. The villages may not need high level engineering tools, but may require an improved package of animal husbandry and agro-horticultural practices, tiny agro-industries and cottage industries. For instance, a secluded but scenic spot may be revived by promoting tourism alone. Thus, supplanting the technology with the more appropriate 'methodology' will help to shed fixation with mechanization and industrialization.

A nationwide effort has to be evolved in the new millennium for adopting a rural technological know-how by emphasizing the following considerations, namely: (i) reviving old technology/village crafts; (ii) improving and upgrading the indigenous skills/tools; (iii) simplifying/ adapting current technology to suit the village needs; (iv) investing low cost new techniques/machinery, which in no way displaces human labour.

Irregular Power Supply

In the Indian context, the Rural Electrification Programme with an enormous financial involvement has not been able to generate electricity in a comprehensive manner for villages of all the states. Rural areas have been provided with the electric poles, yet in certain areas the supply has been irregular. In particular, the irrigation facilities and small scale industrial development has been hard hit owing to the irregular power supply in the rural settlements.

An effort has to be made for providing the top priority to a massive rural electrification programme in the Ninth Five Year Plan through the active participation of private sector. The State Electricity Boards have not been able to cater to the demand of electricity in all the rural settlements. Presently, an alarming number of villages are deprived of electricity which is vital for accelerating the tempo of agro-industrial development. Electricity is largely available to the urban settlements however, the power supply is frequently cut in the rural and small town settlements.

Lack of Amenities

On the whole, large number of villages are ill-equipped with the medical, education and financial facilities.

Rural and Urban Population : 1901 - 1921

Census Year	Population (Million) Rural	Urban	Percentage of Total Population Rural	Urban
1901	213	25	89.2	10.8
1911	226	26	89.7	10.3
1921	223	28	88.8	11.2
1931	245	34	88.0	12.0
1941	274	44	86.1	13.9
1951	298	63	82.7	17.3
1961	360	79	82.0	18.0
1971	439	109	80.1	19.9
1981	525	160	76.7	23.3
1991	629	217	74.3	25.7
2001*	657	231	77.3	22.7
2011*	687	247	73.5	26.5
2021*	723	291	71.3	28.7

Source: Census of India, 1991, Paper 2, Cited from A.N. Aggarwal, H.O. Varma and R.C. Gupta {India Economic Information Year-Book, 1995,' National Publishing House, New Delhi.

Includes projected population of Assam and Jammu and Kashmir.

* Projected Population

The rural settlements have not been provided with sufficient infrastructural and socio-economic facilities. Thus, the lack of employment opportunities have forced the rural inhabitants to migrate towards the metropolitan and large cities.

Rural and Urban Dichotomy

In the 20th century owing to the inadequate financial institutions and lack of an effective administrative set-up, the rural settlements have witnessed stagnation in agricultural productivity and allied sectors. With the adoption of sophisticated technological developments the urban areas are geared for boosting the optimal production, income and employment prospects. In spite of huge investments in rural areas there exists a picture of neglect in terms of developmental progress. This lacuna needs to be corrected in the 21st century.

Presently, a large number of villages are faced with a rising trend of unemployment, under employment and disguised unemployment situations. It is evident that the growing magnitude of rural poverty is due to the economic concentration of developments in the big urban settlements. There has arisen a dichotomy between rural and urban settlements due to differentiations in the level of economic developments. The village economy is harnessed for satisfying the needs of the urban population. Thus, the rural sector has become a vital stimulant for promoting economic prosperity in the urban areas, yet it is subjected to poverty, low income and vast magnitude of unemployment. In the 21st century an effective process of rural development has to be given a top priority of development and planning for generating adequate employment opportunities.

Road Network Requirement

If rural India is to be launched on the path of economic emancipation and is to be brought in the mainstream of national growth and development, then each and every village would have to be linked to nearby urban settlement. Roads are like human arteries through which the vital blood in the shape of men and material flows and accordingly these arteries have to be made efficient channels for bringing in and out the raw material and finished goods.

Punjab and Haryana have shown enormous growth and development which is mainly due to the fact that an excellent road network has been created in these states, covering all the urban and rural settlements. The backward states have recorded slow rate of road development.

In the 21st century, the rural settlements need to be linked to the nearest market centres, so as to enable the villagers to fetch the optimum returns of their produce. Roads also help in making optimum use of available infrastructures of the nearby urban centres besides free flow of information and technology from one area to another. Thus, for an efficient road network it would be desirable to prepare a Master Plan of rural roads on the state and district level basis. This would help in minimizing the overlapping, duplication and multiplicity of roads in certain areas and absence of such roads in others. However, the basic premise while planning the road network in the 21st century should be done in a manner that it involves minimum of road length while covering the entire state, thus minimizing the need for fiscal resources.

Agro-Industrial Development

There is need for developing the entire rural settlements in the Ninth Five Year Plan framework. For the optimal exploration and mobilization of rural resources an integrated spatial and economic process of agro-industrial planning needs to be emphasized. The intensive farm technology, animal husbandry, poultry development and food processing industries are capable of boosting the economic developments of rural settlements.

The type of industries which are conducive to the rural settlements are, namely : (1) sport goods, (2 glassware, (3) footwear and leather goods, (4) leather tanning, (5) brass manufacture, (6) cutlery, (7) bicycle parts, (8) carpentry, (9) woodwork, (10) locks, (11) steel wire products, (12) simple type of mathematical instruments. The small scale industries should be encouraged for providing adequate incentive for developing the rural economic base.

The influence of small town settlement embodying the score of. villages can boost the agro-industrial development through the (i) transmission of power grids, (ii) flow of resource movement and (iii) the appropriate technological know-how. The rural growth centres and small town settlements should have the adequate supporting economic base and inputs of infrastructural developments by embodying the score of villages. The small and medium town settlements are required to function as growth centres for boosting an effective process of transformation in socio-economic structure, scientific innovations for transforming the productive potentialities of the rural settlements in a comprehensive manner. This is an important strategy for rural development which needs to be adopted in the new millennium.

Consolidation of Rural Holding

The rural development in its physical and economic efforts has to be administered for consolidating the fragmented land holdings. The rural cooperatives have to be promoted in the Ninth Plan, 1997-2002 with the adequate financial institutions and consolidation of land management. Secondly, the motivations and mass media of communication should be emphasized for enabling the success of population control programmes in the comprehensive rural settlements. However, owing to the increasing population pressure in the village settlements there has emerged the alarming number of landless labourers and the migration towards the big urban settlements. The appropriate rural technology needs to be emphasized for effectively mobilizing the rural manpower resources.

Surprisingly, the process of urban development has given the due planned recognition, with an enormous financial outlay, for the provisions of infrastructural and socio-economic facilities. The rural areas have lagged behind the adequate provisions of a massive phase of planned programme of infrastructural facilities like power, road and transport and so on. Further, the socio-economic facilities like higher secondary school, hospital and recreational centres are not satisfactory in rural areas as compared to the urban centres.

The villages should integrated as a viable socio-economic unit, so that the pace of agro-industrial development can be accelerated. Subsequently, the role of planning should be recognized by selecting the growth centre settlements the spatial interactions and economic interdependence of agro-industrial development needs to be linked with the score of villages in a statewise perspective. These settlements need to be grouped into integrated clusters comprising villages for promoting the spatial and economic transformation into a process of planning and development. Such an action of rural planning and development should be the watchword in the 21st century.

India is at a decisive phase marching towards the stage of a developed economy. The breakthrough of planning in agriculture and the implementation of massive development programmes in the rural areas has to be aided by scientific, technological and managerial inputs, for promoting the pace of industrial development. As such, India is likely to be poised for ushering into an era of progressive development inclusive of social justice for bringing about a significant improvement in the quality of life of its rural people in the 21st century. Thus, the rural developmental programmes assume importance for promoting the social welfare objectives of the masses in the near future.

The approach of rural planning should be formulated to ensure an effective process of economic system and for transforming the application of scientific and appropriate technological know-how. Apart from these prerequisites of development, the rural prosperity will depend on the provision of adequate power, irrigation, credit, marketing, road and transport facilities.

The easy accessibility of raw materials to the rural areas would create economic viability in the scores of villages for generating the marketable and exportable surplus. Such a phenomenon would accelerate the tempo of employment prospects in the rural settlements. Further, India's rural settlements are required to promote self-reliance in terms of foodgrain production.

The idea of India's rural development has been advocated by the Indian Planners as a basic strategy of national development. It is evident from the resource allocations and increasing emphasis on modernizing agriculture in the Five Year Plans.

In context of spatial development of rural areas the interdependence of rural and urban settlements has been recognized as an important factor of economic development. Rural development and urbanization are basically two facets of the same coin and there is need for developing a harmonious hierarchy of rural and urban settlements by establishing functional linkages. The need for an integrated rural-urban nexus that is egalitarian and productive and not discriminatory and exploitative can hardly be over emphasized.

The integrated rural development aims at accelerating growth. The main goals of such a programme are 'growth with redistribution' for balanced development of economy to be achieved through a two pronged strategy.

(i) Enlargement of employment opportunities for surplus labour absorption.

(ii) Improvement of standard of living of people through physical and social infrastructure development, namely rural accessibility, electricity, water supply and sanitation, housing, health, education and social welfare programmes.

The interdependence of India's rural economy on the urban industrial developmental prospects is a concept of recent appreciation in the Indian context. Industrialization and urbanization can create opportunities and new avenues of employment for the villagers in the vicinity. Rural and urban integration rather than isolation should emerge as an important aspect in planning for rural development in the 21st century perspective.

Rural Planning Perspectives

In a paper, 'Rural Efforts in India' Abdul Qaiyum observes in a comprehensive manner that with the two fold objectives of development of the rural economy and improvement of living conditions in the rural areas, a number of projects have been implemented over the seven plan period. In the earlier years, it was widely thought that programmes of development would raise the living condition of the poor through trickle down process, that agricultural growth without major institutional reforms will alleviate poverty. The Community Development Programme (1952), Intensive Agricultural District Programme (IADP, 1960-61), Intensive Agricultural Area Programme (IAAP, 1964), and High Yielding Varieties Programme (HYVP, 1966-67) were started to raise agricultural production. But this strategy did not work for many reasons including the slow pace of growth.

The rural developmental schemes like IADP, IAAP and HYVP by their very nature, had to be concentrated in areas expected to make quick and good response; areas which involve better endowments in terms of land, water, where farmers possessing large holdings and financial resources, could come forward and benefit from these programmes. Such a programme, had left the areas with poor resource endowment and lack of other essential agricultural infrastructural facilities and they lagged far behind. Further, the small and marginal farmers did not benefit due to the inadequate resources. It was realized that efforts at development of villages made under the Community Development Programmes were inadequate and that they were insufficient for meeting basic needs of the rural areas.

The Fourth Five Year Plan (1969-74), had adopted a new direction in the strategy of poverty eradication, known as 'direct attack' on poverty. Under this programme, the specific poverty eradication programmes for target groups and specific areas were started. Since 1970s, these schemes have passed through a number of phases and ultimately resulted in the emergence of self-employment programmes and wage-employment programmes.

Interestingly, the Fourth Plan had highlighted the need for employment creation and a more even distribution of income. It showed greater awareness of the need to alleviate poverty through direct means and identified that the poor comprised the landless agricultural labourers, small and marginal farmers and village artisans. The scheduled castes and scheduled tribes did constitute the principal segment of the poor. The Plan had observed that there were backward areas located mainly in areas with scanty rains, hill areas, some coastal regions, forest areas, so on.

Keeping these facts into consideration, the poverty eradication programmes for the target groups and specific areas were initiated. The important projects were envisaged, like Small Farmers Development Agency (SFDA), Programme for Marginal Farmers and Agricultural Labourers (PMFAL), and Drought-prone Area Programme (DPAP). These beneficiaries oriented programmes were launched initially between 1969-70 to 1971-72, which were duly considered for helping the small farmers (farmers with holdings between 2.5 to 7.5 acres), marginal farmers—land below 2.5 acres and agricultural labours, farmers in tribal dry and drought-prone areas for raising their income level. This was to be achieved by helping them in adopting improved agricultural technologies; to acquire means of increasing agricultural production like minor irrigation sources; and to diversify their farm economy through subsidiary activities like animal husbandry, dairying and horticulture, so on.

The two schemes, namely SFDA and PMFAL were merged into a single programme during the Fifth Plan period as recommended by the National Commission on Agriculture in 1973. The basic approach of the merged programme was to implement intensive agriculture, multiple cropping, applications of the high yielding variety (HYV) of seeds, fertilizers, minor irrigation, etc., for the identified beneficiaries with special emphasis on dry farming practices and better management techniques. The combined agency, called SFDA, was later merged with IRDP.

The DPAP—an integrated area development programme has an objective for developng the land, water, livestock and human resources of the area. In fact, it is an enlarged and redesignated version of the earlier Rural Works Programme (RWP), started in 1970-71 in areas chronically affected by the drought. The scope of RWP was enlarged because it was thought that a mere rural works programme will not go a long way in solving the problems of these areas and in mitigating the drought conditions. The objective was to enable productive dry land agriculture by better soil and moisture conservation, more scientific use of water resources, afforestation and livestock developments, along with the fodder and pasture resource utilization on a long-term perspective for restoring the ecological balance.

The most important programme of the Fifth Five Year Plan (1974-79) was the adoption of Minimum Needs Programme (MNP). It was specifically directed towards an investment on human resource development and by establishing a network of essential services in the entire country on a coordinated and integrated basis; so that the facilities such as elementary education, health, nutrition, drinking water, provision of housing sites, slum improvement, rural roads and rural electrification could be provided in all the states. The MNP was mainly referred to the backward states which were able to undertake these programmes on a sufficient scale on account of non-availability of resources. Subsequently, the programme was enlarged for achieving a definite social purpose by fulfilling certain basic needs of the poor and was known as the Revised Minimum Needs Programme (RMNP). It comprised nine components, namely the elementary education, adult education, rural health, rural water supply, rural road, rural electrification, housing for landless labourers, and environmental improvement of urban slums and nutrition. There are two distinct sets of activities under the MNP. One set comprises human resource development activities covering the elementary adult education, health, drinking water supply, nutrition and rural housing.

However, another set of activities relate to the area development like roads and village electrification programme.

The various components of MNP seek for enhancing the impact of both beneficiary-oriented and area planning programmes of rural development. While MNP increases the productive capacity of the community as a whole by indirect impact, the rural development programmes improve the economic conditions of the individuals with a direct and personalized approach. All the programmes, except the environmental improvement of urban slums are designed for meeting the rural needs alone.

In the context of the Sixth Plan (1980-85), the adult education was added. In the Seventh Plan, the list was further expanded with three more components, namely, rural domestic energy, rural sanitation and public distribution system. These components form part of the programmes of individual sectors and the allocation for these are part of the sectoral allocations. A review of the programme reveals that in most cases the physical and financial targets have been achieved satisfactorily except in the area of rural sanitation. The quantitative achievements do not mean much in themselves. The selective components are required to be monitored and implemented in an effective manner.

The Integrated Rural Development Programme (IRDP) had become the central pillar of poverty eradication scheme in the Sixth Plan period. The concept of an integrated rural development was first proposed in the Central budget of 1976-77. Presenting the budget, the then Finance Minister had emphatically observed that "an effective attack on rural poverty and under development can be planned in the framework of an integrated programme of rural development based on detailed knowledge of local needs, resource endowments and potentialities. The focus should be directed towards the maximum utilization of locally available resources, including local manpower, rather than the dependence of large inputs from outside. There is a need to evolve operational district plans which fully take into account the precise and separate requirements of each area." A sum of Rs 15 crore was earmarked for the integrated rural development and a beginning was made. The programme was intended for assisting the rural populatin to derive economic benefits from the developmental assets of each area. It was introduced on an extended scale with some modifications in 1978-79.

The focus on IRDP was the target group comprising small and marginal farmers, agricultural labourers and rural artisans. It aimed at integrating the field programmes and proposed to achieve it by developing the primary, secondary and tertiary sectors. All these activities were to be integrated. IRDP had been conceived essentially as an anti-poverty programme with the objective of enabling the poorest families in acquiring the productive assets, technology and skills, so that their economic activities become viable. Thus, it is a programme of assets endowment for developing in a comprehensive manner.

IRDP is a comprehensive scheme under which besides the merging of SFDA, a number of other schemes, like the scheme of Training Rural Youth for Self-Employment (TRYSEM), programme for the Development of Women and Children in the Rural Area (DWCRA), the Special Livestock Productive Programme (SIPP) were recognized.

The assessment of the scheme at the end of the Sixth Plan period has revealed that there are several shortcomings. Keeping this fact in view and the feedback received from the State Governments, suitable changes were introduced in the guidelines for the IRDP in the Seventh Plan. The poverty line was based at an annual income of Rs 6,400, but hose eligible for assistance under the IRDP were to have an average annual income of Rs 4,800 or less. It was assumed that those households with income levels between Rs 4,800 and Rs 6,400 would be able to rise above the poverty line in the process of growth itself.

During the Seventh Plan, the subsidy expenditure on IRDP was Rs 33.16 crores which was in excess of the target of Rs 3000 crores. The total investment, including the institutional credit, amounted to Rs 8,688 crores. As such, in the quantitative terms, the physical achievement of about 18 million households fell short of the original target of 20 million households but exceeded the cumulative target which was only 16 million families. Thus, the sectoral composition indicates that of all the schemes selected under IRDP, 44 per cent were in the primary sector, 18.5 per cent in the secondary sector and 37.5 per cent in the tertiary sector.

A system of concurrent evaluation of the IRDP programme was also introduced by collecting data from the independent research institutions for the entire country on a sample basis. The findings had suggested that the IRDP was quite successful in terms of providing the incremental income to poor families. The number of households able to cross the poverty line was relatively small. However, this was partly due to the low levels of initial investment and also imposing difficulty on the part of the banks for raising the per capita loan assistance.

The Training of Rural Youth for Self-Employment (TRYSEM) was introduced in 1979 for providing the technical skills to rural youth belonging to families below the poverty line. Its main aim was to enable the rural youth to take up self-employment ventures in different spheres across sectors by giving them assistance under the IRDP. Subsequently, in 1987 the scope of the programme was enlarged for the improvement of employment also for the trained beneficiaries.

During the Sixth Plan, about 10 lakh youths were trained under TRYSEM, of which 47 per cent took up self-employment and 12 per cent wage employment. The remaining 41 per cent could not avail of either. Subsequently, a sizeable proportion of the IRDP beneficiaries, who needed training, could not receive it. In fact, only 6 to 7 per cent of IRDP beneficiaries were trained under TRYSEM. During 1990-91, the number of youth trained were 2.6 lakh, of which 70 per cent got employed.

The DWCRA, an exclusive scheme for women, was launched in 1982-83, as a pilot project in 50 districts. In the Seventh Plan, it was extended to more districts. However, at the end of the Seventh Plan period the scheme was in operation in 161 districts.

Under DWCRA, a group of women are granted assistance to take up viable economic activities with Rs 15,000 as a one-time grant to be used as a revolving fund. In the Seventh Plan, about 28,000 groups could be formed against the target of 35,000 with a membership of 4.6 lakh women. During 1990-91 against a target of 7,500 groups, 7,139 were actually formed. Presently the scheme has not shown a significant progress.

While in principle, such a scheme is a sound one but in practical the impact has been inadequate. This is perhaps owing to a lack of cohesion among women groups formed under DWCRA and their inability to identify activities that could generate the sustained level of income levels. However, in this sphere the role of voluntary organizations would be crucial for organizing women for undertaking group-based economic activities which are viable within the context of an area development plan. This should be emphasized in the Five Year Plans of the 21st century.

Among the wage-employment programmes, the National Rural Employment Programme (NREP), and Rural Landless Employment Programme RLEP are important from the rural developmental perspective. The NREP aims at (i) generating employment opportunities in the rural areas; (ii) creating durable community assets in the process of strengthening rural infrastructure and (iii) improving the nutritional status and living standards of the rural poor. The basic objectives of RLEP were (i) to improve and expand employment opportunities for the rural landless for promoting a guarantee of employment to at least one member of every landless labour family upto 100 days in a year and (ii) creation of durable assets for strengthening rural infrastructure leading to the rapid growth of rural economy.

In 1989, the NREP and the RLEP were merged into a single rural wage employment programme spelt out as Jawahar Rozgar Yojana (JRY). The primary objective of the programme was to generate additional employment on productive works which would either be of sustained benefit to the poor or contribute to the creation of rural infrastructure. Under this programme, the Centre's contribution was 80 per cent, 20 per cent being the share of the state government. JRY is implemented in all villages in the country and a significant progress has been achieved.

The Central assistance is provided to the states on the basis of proportion of the rural poor in State/Union Territory to that of the district. The allocations are made on an index of backwardness which was formulated on the basis of (i) 20 per cent weightage for the proportion of agricultural labourer and the total workers in the rural area, (ii) 60 per cent weightage to the proportion of rural scheduled castes and tribes population in relation to the total rural population and (iii) 20 per cent weightage to the inverse of agricultural productivity.

Of the total allocations at the state level, six per cent of the total resources was earmarked for housing under the Indira Awas Yojana (IAY) which are allotted to the Scheduled Castes, Scheduled Tribes and bonded labourers. In addition 20 per cent had been earmarked for the million wells free of cost to the poor Scheduled Castes/Scheduled Tribes farmers. Twenty per cent of the remaining funds was retained at the district level and 80 per cent was allocated for the village panchayats. The responsibility of implementation of JRY in respect of district share of funds is that of DRDA/Zila Parishad, but at the village level it is that of the Gram Panchayat.

During 1989-91, the rural road construction was the primary activity, while minor irrigation, housing, construction of schools and community buildings, wells and social forestry were the other sectors where JRY funds flowed in a big way.

Some of the State Governments had run their own special employment generation schemes. In this context, the Employment Guarantee Scheme (EGS) of Maharashtra operating since 1972 and a Special Employment Programme in Gujarat may be mentioned. The scheme in Maharashtra was intended to provide employment on productive work to the workers who had rendered an unskilled manual work. In this, it did help in reducing the incidence of unemployment, under-employment and poverty in rural areas. The scheme in Gujarat was introduced in the year 1990-91, under which two districts, Dang and Gandhinagar were selected for the achievement of zero unemployment. Thus the additional employment opportunities had been created.

Rural Development: Lack of People's Participation

The Government has spent million of rupees on rural development since independence. The financial outlay in 1995-96 budget was raised to Rs 7,700 crores from Rs 7,100 crores in 1994-95. The combined outlay on rural employment programmes like JRY and the Employment Assurance Scheme (EAS) had been Rs 5,505 crore in 1994-95 and Rs 5,432 crore in 1995-96. Despite such an expenditure in the field of rural development nothing concrete has come out in terms of developmental prospects.

The rural development programmes and schemes in the Ninth Five Year Plan, 1997-2002 and subsequently in the 21st century has to be followed effectively, keeping in view the cost benefit analysis and effective developmental impact.

Critical Evaluation

The basic reason has been lack of people's participation in Government programmes. There is a wide gap between what the villagers expect from the Government and what they get. As such, the Government programmes are more bureaucratic rather than participatory. They are made by keeping Government policies in the perspective rather than the villager's demand.

Benefits of the Government schemes are generally pocketed by a group of big farmers who are literate and control the commercial activities of the village. Many a time, it is seen that a big farmer owning almost about 100 acres of land gives a very small plot of land to a landless farmer and takes the benefit of the Government seheme in his name. Many of these literate farmers take loans before elections because it is generally seen that they are waived after election as a populist measure. The Government is keen to give loans to show the people that it cares for farmers, but this keenness is absent at the time of loan recovery.

Due to absence of concrete steps, loan recoveries are greatly hampered which decreases the enthusiasm of credit cooperatives and rural banks to invest more for rural development.

What should be done for initiating the concrete steps for rural development and how can the people be involved? The first and foremost task is to increase the literacy level of villagers. 'Operation Black-board' is already in operation to provide basic amenities in primary schools and a second teacher in single-teacher schools.

Moreover, the allocation for primary education should be more because the basic aim is universalization of education. In keeping with this, the outlay on elementary education in the Eighth Plan was 45.6 per cent of the total education budget compared to 32.1 per cent in the Sixth Plan and 37.5 per cent in the Seventh Plan. The mid-day meal scheme introduced on August 15, 1995 was directed to motivate poor children to attend schools. Steps are required to be taken for introducing the scheme in rural areas, especially in remote, hilly regions. But there is possibility that the officers involved may distribute substandard or inadequate meals due to lack of fear of any watch dog, especially in rural areas. Therefore the panchayat in which the school is located should be made a monitoring agency for the implementation of the mid-day meal schemes.

One of the main thrusts of rural development programmes has been to make a frontal attack on poverty through special employment generation programmes. The Ministry of Rural Development has introduced an 'employment assurance scheme' which aims at providing the assured employment of 100 days of unskilled manual work to the rural poor who are in need and seek it. To give impetus to this development programme a sum of Rs 30,000 crore was earmarked in Eighth Five Year Plan.

The Maharashtra Government introduced the Employment Guarantee Scheme (EGS) in 1972-1973, the first of its kind to give recognition to the 'Right to work' enshrined in the Constitution. The scheme was particularly designed to help the economically weaker sections of rural society. A review of progress of the schemes during the 10 year period (1972-73 to 1982-83) revealed that while the expenditure incurred on the implementation of various programmes under EGS had been increasing, the number of mandays of employment generated as a result of these programmes had declined continuously during the last four years. Such a failure was due to lack of people's participation in the implementation of EGS. Instead of using such a wide range of officer for implementation of these schemes if more rural people involved, then obviously more mandays of employment could have been generated.

Provision of drinking water and sanitation is important for rural development in terms of social progress. In order to accelerate the pace of coverage of villages without water supply, the Government introduced the Accelerated Rural Water Supply Programme (ARWSP) in 1972-73. The total outlay provided for rural water supply during the Eighth Plan was Rs 5,100 crores under the Central Sector and Rs 4,954.52 crores under the States Union Territories for providing potable drinking water to the entire uncovered rural population during the Eighth Plan period. In addition, Rs 380 crore has been provided for the centrally sponsored rural sanitation programme. Lack of people's participation has left all the scheme in red. Thus in the 21st century, planning effort has to be directed to initiate a specific people's participation for upliftment of rural India.

Land Reform

The need for land reforms was recognized at the time of independence and has been reiterated in the successive Five Years Plans. The Seventh Plan had enunciated land reforms to be an intrinsic part of the anti-poverty strategy. The importance of land reforms continues to be significant. The aim of land reforms in the Eighth Plan was concerned with the fulfilment of all the five principles of National Land Reforms Policy, that is, abolition of intermediaries, tenancy reforms with security to actual cultivators, redistribution of surplus ceiling land, consolidation of holdings and updating of land records. As such, the landlessness is the root cause of rural poverty and land reforms should be the watchword of 21st century.

In a country where agriculture is the principal means of livelihood, access to land is a major source of employment and income. This access could be achieved in two ways either by a more equitable redistribution of land or by providing security of tenure to tenants and sharecroppers who are the actual cultivators. The scope with respect to redistribution is limited. After the imposition of the ceilings, 7.23 million acres of land were declared surplus, of which 4.65 million acres had been distributed by the end of the Seventh Plan. Of the remaining, a large proportion of land is under litigation dispute. With the average size of holdings declining, there is no possibility of fresh ceiling limits.

Subsequently, efforts will have to be made for detecting the surplus land to distribute the existing surplus expeditiously and ensure that allottees retained possession of land. In the context of the Ninth Plan the rights of tenants and sharecroppers will have to be emphasized with the objective of giving them security of tenure. In some states, such an experiment has already been done and it has led to an increase in both employment and agricultural output. The allottees of the surplus land and the tenants were provided a package of modern land inputs for increasing the yields from land. This strategy had met the twin objective of poverty alleviation and output growth.

Energy Requirements

Presently, the rural energy consumption is dominated by non-commercial energy sources such as firewood, agricultural waste and cowdung which formed nine-tenth of the total energy consumed in the rural areas.

The growing energy requirements of the rural areas has been a challenging task in the 21st century. For tackling such an uphill task, the need is the adaption of the technique of energy generation to varied requirements. It is as much important as the generation and augmentation of the total available resources.

As the Indian rural society is predominantly agricultural, wind energy can be helpful in (1) pumping fresh water for livestock and human consumption, (2) irrigating fields, (3) powering agricultural operations such as grinding corn, wheat and sugarcane and threshing chaff, cutting and winnowing, (4) cutting wood, (5) generating electricity the usefulness of which could be restricted to domestic lighting, radio, television, space heating or cooling etc.

The Integrated Rural Energy Programme (IREP) which was taken up during the Seventh Plan had become a major effort in the direction of planning in energy for rural development, by taking into account the concerns for equity and social justice. The IREP was developed as a plan scheme on the basis of experience of a pilot rural energy planning exercise taken up in the Sixth Plan. During the Seventh Plan and the subsequent two annual plans in 1990-91 and 1991-92, around 25 blocks had been covered under the programme. In the Five Year Plans of 21st century efforts has to be made for emphasising the rural energy developments in the comprehensive rural settlements.

Developmental Administration

During the Seventh Plan, various rural development programmes were planned and implemented by a single agency at the district level called the District Rural Development Agency (DRDA). The Committee, set up to review the existing administrative arrangements, re-emphasized the need for decentralized planning at the district level and below. This had ensured the effective participation of local representatives in the developmental planning. Further, it was realized that this would reflect the needs and aspirations of the local people. The programme would have accountability. Such an approach should be a guidelines of the rural development in the 21st century perspective.

In the states where Zila Parishads were not in existence, the setting up of District Development Councils with Government officer as a chief executive was suggested. In either case, it was envisaged that planning and implementation of sectoral activities would be decentralized and integrated into a unified activity with horizontal coordination at the district level. Similarly, at the Block level too, an integrated area plan was imperative based on the availability of local skills and resources. No uniform pattern was adopted across the states. In 1989-90, with the introduction of JRY it was stipulated that the funds would be placed at the disposal of the village panchayats, which would mark a shift towards democratic decentralization with certain funds and powers vested in the Gram Panchayats for development.

Panchayati Raj Institutions

The Panchayati Raj Institutions (PRI) are in existence in almost all the states and Union Territories but with considerable variations in their structure and mode of elections etc. At the end of the Seventh Plan, there were 2,17,300 Gram Panchayats, 4,525 Block Panchayat Samities and 330 Zila Parishads in the country.

The Constitution (Seventy-Third Amendment), Act, 1992, has provided a firmer basis for the establishment of democracy at the grass roots level by conferring on panchayats the constitution and composition of panchayats, reservation of seats, duration of panchayats, power, authority and responsibility of panchayats, power to improve taxes and funds of the panchayat, audit of accounts of panchayats, elections of the panchayats.

Constitution (Seventy-Third Amendment) Act, 1992, enables the provisions of administrative, executive and judiciary powers. All the seats in a panchayat shall be filled by persons chosen by direct election from territorial constituencies in the panchayat area. For this purpose, each panchayat area shall be divided into territorial constituencies in such a manner that the ratio between the population of each constituency and the number of seats allotted to it shall, so far as practicable, be the same throughout the panchayat area.

One of the important provisions endowed to panchayats is the power, authority and responsibilities subject to the provisions of the Constitution. The Legislature of a State may, by law, endow the panchayats with such powers and authority as may be necessary to enable them to function as institutions of Self-Government. Such law may contain provisions for the devolution of power and responsibilities upon panchayats at the appropriate level, subject to such conditions as may be specified therein, with respect to (a) the preparation of plans for economic development and social justice, (b) the implementation of schemes for economic development and social justice.

Past Planning Efforts

In spite of the fact that high priority has been given in the successive Plans to the development of rural areas, the quality of life in the areas continues to be much below the desired standard of living. Special employment programmes like IRDP and JRY have succeeded in providing a certain quantum of employment to people and have led to the creation of some durable assets in the villages, there is a feeling that the achievements have not been commensurate with the resources spent on them.

As reported in the Eighth Five Year Plan, 1992-97 (document of the Planning Commission, Government of India), that about half the number of beneficiaries under the IRDP have overdues. This raises doubts about their ability to come out of the debt syndrome due to a low level of subsistence which does not generate enough income to repay the loan. As such, the banks are reluctant to raise the credit limit because of scepticism regarding the repayment capacity of the target groups. It is estimated that about one-third of them do not even have the original assets that was given to them. Even those beneficiaries who have generated sufficient additional income to cross the poverty line may relapse into the category of poor, with additions to the family, loss of assets and non-availability of the activity chosen by the individual.

Similarly, under the JRY, as reported in the document, some employment was provided in the lean season and the supplementary income thus generated was not sufficient for the survival of many poor families. As such, under DWRCA the results have not been satisfactory mainly because of lack of adequate investment and selection of unviable activities.

Rural Development in the Eighth Plan

The eradication of rural poverty will continue to be a major objective of the rural development in the context of the Five Year Plans. Greater emphasis has to be given for the self-sustainability of employment opportunities.

During the Eighth Plan, the Integrated Rural Energy Programme (IREP) had focussed the following two major areas, namely : (a) provision of energy for meeting the basic needs of working, heating and lighting, especially for the weaker section, by utilizing locally available energy resources to the maximum extent possible; (b) provision of energy as the critical input in the economic development of the rural areas was visualized to realize the creation of employment opportunities by enhancing the productivity and income and accelerating the process of decentralized development. Thus, the sustainable agriculture production prospect was visualized for realizing the self-sustained rural developmental activities.

In keeping with above directions, the IREP in the Eighth Plan had envisaged the following major features:

(1) Extension of the programme to cover at least 100 blocks per year; (2) provision of minimum energy needs of cooking, heating and lighting in each IREP block, so as to ensure 100 per cent coverage for the economically weaker sections; (3) provision of the most cost-effective mix of various energy sources and options for meeting the requirements for sustainable agriculture and rural development by giving due weightage to the environmental factors; (4) ensuring large-scale people's participation in the planning and implementation of the programme by the direct involvement of panchayats, voluntary and non-official bodies and institutions and the establishment of self-managed organizations and other appropriate people-oriented arrangements wherever feasible at the micro-level for the implementation of the IREP projects, (5) setting up and strengthening of the mechanisms and coordination arrangements that would effectively link micro-level planning for rural energy with the national and state level planning and programmes for energy and economic development, so as to ensure regular and planned flow of energy inputs, the commercial energy sources for meeting the requirements of various uses in the IREP projects; (6) financing of the programme by supplementing available Central and

state budgetary support mobilized by the panchayats and other local bodies and people's participation. The financial institutions and the banking system were to be actively involved in financing the IREP projects and its components for which suitable new schemes was developed in the Eighth Plan.

Interestingly, the Eighth Plan had recognized the need for integrated approach to rural development where the poverty alleviation programmes, the area development programmes and sectoral schemes were emphasized. To achieve this, taking district as a unit of planning and the district plan were required to be prepared. The plan visualized the physical and human endowments of the area with respect to the felt needs of the people and the funds available. The viable activities, particularly in agriculture and allied sectors including animal husbandry, horticulture, forestry and agro-processing were selected in developmental programmes. Village and small district industries with potential had been identified on the priority basis. In addition the development of infrastructural support and backward and forward linkages had been spelt out as the essential prerequisites for the viability of the selected activities. Emphasis on human resource development was recognized. Therefore, the social aspects of development had been linked with the plan for economic development. The strategy of approach towards interlinks of industrial development with the transport network system in rural areas has to be worked out in the Five Year Plans of the 21st century.

In the Eighth Plan a district per state had been selected for the implementation of this programme. The various governmental departments with specialized expertise and banks should work in close cooperation with the district planning unit in order to have a coordinated and scientific plan, assessing the needs of the people, the availability of local resources, the potential for alternative productive works and for viable schemes.

The greater self-help by the people and their participation in programmes of the Panchayati Raj institutions, cooperatives and other self-managed institutions' role is recognized as an important factor for planning and implementation of the rural developmental programmes. This should be followed as an effective economic strategy in the Ninth Plan Perspective, 1997-2002, and India's Five Year Plans of the 21st century.

Rural Settlements: Case Studies

The unemployment, underemployment and disguised employment problem in rural India has assumed alarming proportion and has presented a serious challenge to the Indian economy. Besides there are glaring inadequacies and irregularities in whatever facilities that have been provided to the rural areas aiming at their development.

At the first instance, the irregularity and insufficiency in provision of electricity in the rural settlements needs to be done away with. The rural banks are existing but are mobilizing savings mainly for urban development. As such, the loan sanctioned under the IRDP have not been able to specify the eligibility of assistance to beneficiaries. There is caste based politics and therefore, the rural development has been hampered in a big way. Even though sufficient period has passed after independence many villages throughout the country do not have the adequate dispensary, police post, transport, educational facilities and post office facilities. Keeping these facts in view, it has been visualized that the emphasis in the Ninth and the subsequent plans needs to be directed for providing socio-economic and infrastructural facilities to the viable rural settlements.

Rural Survey Studies

A research oriented study had been undertaken of selective villages of Uttar Pradesh, Haryana, Delhi and Tamil Nadu. The survey based empirical observations are analysed in statewise perspective.

Aggarwal Mandi Tatri (Uttar Pradesh)

The village is urbanized and located within a distance of 5 kilometres from Baghpat. Having a population of more than 10,000, this village is in the district of Meerut. The main occupation of 60 per cent of the population is agriculture. Wheat and sugarcane are the main crops grown in the area. There are five primary schools and two intermediate colleges. The roads are *kutcha* and *pucka.* Though there is supply of electricity, it is irregular and on an average it is available only for six hours in a day. Farmers demand more electricity but due to non-availability it has affected the pace of rural development.

There are more than 1000 commuters to Delhi. 80 per cent of them having done graduation work as clerks and teachers, the remaining have studied upto matriculation and are identified as class IV employees, namely peons and chowkidars. Surprisingly, the urbanized village with such a considerable population does not have a dispensary. For availing the hospital facilities, the people of the village have to go either to Meerut or to Delhi.

The district and session courts are located at Meerut, lower court at Baghpat, High Court at Allahabad and lower revenue court at Ghaziabad and Meerut. Thus, there is no legal service in the urbanized village.

There is the availability of loan facility under the IRDP. The loan is available to the *chamar* within the category of Schedule Castes. Beneficiaries number is meagre and the loan ranging from Rs. 4,000 to 5,000. Surprisingly, to get the loan, roughly 10 per cent of the amount is to be given away as bribe to the bank officials. When the buffalo or the buffalo-cart is purchased with the loan, the beneficiaries declare theft or death of the buffalo and thus no loan recovery is made by the banks. Surprisingly, the insurance claims and theft cases have increased with the opening of police posts. The people of the village, for reporting FIR, have to travel a distance of 5 kilometres at Baghpat.

At the time of distribution of fertilizers too, it is noticed that the better quality fertilizers and high yielding seeds have been pocketed by the rich farmers.

Gothina (Uttar Pradesh)

The village Gothina, *tehsil* Baghpat in Meerut district consists of more than 2,000 population. It is a backward village settlement. The main occupation is agriculture and the crops cultivated are wheat and sugarcane. The per capita income is meagre. The village is backward in terms of economic development. It has not got the rail and transport linkages. As such, the roads are *kutcha* and during rains they are flooded. The electricity poles exist but subsequently there is no supply. There is no primary school nor intermediate education facility nor any dispensary in the village. Naturally from this village the class IV employees and babus shift to Delhi, setting up a pattern of migration trend.

Kapholi (Uttar Pradesh)

The Kapholi village is located in the district of Almorah. The nearest town is Bageshwar, at about 10 kilometres and the nearest railway station is Kathgodam, 200 kilometres from the village and, the nearest bus stop is 2 kilometres away. The village and the district road is *kutcha* and *semi-kutcha* respectively.

The village does not have the provisions of medical and dispensary facilities. However, the primary health centre is located at a distance of 10 kilometres from the village. The fertilizer and seed distribution centres is two kilometres away. The primary school is at a distance of one and a half kilometres, high school at two kilometres distance and college is ten kilometres away from the village. The police post is ten kilometres away and post office at a two kilometres distance and telegraph facility is ten kilometres away from the village.

As such, 80 per cent of the population is engaged in agricultural activities. The main crops grown are wheat, barley, gram, oilseeds, tobacco, rice, dal, pulses etc. Though there is supply of electricity, it is irregular which has hampered the agro-industrial productivity.

For servicing litigation purposes the *tehsil* level court is located at a distance of 10 kilometres from the village.

The village income level is low and cannot meet a substantial standard of living. Further, the migration of educated and uneducated is mainly towards metropolitan cities of Delhi, Lucknow, Mumbai, and Calcutta.

One of the most prosperous rural settlements of Uttar Pradesh in Nainital zone is Rahmetgunj Adresh village located in the district of Rampur. The houses are *pucka* and has a significant per capita income. There is regular supply of electricity and the village has recorded significant industrial progress. The notable industries are cotton, cardboard manufacture, breweries and rice mill. There are potato godowns in a significant number.

The migration pattern of working population is 25 per cent towards Delhi, 25 per cent in the state of Uttar Pradesh and 50 per cent to other places.

Jharsa Urban Village (Haryana)

This village depicts fast changing scenario to the vast tracts owing to agricultural land acquired by the Haryana Urban Development Authority HUDA. The urban village is located at a distance of 1.5 kilometre from Gurgaon town. The village is highly urbanized and is well connected with the Gurgaon township. There is a proposal to promote effective transport and electrification programme for Jharsa.

Sector-wise housing development in Jharsa by the HUDA has brought an effective socio-economic and infrastructural developments.

As Jharsa village land on a large-scale has been acquired, therefore it is visualized that the HUDA will provide an effective plan for sewerage and sanitation. It is recognized that the village has lost its character of agrarian origin and will become the vital project of HUDA in terms of innumerable housing schemes of different income categories.

Malhamajara (Haryana)

The village is situated near Sonepat and is about 35 kilometres from Delhi. The population of the village is 4,500 and the average per capita income is around Rs 600. The working force is either engaged in factories or in transport sector. The village has a high percentage of literacy.

The break-up of educational level constitutes—M.A., 18 per cent,

B.A., 25 per cent and High School, 57 per cent. More than 50 per cent of the working force has migrated to Delhi. Surprisingly, there is no dispensary in the village to look after medical requirements of the inhabitants.

Sundararajapuram (Tamil Nadu)

The village Sundararajapuram is located in the district of Kamaraj in Tamil Nadu. The nearest town is Rajapalayam, at a distance of eight kilometres. The population of the village is more than 10,000 and the main occupation is agriculture. The main crops grown in the village are paddy, cotton, groundnut and sugarcane. The average per capita income of an agricultural labourer is very meagre and as such the village is under the grip of severe poverty.

The roads in village are *pucka*. There is no dispensary and for medical facilities they have to go to the nearby town. There is drinking pipe water facility with about 15 common taps. Electricity is available with regularity. The village does not have factories.

There is a school in the village upto tenth standard. Higher educaiton is available only in the town. People are recognizing the importance of education due to spread of media and awareness.

The distribution of seed and fertilizers is done through cooperatives. The rich farmers have the easy accessibility to the agency. Consequently the poor farmers are ignorant about the facilities rendered by the cooperative and also unable to afford.

Interestingly, there is a Cooperative Bank in the village. The loans are sanctioned by the agricultural field office under the IRDP. But about 10 per cent of the loan amount goes towards bribing for obtaining the loan. The loan is not properly used and assets are not created for ensuring the economic gains for the village community.

The entire village population belongs to the Scheduled Castes. The nearby village Krishnapuram within a distance of one kilometre and having a population of about 10,000 has adequate facilities as compared to Sundararajapuram village. The businessmen of Krishnapuram village acting as moneylenders are in the habit of exploiting the people of Sundararajapuram.

The police station is located at a distance of two kilometres. The bus stop is at a distance of one kilometre. Casteism is the main hurdle for the extension of bus facility to the village. There is no railway station in the village and this facility is available at a distance of eight kilometres.

Since the last ten years elections for panchayat has not taken place in the village. The Government officials are running the administration

Sawada (Delhi)

The village is located at a distance of 25 kilometres from Delhi. There are 50 houses and the village does not have a dispensary. The medical facility is available in the Ramrup Health Centre, at a distance of two kilometres.

The village has supply of clean drinking water though, irregular. The drainage and sanitation facilities do not work during the rainy season and the roads are flooded. There is no arrangement for spray of DDT for the prevention of malaria which is widespread in the village area.

The main occupation is agriculture and the crop cultivated is wheat. However, there is no factory. The village has electricity but is not well linked. There is lack of transport facilities. Seventy per cent of the working force has moved towards Delhi.

Planning Action

The rural settlements need to ensure a dynamic reformulation in the planning and organizational system. Then only the credit facility, road and power development would assume significance for vitalizing the tempo of rural development. As such, village planning is devoid of an integrated organizational set up for monitoring the developmental projects in the comprehensive rural settlements.

The notable schemes for rural development are, namely (i) IRDP, (ii) NREP, (iii) Rural House Sites and Rural Water Supply Programmes. These programmes involve huge financial outlay which are leaked due to mismanagement and rampant corruption prevailing in the rural administrative set up.

In an interesting book, *The Challenge of the Cities* Mr Jagmohan, has rightly pointed out that "undoubtedly, rural development is necessary for our progress. The dramatic increase in the size of the metropolitan cities has not reduced the pressure of population or poverty in rural areas. We are facing problem not only of 'teeming cities' but also of teeming countryside. During the last 30 years, our rural population has increased by 74 per cent while during the same period rural areas lost 15,000 square kilometres of land to expanding cities". Thus, there has been a widespread emphasis on rapid urbanization and neglect of rural development and planning. There is need for ensuring an effective process of economic development and employment opportunities in the rural settlements for promoting the integrated process of agro-industrial prosperity and generating thereby the marketable and exportable surplus. Country's rural economic prosperity is mainly dependable on the transportation and financial institutions.

Growth Centre, Developmental Strategy

A harmonious rural-urban balance is essential for a healthy growth of both. In the absence of integrated planning of rural growth centres and the development of small and medium-sized towns, the large metropolitan areas may develop the excessive concentrations of population with their attendant problems. The small and medium-sized towns may, on the other hand, fail to develop into growth centres supporting and stimulating the rural hinterland. Therefore, an essential part of area planning would have to be directed towards the development of rural growth centres. These would consist of centres provided with necessary economic infrastructure and services whose locations would have to be determined by the criteria of maximum efficiency and accessibility. The growth centres, rural and urban, will have to be linked in a graded hierarchy, which would help in overcoming the constraints to development in rural areas, which have been responsible for the scattered distribution of rural settlements and diffused disposal of rural wealth.

The rural development through growth centres has a vital importance in the context of the national planning. As such, the Indian villages settlement pattern is scattered and lacks and economic viability benefit. However, on the basis of spatial and economic advantage it is difficult to link the villages. The possibility of providing all the villages with adequate infrastructural and socio-economic facilities, however, rules out the planning proposition. Moreover, it is indeed possible to have an inducement of development activities in the viable growth centres of rural areas to cater to the needs of the village economy. These viable spatial and economic settlement pattern require a demographic and social viability set up. Subsequently, the rural economy can be accelerated for promoting the agro-industrial based marketable and exportable surplus. The self-sustained growth can be visualized in the national perspective by developing the rural areas in an integrated manner for ensuring the balanced process of regional development.

The growth centre planning formulation in the context of rural settlements must provide a well-regulated market, which could be able to stimulate the two-way flow of agricultural produce for generating the effective pace of industrial production. Thereby, the agricultural sector will have to be integrated for accelerating the tempo of industrial activities. It is pointed out emphatically that the rural growth centre has to play an important role for vitalizing the score of villages having the adequate economic potentialities. The rural growth centre through its physical proximity, will have to transmit in its influential planning area the infrastructural and socio-economic requirements in the entire adjoining village areas. Therefore mechanization, skill, technology, capital and administration can be transferred from growth centres having the built up development in small town to backward village settlements. The higher rate of rural productivity and market surplus can be achieved by integrating the rural growth centre with score of adjoining villages. An effective transport planning assumes a great significance for boosting the rural growth centres, economy and exploration of physical potentialities in a comprehensive manner.

The rural settlements have lacked in the absorption of employment opportunities. Owing to the alarming migration towards the urban areas it is a cumbersome task for urban planners to provide the excessive demand for public utility services. If the comprehensive village settlements have to be developed, then the rural growth centres and small towns must be given the provisions of transport, power, water, efficient administration and techno-scientific personnel facilities for exploring the potential agro-industrial resources of the adjoining village economy in a regional perspective. Thus, India's economic planning has to be resource, based by exploring the optimal agro-industrial potentialities. Therefore, the rural areas have to be developed in a comprehensive manner of planning for promoting the production, income and employment prospects.

The incoming technological revolution in India has been followed by the haphazard growth process of industrialization and urbanization. The attraction of industry, trade, commerce and service sectors in the urban areas has created regional imbalances in terms of spatial and economic development in rural areas. As such, the rural areas have not been developed and the migration has increased in urban settlements in a big way.

Objective of Growth Centre

In the context of the Ninth Five Year Plan and the 21st century India's economic planning, emphasis has to be given for selecting the viable rural growth centres. This would create condition for rural self-sustained growth and generate an accelerated tempo of economic development, thereby checking the growing trend of village migration towards the metropolitan and large cities.

For developing the ago-industrial planning the objectives of rural growth centres in the Ninth Plan framework and the subsequent plans are as follows:

1. To have larger agricultural inputs into the farms to facilitate the movement of larger marketable surplus in agriculture and horticulture through the regulated markets and to provide a larger flow of goods and services both ways.

2. To stimulate higher agricultural productivity with agricultural services units and better provisions of marketing facilities.

3. To set off a catalytic development process, which will lead to larger employment prospects, higher consumption of goods and services and better housing facilities.

4. To provide rural employment through the works envisaged in the farms, at the regulated market and in the transport system. The market centre could generate new tertiary sector.

5. By the development of the growth centres, the pressure on the metropolitan cities for the provision of employments to the rural migrant population would ease to a considerable extent.

Identifying Growth Centres

The basic argument in development of the growth centres and meeting the needs of the rural inhabitants living in the hinterland through agricultural development is followed by the following phenomenon, namely higher productivity and greater attention to agricultural means, a greater purchasing power and more intensive use of labour available. This, in turn, requires a market for consumer services and inputs plus some public financial institutions mobilizing savings and providing credit. However, this in turn would be able to stimulate the local industries using intermediate technology for increasing the marketable prospects for the agriculture produce.

For identifying growth centres scientifically the pattern of primary, secondary and tertiary activities has got to be spelt out in a comprehensive manner. More important is study the prerequisites of developmental possibilities such as communication marketing, storage and processing facilities, irrigation, power network, banking and credit, medical and recreational facilities. As such, for evaluating the rural growth centres, the specific points of study could be the problems, potentials and prospects and, above all priorities in respect of meeting the targetted goals of national planning.

The selection of the growth centres necessitates a detailed techno-economic survey of the entire rural planning areas. A comprehensive a possible line of action programmes for boosting the planning areas with the potential locational advantages. Further, the need will arise for a profile of the town or village selected in a regional perspective.

Requisites of Formulating Growth Centres

After having the comprehensive evaluation of adjoining score villages, the growth centre settlement pattern has to be ascertained. A well-planned market organization with storage facilities for grain and fertilizers seems to be an imperative necessity. Moreover, the follow up of industrial development in growth centres must have the locational rationality and the local finance availability with high quality of entrepreneurial skill.

The transport effectiveness, the adequate labour availability, capital requirements, scientific technical know-how, entrepreneurial skill and banking facilities with loan incentive concessions are some of the vital requirements of a growth centre planning area. The infrastructural and socio-economic facilities like power, water supply, transport, medical, education and recreational amenities necessitate the per capita availability. However, such economic functions need to be formulated within the growth centre planning area in the Eighth Plan perspective.

It is desirable to have the following data village wise for vitalizing the effectiveness in the rural growth centre settlements with the development of economic potentialities.

1. The level of agricultural production in villages.
2. The level of consumption pattern in each village.
3. The availability of surplus available which could be turned as raw material within the centre villages for producing agro-industrial products.
4. The existing and future assessment of power and water supply availability and requirements.
5. Existing industries have to be assessed in the light of the adjoining villages. The raw material procurement process has to be known.
6. Availabilities of the village wise socio-economic amenities such as education, medical, transport and commercial activities.

There is need for assessing the existing functional, organizational set up of the market mechanism in the rural growth centres. Such a process would accelerate the trade and commercial activities within the adjoining villages.

An efficient administrative set up would have to be formulated for promoting an effective system of distribution with reference to the inflow and outflow of goods and services in the context of planning the growth centre settlements. Thus, the rural and small town settlements would become the economically viable centres.

The adequate socio-economic facilities in growth centres with better equipped links of transport system necessitates the development of the adjoining villages. The entire rural spatial settlement should be developed for vitalizing the effectiveness of economic activities, so as to asborb the huge idle manpower resources.

Rural-Urban Integration

It is realized that "agriculture can be combined with industry without undermining the age-old social asset—the village". With the adequate infrastructural and modernized administrative set up the village outlook can be transferred into the outlook of modernization.

The rural family is larger than the family in the city. It has a surplus of labour. Such a vast rural surplus must find an outlet in other non-agricultural sectors of the economy. But why should the village population be compelled to leave their homes? Why not develop non-agricultural sources of employment and livelihood in the immediate neighbourhood? In the 21st century perspective, the agro-based industrial growth centres of small town settlements will have to function for catering to the needs by clustering a score of villages with the modernized technological socio-economic facilities.

It is understood that by formulating the rural-urban integration, a rural family which has its income from agriculture can also do so from industry, commerce and, thereby enjoy a higher standard of living. Such facilities must be formulated in growth centres of rural settlements. "The flight from the village will be checked and the deep-rooted and closely-knit rural society, which, at the moment, has a more definite image than the amorphous urban conglomerate, will be preserved". The urge, so deeply rooted in our present day national planning of "balanced regional development" and "growth with stability" can be achieved through an effective selection of growth centres. Such agro-industrial small towns must boost the production, income and employment prospects of the adjoining economy having a reach within the physical proximity.

According to the 1991 Census, there has been the economic concentration in urban areas, however, the small town and rural areas have remained without the requisite developments of socio-economic, infrastructural and financial institutions. The establishment of agro-industrial growth centres of small town and rural growth centre settlements area has to evolve a criteria where demographic, occupational, socio-economic and basic infrastructure functional characteristic is highlighted in respect of resources endowment.

Criteria of Selecting Growth Centre

To establish the agro-industrial oriented centres, it is important to know the possible scientific assessment for evaluating the socio-economic and infrastructural potentialities. Thereby the standards requirements have to be worked out in respect of per capita population availability. Below has been outlined a tentative list by which we can select the potentials of the agro-industrial small town growth centres which can cater to the needs of the adjoining village economy and thereby check the rural migrants flow towards urban areas.

Demographic Factors

A small town having a demographic viability with a population between 5,000 to 10,000 and 10,000 to 20,000 i.e. class IV and V towns, should be taken up for a purposeful developmental planning. As such, there is a planning need for diagnosing the structural pattern of occupational activities existing around the villages and small towns. The infrastructural requirement assessment would indicate the need based action oriented planning programmes.

It is visualized ideal occupational composition that the small town settlement, oriented as growth centres would constitute about 60 per cent in the primary and 40 per cent in the combined secondary and tertiary sectors. Such a selection indicates that the agricultural and industrial economy has a significant level of productivity. Moreover, the imperative need is to adopt, for vitalising growth centre economy, labour intensive and capital saving based agro-industrial planning.

Urban Proximity

However, the viable small towns should have two functional dimensions in the 21st century perspective. Firstly, it should have an adequate transport network links with the adjoining areas and secondly, it should be near the unbanized industrial centres. This latter provision would accelerate the small town settlements, growth prospects in terms of socio-economic and infrastructural facilities. Thereby it would be able to accelerate the tempo of production, income and employment prospects.

Power Advantages

However, the use of electricity in the context of modern industries has opened up the enormous potentialities, particularly in the national planning programme for decentralized electric power generation. Electricity to agro-industrial small towns and rural growth centres through the transmission grid has to be generated from the urban industrial areas having the physical proximity to it. This would eventully lead to the setting up of factories and agricultural processing establishments away from the congested urban centres and, in this way the migration that takes place in an alarming magnitude would be checked to a considerable extent.

Administration and Economic Motivations

The economic inducement of activities for boosting the agro-industrial small town growth centres, should be aimed in India's planning for the optimal achievements of employment and income prospects. There is also an imperative need for involving an effective decentralization policy, so that the urban economic activities and Government offices can be shifted in growth centres of small towns for boosting capital-cum-technology prospects. This requires an effective administrative machinery which can effectively mobilize the rural resources in the 21st century.

Moreover, the selection of technical personnel would enable the viable ago-industrial small towns to function as the specilized productive units. They should become the centres of training for unskilled labour, so that they can spontaneously yield higher productivity in the continum of rural and urban settlements.

The growth centre has to be located in such a manner that it abides adequately the socio-economic and infrastructural facilities to boost agro-industrial developmental possibilities.

Policy Perspective

The Indian Rural Development Report points out that more than a third of the Indian population in the nineties were poor. The agrarian reforms begun in the 50s remained unfinished and long overdue; direct anti-poverty programmes achieved only limited success. The rural development has been ineffective, as central to the overall failure are excessive reliance on a top-down centralized bureaucracy and scarcity of funds. It is paradoxical that a bureaucracy created to govern a colonial—feudal system was entrusted to implement agrarian reforms and elements of all those policies that were inherently anti-feudal, progressive and democratic.

It is revealed in the report that an elaborate system of patronage thriving on the disempowerment of the poor and hapless, distributes thriving on the disempowerment of the poor and hapless, distributes large to the chosen few at the cost of multitudes. As for the funds, rural development, meaning the development of about half the country's population, has attracted less than tenth of the expendable funds of any time. An acute urban bias is all pervasive. The report warns that goals like participation of the poor in governance, reduction of inequities, social cohesion, control that the poor exercise on their lives and empowerment are no longer considered important in the wake of the new philosophy of liberalization.

While the Government of India has been spending plenty of money in implementing several rural development programmes, they are based on a belief that "spending money is in itself a necessary condition for poverty alleviation". The problem with this belief is that it 'underplays' the role of non-monetary policies and the impact on the lives of people. A solution suggested by the report is the possibility of localizing tax collection, transferring funds to districts from the Centre or a transfer from the state under a different Finance Commission or a new statutory authority.

The approach of rural development strategy should be given top priority in the five year plans of the 21st century. The massive electrification programme should be emphasized in the plan as an important factor for promoting the marketable and exportable surplus. As such, the rural settlements have tremendous rural manpower surplus which can be employed gainfully through the massive agro-industrial programmes.

The cooperative institutions have to play a vital role of accelerating. the tempo of agricultural productivity and small-scale industrial development. Further, the spread of education and road transport development have to be duly recognized as important action programme in the 21st century oriented Five Year Plans. Then only an effective process of rural development would have a meaningful approach of planning from the regional and national perspective.

REFERENCES

1. Bepin Behari: Energy Needs of Rural Development, *The Financial Express,* June 11, 1986.
2. ____________ Rural Industrialization in India, Vikas Publishing House, New Delhi.
3. Government of India: First Five Year Plan, Planning Commission.
4. ____________ Second Five Year Plan, Planning Commission.
5. ____________ Third Five Year Plan, Planning Commission.
6. ____________ Fourth Five Year Plan, Planning Commission.
7. ____________ Fifth Five Year Plan, Planning Commission.

8. ____________ Eighth Five Year Plan, Planning Commission.
9. Bepin Behari: Ninth Five Year Plan, Planning Commission.
10. ____________ The Constitution (Seventy-Third Amendment) Act, 1992.
11. Gupta, J.K.: Economic Initiatives and Employment Generation in Rural Areas: Agenda for action, paper presented at the 44th National Town and Country Planners, Congress, Planning for Rural Development held at New Delhi, January 31 and February 1, 1996 organized at the Institute of Town Planners, India.
12. Gupta, M.M.: Regional Demographic Situation in India, paper presented in the seminar on Regional Dimension of India's Economic Development held at Nainital, April 22-24, 1982.
13. Gupta, R.G.: Rural Development Planning, *Journal of the Institute of Town Planners*, India, Volume 9, No. 2 (144) January, 1991.
14. Jagmohan: The Challenges of the Cities, Vikas Publishing House, New Delhi.
15. Javed, Qamar: For the People by the Government, *The Hindustan Times*, December 14, 1985.
16. Mahapatra, Satyen: Rural Development Long Postponed, *The Hindustan Times*, February 15, 2000.
17. Qaiyum, Abdul: Rural Development Efforts in India, *Journal of the Institute of Town Planners, India,* 1993.
18. Rao, B.V. Venkata: Rural Development, Letter to Editor, *The Hindu,* February 9, 1996.
19. Sharma, D.P. and Desai, V.V.: Rural Economy of India, Vikas Publishing House, New Delhi, 1980.
20. Siddiqui, Agha M.A.: Rural Roads Planning Vis-a-Vis Rural Development, *Journal of the Institute of Town Planners,* Volume 13, No. 2 (160), December, 1964.
21. Singh, Radha Raman: Studies in Regional and Rural Development, Associated Book Agency, 1982, Patna.
22. United Nations: Economic and Social Commission for Asia and the Pacific, Guidelines for Rural Centre Planning, New York, 1979.

CHAPTER 9

DEVELOPING THE SMALL AND MEDIUM TOWNS SETTLEMENTS PLANNING AND POLICY OPTIONS

The Planning of small and medium town settlements in India has assumed importance as metropolitan and other large cities are becoming congested and there is a marked deterioration in the quality of life. The Indian metropolitan cities, in particular are confronted with population explosion. Such a situation has led to the distortion of planning and management in the urban centres. To avoid the urban crisis in the 21st century, it is imperative that the approach of decentralization should be emphasized while planning for the small and medium town settlements, in a comprehensive manner.

Migration has been rising at a spectacular rate causing constraints on scarce financial resources for providing the housing, medical, educational and recreational facilities. However, the per capita investment on public utility services in large cities is enormous with reference to water, power and transport facilities.

In the metropolitan and other large cities in India there is a heavy pressure of industrial development, concentration of economic, commercial activities and office establishments. The 1991 census had observed that class-I cities had grown in population whereas the small towns had not shown any significant level of progress in economic development. Presently, there is an excessive stress on spatial, economic, trade and commercial developments in the large urban centres. The small towns can be classified with a viable population size ranging between 5,000 to 50,000; the medium town ranges from 50,001 to 1,00,000.

Neglected Small and Medium Towns

In the process of rapid urbanization, the mega cities are exploding and large cities are growing by leaps and bounds, while the small and medium towns are limping and many of them are stagnating or even decaying. It is a sad state of affairs. In 1991, the small towns, having less than 50,000 population, accounted for 82.3 per cent of the total number of urban centres in India. In spite of this large number, the share of total urban population living in these towns was only 23.9 per cent. The share for medium towns (50,000–100,000 population) was a stagnant 11 per cent during the three decades, 1961-91. On the other hand, merely 300 class-I (more than 100,000 population) cities accommodated as high as 65.2 per cent of total urban population. During 1981-1991, the decadal rate of growth of population of class-I cities was 46.9 per cent, whereas the corresponding figure for small towns having 20 to 50 thousand population was 35.4 per cent and for towns, with less than 20,000 population, it was as low as 6.1 per cent. In case of medium towns it was 28 per cent.

Such a plight of small and medium towns has resulted in a mass rural-urban and urban-urban migration to large cities which are unable to absorb the influx by providing gainful employment, housing and civic services. The consequence of this is a well-known phenomenon. However in such a situation people living in both towns and cities suffer.

Towns, small or medium, play a major role in the rural-urban continuum. They provide a variety of easily accessible services to the rural areas. When located near a metropolis or a mega city, they provide alternative locations for economic activities, extending full advantage of agglomeration economies and if well planned they can serve as a vital potential growth centres in the metro-regional context. Such towns are thus an important link between the villages at the lower end of the ladder and the metro cities at the top. As such, the development of these towns should not be neglected. If developed timely, these settlements can be instrumental in providing environmentally sustainable quality of life to the people.

By 1991, the number of million-plus cities had nearly doubled to 23, with a total population of 70.7 million and 8.4 per cent of the Indian population. Thus, the process of urbanization in India has essentially been the growth of large number of towns and metropolitan cities at the cost of small and medium town settlements. While the pace of urbanization in the country as a whole has been slowing down, the pace of metropolitanism has been accelerating.

It is learnt that 'the projected increase in urban population and labour force suggested that provision of adequate employment and infrastructure facilities in urban areas is going to be the main challenging problem in the immediate future. These assume urgency because in the absence of effective interventions in terms of appropriate strategies and resource allocations to meet the persistent problem of increasing urban poverty'.

In the present context, while deficiencies in infrastructure facilities and resources affect practically all categories of towns and cities undergoing rapid population growth, the situation of small and medium towns, because of their weak financial and management capacity, is particularly vulnerable. One of the side-effects of the new liberalization policy with its emphasis on export led growth will be to edge out the Indian small and medium towns in favour of large and metropolitan cities.

Though the small and medium towns have till recently not received much attention in public and private investments, there are several instances of towns in this category doing very well in economic growth. Judicious use of such investments can help to capitalize their potential in the overall interest of country's economic development.

The Government of India has been committed to promote the growth of small and medium towns and since December 1979 till March 31, 1995 invested over 230 crores in 749 towns under the Centrally sponsored scheme of Integrated Development of Small and Medium Town (IDSMT). However, the Indian experience in the implementation of the IDSMT scheme has revealed a number of operational snags, a major limitation is the weak institutional and management capacity at local level. A number of initiatives have been taken to improve the performance of the scheme through revision of guidelines including, among others, increase in the upper limit of town eligible for assistance, changes in the pattern of financial assistance, rationalization of selection of towns through mandatory preparation of states-urban strategies and involvement of institutional financing agencies in the scheme''.

It is realized that every effort must be made to ensure that towns and cities stimulate the economic development of rural areas instead of impoverishing them, which means taking more account of the interdependence of towns and countryside. The policies of decentralization must acknowledge the expression and mobilization of local energies, help people to take responsibility for their own affairs and establish the physical and institutional framework necessary to local development, in conjunction with the state and other sectors.

The notable characteristic of small and medium town settlements is that they have physical proximity with rural hinterlands. As such, the small towns' development are conditioned with the lack of socio-economic and infrastructural facilities. The small town settlements have a weak economic base and eventually they are starved of credit facilities due to the absence of inadequate number of financial institutions. The small town development requires the provision of adequate infrastructural facilities like road, transport and power.

The main economic factor of population growth in the metropolitan cities is the attraction of higher income and employment prospects. Therefore, the small town will have to be developed with the adequate infrastructural and a well supported financial institutional facilities.

The Fourth Five Year Plan had rightly pointed out that beyond certain limit unit costs of providing utilities and services increases rapidly with rise in the size of cities. The ultimate analysis of the problem is that of planning the spatial location of economic activity throughout the country. The document of the Fourth Plan had rightly recommended that the "future planning must be oriented for the stabilization of population at desirable optimum figures and towards planning suitable new centres in the region for a likely spill over". As such, the Fourth Plan had indicated that in the regional context the population should be distributed in a balanced manner.

At present, the concentration of population has been mainly in the metropolitan and large cities. Thus, the attention of planning has got to be directed for ensuring a decentralized process of urban economic activities in the small and medium town settlements.

It is visualized that with the proper approach of small and medium town planning, the marketable and exportable surplus can be utilized for the Indian economy by effectively promoting the agro-industrial development.

The one sided process of urban growth alone cannot effectively generate the self-sustained potential exploration of economic developments. The excessive growth of urbanization with large number of cities cannot ensure a balanced process of regional development.

The migrants in urban areas, even though with a job, have been subjugated to a slum-living condition where there is the denial of fresh air, light and privacy. These migrants have to accept either jobs without homes in urban areas or homes without jobs in rural areas. Thus, the economic, commerce, trade industrial, infrastructural and socio-economic amenities need to be emphasized in the small town settlements.

Village-cum-Town Developments

The villages have to be linked with the towns in terms of flow of raw material and finished products and transfer of technological developments. Dr. Douglas Ensminger "Growth and Viable Rural Urban Communities" has made the following observations on rural-urban integrated development that not village development alone, nor town development alone, but village-cum-town development linking clusters of villages to town growth centres in the context of India should be adopted for future planning of the countryside. Over a period of perhaps twenty years, viable rural-urban communities can be expected to emerge for offering the people, both in the centre and the surrounding cluster of villages, most of the social and economic institutions and services required. However, such a process can be hastened and guided by the integrated area planning and development of suitable small town settlements. The connotation of an integrated planning for a given geographic area with respect to all aspects of development includes transportation, communications, education, agriculture, banking, industry, health and family planning, recreation and other services which have to be adopted for modernizing rural living conditions.

The small and medium towns in integrated area planning can vitalize the adjoining rural economy. It is understood that "India's agricultural development can be achieved only in addition to increased production, there is a policy and action for involving all who work on the soil in the benefits of increased production". Plans and programmes mobilizing effectively the agricultural resources for industrial purposes needs to be highlighted. This will improve the living standards of all village people.

Policy for Small and Medium Towns

Growing urbanization in India is gradually witnessing many basic inequalities that have come into being during the period of rapid change. A change from an agrarian economy to the pre-industrial economy and subsequently to a well-balanced agro-industrial economy which has not carried along side its transformation of the human settlements from purely agricultural to urbanized ones. That would fully meet the needs of the population living in them and at the same time establish backward and forward linkages with the surrounding regions in tune with the overall development of the region. This problem has, with the passage of time, assumed large proportions and complex character, but notwithstanding the current problems of urban development in the country, it has now been an accepted fact that urbanization is an important promoter and supporter of economic and social development and as such, must be sustained.

The policy for developing the viable small and medium town settlements should constitute the spatial and economic linkages through an effective administrative and planning set up directed for implementation of socio-economic and infrastructural facilities. There are prerequisite issues which need to be spelt out while formulating a comprehensive action plan as a strategy for decentralizing the urbanized economic and commercial activities.

The urban local bodies have to be oriented in their administrative structure for promoting a meaningful small and medium town development and planning through the efficient mobilization of civil taxes. The octroi taxes need to be rationalized as the production activities of small and medium town settlements are hampered. This emphasis should be given to the single entry point of collection of octroi taxes within the same state boundary.

There is a need for specifying the landuse development through environmental and ecological legal rules and regulations. The proper drainage and collection of garbage in small and medium town settlements assumes importance in creating a congenial environment.

As an action proposal for small and medium town settlements, the emphasis has to be given for the priority of power and transport facilities. This would enable raising the production, income and employment prospects to the proximity of metropolitan and large cities.

Given these broad-based urbanization policy imperatives for India, the planning and management of human settlements with special stress on small and intermediate towns and growth foci with appropriate institutional and legislative supports holds the key to the goal of a decentralized urbanization.

Trade and commerce constitute a major economic activity in a fairly large number of small and medium towns, which together with household industries usually shelter the bulk of informal growth of economy. Agricultural activities also engage a substantial proportion of working force in a large number of these towns. Wholesale marketing of agricultural and other primary produce provides an opportunity for commercial development in greater or lesser degree in most of the towns. Considering the predominantly agricultural character of the economy, importance of vigorous marketing for hinterland to provide the initial impulse for growth can hardly be overemphasized in the case of small and medium towns and cities. A sprinkling of manufacturing including household exists in most of the urban settlements but the workers in manufacturing sector account for a very small percentage of the total.

The fringe of small and medium towns is mostly utilized for cultivation of paddy and wheat crops in place of sugarcane. The fringe is thus predominantly agricultural, while the industrial development may extend beyond the municipal area along rail and road routes. The fringe is also used for spot location of industry in most of the urban settlements.

By and large, it is evident that the development of these urban settlements has not influenced the urban fringe to any extent and almost next to the boundary of the urban settlements, the area remains to be rural. The development of urban fringe is essential for an integrated development of the surrounding areas under the urban dominance. The gross town density is, by and large, low and in medium towns it is less than 20 per ha. On an average, in the large towns the gross town density is between 50 to 60 per ha. This indicates a low utilization of urban land. In the small towns, the highest gross density is 72 and the lowest 54 per ha. In medium towns the range varies between 13 and 125 per ha.

About 85 per cent of the small and medium towns have some kind of protected water supply and connected to the regional grid. On an average, though 80 to 97 per cent of the municipal area of the towns and 75 to 92 per cent of the population are covered by the power supply network, the number of connections per thousand of the population is low. Generally speaking, the available facilities of education in small and medium towns are fair. For every 1,500 to 2,500 population, there is primary school and for every 5,000 population of the town there is a higher secondary school. But the situation varies widely from one urban settlement to another. Those which have a central location and command a large rural hinterland also involve a higher level of educational facilities particularly higher secondary schools and colleges. But there is lack of vocational centres and other work-cum-training institutions in nearly all the small and medium towns. The urban settlements which are near large cities or metropolies cater the increasing demand for educational facilities and in such towns many improvised institutions emerge for commercial gains.

Cities and large towns function as the important centres of medical care, but in small towns the medical facilities are grossly inadequate. Surprisingly, in many of the small towns of India, except for a dispensary there are no other medical facilities.

In short, all the smaller towns suffer from lack of basic facilities such as drinking water, sanitation and low level of social services. All the settlements uniformly suffer from poor infrastructural development, inadequately organized distributive services and even more poorly organized economic services which have inhibited their economic growth. The programme for improvement of small and medium towns has attempted to make these aspects economically more attractive for the prospective rural migrants, by establishing new industrial, commercial and agro-industrial centres. The quantum of this diversion may be much low because no planned area wise programme of development of the small and medium urban centres is envisaged within a time bound programme.

Vital Linkages for Rural Development

Small and medium town settlements should embody the physical links with the whole cluster of villages for the developmental purposes. New economic schemes, and in particular, the transmission of power to adjoining rural areas should be provided for ensuing the new services demanded by the process of rural modernization. The small town should act as a source of production, income and employment linkages with the villages for vitalizing an effective relationship of trade, industry, finance, education and various other activities. The rural areas, having physical proximity with small town settlements should provide for rural people, all the modern services and amenities like that of urban areas. Further, it should also provide the sufficient employment opportunities. Such a process necessitates a well-built infrastructural and socio-economic network of facilities.

The growth of small and medium town settlements within the physical proximity of a large urban centre are required to promote rural developmental prospects which are advantageous in terms of locational characteristics. Thus, there is likely to be rural-urban integration in terms of resource flow movement for accelerating the tempo of production, income and employment prospects.

In the context of India, it is visualized that the small town settlement would be able to absorb the rural surplus manpower resources. Further, the employment prospects necessitate an effective process of industrialization programmes for the small and medium town settlements. Agriculture has got to be linked with the industrial development by coordinated it through marketing management and financial institutions.

Plan for Economic Prosperity

In the context of Indian economic scenario it is realized that there will be a need for human resource development. A significant volume of investment with efficiency will have to be directed for planning the rural areas. The increasing tempo of agricultural development is expected to create adequate job opportunities in the primary and secondary sector.

Such a process of small town settlements has to be spelt out with reference to the locational advantages. Accordingly, its level of economic prosperity can be transferred to the lesser developed area. The inducement of infrastructural facilities in it will vitalize the adjoining planning areas.

Thereby it will be able to promote the effective process of rural development in a comprehensive manner.

By inducing the socio-economic and infrastructural facilities in the viable small town settlements, the agro-industrial resource based locational potentialities can be explored to its optimum. Thus, the rural-urban integration can be visualized and the balanced process of regional development can be achieved. These locational centres are required to offer an economic rationality for ensuing an effective flow of agricultural resources for boosting the tempo of agro-industrial developmental prospects.

Integration of Agriculture with Industry

The linkage of agriculture with industry in its workability is, however, economically justified in the growth centres of small and medium town and rural area settlements. This is possible when the growth centres of small town settlements are provided with the adequate educational, medical, transport, power, water supply, administrative and market facilities.

There is need for detailing the spatial advantages in terms of locational characteristics of small and medium town settlements. An evaluation of potential small towns adjoining villages needs to be visualized with reference to the inducement of financial allocations and assessing the developmental requirements for promoting employment prospects.

Employment Prospects

If India's Ninth Plan has to be employment oriented, then the decentralized urban economic planning has to be emphasized within the developmental approach of small town settlements. As such, there is a vital need for selecting viable areas for urban economic type of decentralization within the small and medium towns, which can boost the economic development programmes of rural areas. Thus, an accelerated pace of employment can be generated in the rural areas in the context of India's Five Year Plans.

First of all, it is desirable to assess the raw material producing potentialities of the adjoining villages of small and medium towns for an effective realization of the agro-industrial prospects. Moreover, there is also the need for a comprehensive economic analysis of industrial decentralization in relation to the cost of the input to be compared with its corresponding turnover production quantum. If the input involvement has the economic proposition of maximizing the output at low cost of industrial establishment, then only the decentralized sector would be able to promote an optimal product market saleability in the viable rural, small and medium town settlements. Thereby it would be able to promote the optimal production income and employment prospects. There is need for inducing the accelerated production and income possibilities through industrialization in growth centres of small town settlements, then it would obviously transfer the enormous employment avenues in the score of villages. This process of development has to be supported by the adequate provisions of infrastructural facilities.

Criteria for Small Town Settlements

For establishing the small town settlements it is important to ascertain the various socio-economic components which must be considered in a comprehensive manner. Keeping this fact in view, a tentative potential spatial and economic characteristic has to be ascertained.

Population Factor

The small towns with a population ranging from 10,000 to 50,000 and beyond 50,000 and less than 100,000 can be chosen as viable growth centres for boosting score of villages. Over a period of time, the population would increase and subsequently create conditions for stimulating the economic activities.

Occupational Composition

In the Indian context, the state wise census figures of occupational pattern of small and medium town settlements have to be identified. The occupational structure would reveal the manpower in primary, secondary and tertiary sectors in the context of small town settlements. The ideal occupational pattern would be about 60 per cent in the primary and 40 per cent in the combined secondary and tertiary sectors.

A small and medium town settlement first of all, should have transport linkages with the adjoining areas and secondly, it should be within the proximity of the urbanized industrial centres. The approximation of spatial location would accelerate a rapid pace of socio-economic development, industrial, commercial, educational and medical facilities.

Power and Water Supply

In the Ninth Five Year Plan of India, there is a programme of industrialization for decentralized power generation. As such, electricity can be made available through transmission grid from the urban industrial areas. However, this would open immense possibilities which would lead to the emergence of factories and agricultural processing establishments far away from the congested metropolitan and large cities into the small and medium towns settlements.

Economic development of the small and medium town settlements in the context of 21st century necessitates that the industrial economic base should be administered for accomplishing an optimal level of employment and better income prospects. Thus, rural migration to urban areas can be minimized in a significant magnitude.

In a study "Growth and viable Rural-Urban Communities", Dr. Douglas Ensminger has rightly emphasized the need for road development for accelerating the economic development in the small and medium town settlements. By a road construction programme, four important advances will be made. First, fertilizers, tools and other needs of the cultivators can be met freely from the small town settlements to the score of villages, secondly, the marketable agricultural produce can move easily to the small town, which will then emerge as the natural storage, marketing and distribution centre. Both these processes are essential for modernizing agriculture. A third contribution of the road construction programme to economic growth will come from improved opportunities for the employment of landless labourers, holders of uneconomic units and village artisans. At least in the formal stages of the rural-urban integrated small town development, one would expect those who gain employment in small towns to live in their "home" villages and commute from the centre for work each day. Good roads will shorten the time of travel for potential employees and increase the distance from which they can come. A fourth contribution of roads linking all the villages to the small town will be the interaction among people which breaks the isolation and develops a sense of identification with a larger community.

The transport development in small town settlements is an imperative necessity. It is emphasized that the linkages of small town and rural settlements with the metropolitan and large cities would enable to boost the employment possibilities.

Integrated Development of Small and Medium Towns: A Caste Study

The policy for urbanization in India has to be oriented towards the planning the totality. The human settlements comprising urban centres, villages wherein each size of settlement, be it super-metros, metro cities, towns or rural settlements, has got to play a specific role for ensuring that liveability improves with full access to employment and physical and social infrastructures at affordable cost in different settlements. The framework through legislation and governance is available and, only the priorities in development, finances and interaction between governmental and private initiative and voluntary action groups has to be properly organized. The Seventh Five Year Plan had made attempts to take care of such priorities. In this process, the small and medium towns, population around 1,00,000 and rural growth centres (with population exceeding 5,000) had been recognized as important key factor for planning and development.

The Sixth Plan document had stressed the development of small, medium and intermediate towns, "to ensure continuance of the present balanced distribution of urban population", and also to correct the "tendency to neglect infrastructure provisions in small, medium and intermediate cities in the past which have restricted their role as dynamic growth centres." The specific 'stress on small and medium towns (SMT) was directed to develop them as service centres which would promote the developmental prospects of their hinterlands for a balanced development of rural and urban areas, for an effective rural, small and medium town settlement linkages. Their development was also designed to put a curb on migration towards the large cities, thereby preventing the already strained municipal services. Their growth was as part of National Urbanization Policy for dispersed urbanization by providing the adequate infrastructures in small and medium towns.

The major objectives of small and medium towns' development were for (i) promoting the development of rural hinterlands, and (ii) to restrain migration of rural population. This was the underlying objective of the national programme of IDSMT, initiated in 1979 and continued in the Sixth Plan (1980-85), which made a provision of Rs 960 million in the Central sector for the Centrally sponsored scheme of IDSMT in the form of assistance to the state departments, provided matching contributions were forthcoming from there.

It was anticipated that the selection would be on the basis of regional and state level strategies, so as to identify those centres which had decennial growth rate exceeding 30 per cent; with pronounced facilities to accelerate the process of growth and thereby to absorb new migrants, who would otherwise go to large and metropolitan cities. The regional and state level strategies were, however, not available and therefore, district headquarters and towns with pronounced growth were primarily picked up.

The criteria of selection of towns for integrated development, subject to the population ceiling of one lakh, were with reference to the growth of population, the growth of the region, linkage of employment generation with urban development and the capacity of the institutions responsible for urban development. Subject to these broad criteria indicated in the guidelines, selection of towns was left entirely to the state governments.

The components of the IDSMT scheme were separated into two sets by the guidelines. The first set, which contained those components to be assisted by the Government of India, on a matching basis (50:50), was intended to generate employment opportunities in small and medium towns, so that the rush to the big cities in pursuit of employment could be mitigated. Included here were:

1. Land acquisition and developments. Residential schemes were to include sites and services, with or without core housing, but 50 per cent of the plots were to be allocated to economically weaker sections and 20 per cent to low income groups.
2. Traffic and transportation to serve shelter and employment projects. The projects which need priority are the construction of new roads and the improvement or upgrading of existing roads, but did not include the purchase of motor vehicles.
3. Development of markets/*mandies*, provision of industrial estates and other services and processing facilities for the benefit of agricultural and rural development in the hinterland.

The form of assistance was a soft loan carrying an interest rate of 5.5 per cent per year (7.5 per cent in the Seventh Plan), and it was to be repaid in twenty-five years with a grace period of five years.

The second set of components of the IDSMT scheme was to be funded through the resources of the state government and implementing agencies. They were, however, to be part of the integrated scheme. These components aimed mainly at improving the urban environment of towns by improving slums, and by developing parks and other public amenities. This set of components included:

1. slum improvement and upgrading, urban renewal and small-scale employment generation activity;
2. low cost schemes of water supply, sewerage, drainage and sanitation;
3. preventive medical facilities/health care;
4. parks and playgrounds; and
5. assistance for the purpose of making modifications, wherever necessary, in city master plans to permit mixed landuse.

IDSMT under the Eighth Five Year Plan

While the IDSMT scheme under the Sixth and the Seventh Five Year Plans was felt by the Government of India to have broadly served its objectives and succeeded in creating sufficient infrastructure and other assets in the small and medium towns, paving the way for the much-needed boost to the growth of rural and small town economies. However, the development achieved was compartmentalized and neither created infrastructures in an integrated manner in the selected towns nor had a discernible impact in the surrounding hinterland. The selection of towns was also dependent upon project reports sent by the state governments and was not linked to proper state urbanization strategies. The funds available to the scheme through budgetary support were also inadequate and caused investments to be made at a "sub-optimal level". As a result, the desired objective of reducing migration to the big cities was not achieved.

In a paper IDSMT: Strengthening Infrastructure in Small and Medium Towns, D.S. Meshram has made the following observations as far as physical and financial progress is concerned. It may be mentioned that during the Sixth Five Year Plan the central assistance amounting to Rs 63.57 crores was released to 235 towns. In the Seventh Plan the scheme was continued with the provision of Rs 88.00 crores for covering additional 145 towns and for giving central assistance to the ongoing schemes of the towns covered earlier against which Rs 80.01 crores were released and 145 additional towns were also covered as targetted. During the year 1990-91, and 1991-92 the provision of Rs 21.00 crores and Rs. 15.00 crores respectively was made available, against which central assistance amounting to Rs 19.10 crores and Rs 13.44 crores was released and the additional towns numbering 77 and 60 were also covered respectively.

The total approved cost of the 387 towns covered under IDSMT scheme during the Eighth Five Year Plan amounts to Rs 890.65 crores against which central assistance amounting to Rs 107.81 crores (excluding releases made under Central Urban Infrastructure Support Scheme CUISS) was released by March, 1998. The total expenditure reported by state governments amounts to Rs 91.17 crores for towns covered during Eighth Five Year Plan period. Thus total central assistance released for 920 towns covered so far amounts to Rs 309.95 crores against which an expenditure of Rs 465.72 crores was reported by the close of the financial year, 1997-98.

Number of Towns Covered and Central Assistance Released Plan wise under IDSMT

(Rs in crores)

Plan Period	*Number of Towns*	*Central Assistance (CA) CA Released*
VI Plan	235	63.57
1991-91	145	80.01
VII Plan	77	19.10
1991-92	60	13.44
VIII Plan	387	107.81
1997-98	16	26.02
Grand Total	920	3019.95

Source: D.S. Meshram, IDSMT: Strengthening Infrastructure in Small and Medium Towns (papers) cited from Town and Country Planning Organization, Training Programme, Management of Small and Medium Towns, 10-14 January, 2000. Reading Material sponsored by the Department of Personnel and Training and Ministry of Urban Development, Government of India.

In addition, under the CUISS, Rs 1.99 crores were released for 108 towns during the year 1993-94, Rs 1.46 crores during 1994-95 for 78 towns, Rs 1.77 crores during 1995-96 for 88 towns, Rs 2.00 crores during 1996-97 for 95 towns and Rs 0.80 lakh during 1997-98. Thus, an amount of Rs 7.24 crores has been released for 369 towns under CUISS by March 31, 1998.

For the Eighth Plan the approved proposals under various components in different states and Union Territories are as follows:

— Site and services: Total area to be developed amounts to 1248.84 ha. for carving out 53555 number of plots at the cost of Rs 124.84 crores.

— Commercial schemes (Market *mandies*): The total number of shops/stalls to be constructed amounts to 49717 and 558 offices on a total area measuring 520.55 ha. at the cost of Rs 403.45 crores.

— Traffic and Transportation: The proposal is to construct 307.64 km of new roads, 929.07 km of roads to be improved/upgraded besides constructing 120 bus/truck terminals, 23 rickshaw/car parking and improve 147 round abouts and also to provide street lighting on the roads measuring 525.44 km, at the cost of Rs 175.19 crores.

— Slaughter houses: The proposal include the construction of 49 slaughter houses at the cost of Rs 5.08 crores.
— Construction of drains: The proposal is to construct 270.43 km of drains at the cost of Rs 22.74 crores.
— Parks and playgrounds: The proposal is to develop 208.96 ha. of area under parks and playgrounds at the cost of Rs 31.32 crores.
— Community Centres/ Kalyanamandaps: Total 99 community centres are to be constructed at the cost of Rs 30.53 crores.
— Tourist facilities: An amount of Rs 23.70 crores has been approved for developing tourist infrastructure like dormitories, improvement of fair-grounds etc.
— Slope stability measures: The proposal includes construction of 4.26 km retaining wall at the cost of Rs 1.31 crores.

Thus, it is quite evident that the IDSMT envisages a comprehensive programme for selected towns/growth centres covering various facets of development. This needs to be based on a multi-sectoral/integrated development plan which will take into account the long-term master/ development plan strategy for the town in conformity with state-urban development strategy. As per IDSMT guidelines the State Government needs to prepare a project document indicating the type of urban infrastructure facilities that would be required in the town keeping in view its projected growth profile and functional activities. The project report must also contain the cost benefit analysis in respect of the various components/schemes/programmes identified.

The IDSMT scheme was, therefore revised for the Eighth Plan, with special emphasis given for strengthening the economic base of the towns with the spatial planning of its region. This led to the conclusion that, "the obvious answer is to have a multi-sectoral integrated development programme encompassing all facets of development with adequate emphasis on maximizing employment as well as on the development of infrastructure meant for supporting agricultural and rural development."

In addition, it was recognized that an assured, uninterrupted flow of funds at a higher level was "of utmost importance" to the success of such multi-sectoral development programmes. The scheme as originally formulated suffered both due to the failure of the states to provide matching funds and due to the inadequacy of the total amount of funding available. It was, therefore, acknowledged that the scheme should not depend solely on the Government of India loans and budgetary support, but it should also be supported by institutional finance. Consequently, implementation was reorganized to include infrastructure loans through the HUDCO, as well as from other suitable financial institutions. Thus, budgetary provisions are now to be used mainly for providing seed capital to the institutions and local bodies, for generating the much-required funds and for critical infrastructure which do not have any direct return, but would act as a catalyst for further development. At the same time, it was accepted that the institutional finance must be available to implementing agencies at rates which are "reasonably within their repaying capacity". Under the Eighth Plan, then, funding is split three ways among the Government of India, State Governments/agencies and HUDCO/other financial institutions (OFIs).

By introducing the HUDCO/OFI's, while making more funds available to the IDSMT schemes makes repayment terms more difficult. It is not at all clear that these terms are feasible. HUDCO net interest rates for towns of the sizes range from 14% to 17.5% to be repaid in fifteen years with no grace period. These are substantially harder terms than those offered by the Government of India.

The new financing pattern also involves higher participation by the Government of India, so that the Government split is now 60:40, with the state governments having the smaller share. However, with HUDCO now involved, the three-way financial burden varies according to the size of the town. While the IDSMT scheme initially covered only towns with less than one lakh population, it now includes towns as large as three lakh grouped as follows:

1. Category A : Less than 20,000
2. Category B : 20,000 + to 50,000, the prime target group
3. Category C : 50,000 + to 1,00,000
4. Category D : 1,00,000 + 3,00,000.

The financing pattern also varies with the amount of funding, and the maximum which may be provided to any town rises according to the category of town. Thus, the complete picture is as follows:

- Category A : Rs 100 lakhs—GOI 35%, State 24%, HUDCO/OFIs 40%
- Category B : Rs 200 lakhs— GOI 36%, State 24%, HUDCO/OFIs 40%.
- Category C : Rs 500 lakhs—GOI 24%, State 16%, HUDCO/OFIs 60%
- Category D : Rs 1000 lakhs—GOI 18%, State 12%, HUDCO/OFIs 70%.

The components of the revised IDSMT scheme and the sources of the funds for each can be summarized as follows:

-	Integrated Sites and Services Schemes	:	GOI/State
-	Strengthening of link road facilities	:	GOI/State
-	Provision of bus terminals	:	GOI/State
-	Construction/upgrading of roads and side drains	:	GOI/State
-	Development of shopping centres	:	GOI/State
-	Localized drainage works	:	GOI/State
-	Street lighting	:	GOI/State
-	Slaughterhouse	:	GOI/State
-	Provision of tourist facilities	:	HUDCO/OFIs
-	Cycle/rickshaw stand	:	HUDCO/OFIs
-	Development of parks and playgrounds	:	HUDCO/OFIs
-	Traffic management scheme and social amenities	:	HUDCO/OFIs
-	Construction of retaining walls and slope stability measures in hill towns	:	HUDCO/OFIs

Need for Revision of Existing IDSMT Guidelines

A revision of the existing IDSMT guidelines is called for on the following key considerations:

(a) An appraisal of IDSMT scheme shows that although the Eighth Plan guidelines envisages an institutional finance component ranging from 40 per cent in the case of towns of Category A to 70 per cent in the case of Category D, almost all the towns identified under IDSMT have experienced tremendous practical difficulties in securing loans from financial institutions. There is a general consensus among state governments that the existing financing patterns are not feasible. Moreover, it is felt that since the IDSMT scheme objectives envisage a judicious mix of the remunerative and non-remunerative projects in the selected towns without which the objective of 'integrated' infrastructure development would not be achieved, to enable them to emerge as centres of economic growth and employment there is need for a grant element in the IDSMT financing patterns.

The exercises by the Planning Commission in the context of the newly introduced Mega City Scheme suggest that in the absence of 50 per cent zero-cost capital, it may not be possible on part of the mega cities with more than 4 million population in 1991, to tap institutional finance to the tune of 50 per cent of the costs of a desirable mix of remunerative, cost recover based and social service oriented projects. In this connection, there can be no doubt that the tax bases of small and medium towns are far narrower than those of the mega cities and the need for grant support to the former to enable them to tap institutional finance is considerable.

(b) The Constitution (74th) Amendment Act provides for the constitution of District Planning Committees. Urban Planning including town planning and planning for social and economic development are included as legitimate municipal functions under the 12th Schedule of the Constitution. It is envisaged that the municipalities should prepare Town Development Plans (TDPs) which would integrate landuse master plans and socio-economic development plans and implement them effectively. Moreover, the TDPs would have to be synchronized with the plans of panchayats representing the surrounding rural areas. The statutory District Planning Committees would be required to consolidate the plans prepared by municipalities and panchayats for submission to the state governments (and eventual integration with the state planning process).

The preparation of State Urban Development strategy also envisages the preparation of State Urban Development Plan which would comprise of District/Town Development Plans. In this context, it will be desirable to direct the Centrally sponsored IDSMT scheme primarily at the implementation of the development plans of towns with potential for development as regional growth centres.

(c) Given the past inadequacics of the IDSMT scheme to generate adequate investment in infrastructure in the selected small and medium towns, it is considered desirable that appropriate fiscal reforms to strengthen the municipalities should accompany the implementation of the IDSMT projects. The need for IDSMT emanates from the inability of municipalities to earmark adequate funds for infrastructural development. Therefore, the creation of a capital or infrastructure fund at the state/municipal level (State Urban Development Fund/Municipal Development Fund) as part of a series of municipal reforms is considered desirable. Unless the capital funds of municipalities are separated from the revenue funds and there is proper planning, infrastructure development is bound to suffer and municipalities will have a tendency to spend on unnecessary items such as excessive staff at the cost of basic infrastructure. In this regard, the IDSMT scheme could be used as a vehicle to promote municipal reforms as envisaged in the 74th Amendment Act.

(d) Experience with Nehru Rozgar Yojana (NRY) and Urban Basic Services for the Poor (UBSP) schemes suggests that it may be desirable to have one single agency responsible for monitoring all the centrally sponsored schemes or develop an appropriate institutional framework for monitoring the implementation of urban development projects. The State Urban development Agency/Urban Infrastructure Development Corporation/Director of Municipal Administration/Town Planning or a similar type of institutional arrangement could be appropriate for the implementation of schemes like IDSMT, NRY, UBSP, EIUS programme and Low Cost Sanitation (LCS), etc. The IDSMT funds could be directly routed through this institution which will have specialist staff including those for project formulation/ appraisal, project/financial management, data collection and updating, research and training for municipal capacity building, coordination, monitoring, evaluation and reporting, etc. The institution could eventually maintain a State Urban Development Data Bank and also a State Urban Development Fund.

Some Suggestions for Restructuring of IDSMT

Keeping the above major considerations in view, certain changes in the IDSMT scheme guidelines are suggested as follows:

Scheme Objectives

(a) Improving the infrastructural facilities and helping in the creation of durable public assets in small and medium towns having potential for development as regional centres of economic growth and employment, thereby reducing the incentives for people belonging to rural and smaller urban areas to migrate to bigger cities and towns for jobs.

(b) Decentralizing economic growth and employment opportunities and promoting dispersed urbanization while taking advantage of the functional and spatial interlinkages between villages, towns and cities through a regional planning approach.

(c) Increasing the availability of serviced sites for housing, commercial and industrial uses and promoting the principles of planned and orderly development in the towns covered by the scheme.

(d) Integrating spatial and socio-economic development planning as envisaged in the Constitution (74th) Amendment Act and preparing and implementing Town Development Plans.

(e) Promoting resource-generating schemes for selected urban local bodies to improve their overall financial position and ability to underake long-term infrastructure development programmes on their own as well as to repay the borrowed capital and undertaking necessary reforms in this regard.

(f) Encouraging fiscal and institutional reforms in the urban sector in accordance with the objectives of municipal decentralization envisaged in the Constitution (74th) Amendment Act.

Scheme Coverage

The coverage of IDSMT scheme needs to be extended to towns with population between 3 to 5 lakhs as these towns generally have the capacity for development as regional growth centres and can withstand the strong pulls of metropolitan cities. Moreover, they are not covered under many of the Centrally sponsored schemes. Often smaller towns are unable to generate an adequate employment base to attract migrants vis-a-vis large cities. Towns may be categorized into the following groups for the purpose of coverage under IDSMT:

Population	*Category*
Less than 20,000	A
20,000 - 50,000	B
50,000 - 100,000	C
100,000 - 300,000	D
300,000 - 500,000	E

In the selection of towns having potential for development as regional growth centres under IDSMT, preference should be given to headquarters of districts having more than 90 per cent rural population, followed by mandi towns and industrial growth centres (identified by the Ministry of Agriculture and Industry respectively), tourist places, pilgrim centres, etc. While the Scheme may not cover the industrial estates, industrial growth centres could be covered, taking due care that there is no overlapping in the provision of infrastructure under IDSMT and Growth Centre Scheme of the Department of Industrial Development. The state governments should identify limited number of towns in accordance with their strategies for urban development. The Ministry of Urban Affairs and Employment and the Planning Commission may lay down the criteria for the selection of IDSMT towns for guidance of the state governments.

Scheme Components

The components for assistance under IDSMT should include works needed to implement City/Town Development Plans which may have city/town wide significance. An illustrative list is as follow:

— Strengthening of master plan road facilities including arterial, bypass/link roads and small bridges.
— Sites and services.
— Development of bus/truck terminals.
— Construction/upgradation of master plan drains including stormwater channels.
— Solid waste management.
— Development of market complexes/shopping centres.
— Provision of tourist facilities.
— Master plan street lighting.
— Slaughter houses.
— Major public amenities like city-scale parks, playgrounds, marriage halls, pay and use toilets etc.
— Cycle/rickshaw stands.
— Traffic improvement and management schemes.
— Construction of retaining walls and slope stability measures in hill station towns.
— Social amenities specially for the poorer sections.

Schemes for water supply in the IDSMT towns may be undertaken/ supported under the HUDCO/LIC/externally aided infrastructure lending programmes and the Centrally sponsored AUWSP—Acclerated Urban Water Supply Programme (applicable to towns having less than 20,000 population).

The implementing agencies may be required to adopt a basket type approach so that the expenses incurred on the non-remunerative side and for the weaker sections are made up through adequate returns from the remunerative components like markets, shopping centres, bus and truck terminals, etc., so as to enable the generation of surplus funds for infrastructural development. The indicative ratio between commercial, cost recovery or user charge based and non-remunerative projects may be 40:30:30. However, this could be different for different size classes of towns depending on town priorities and the loan component involved.

Financing Pattern

Keeping in view the impractical nature of the existing guidelines for the financing of IDSMT projects.

The Financial Pattern for IDSMT

Rs in Million

Category	*Project Cost*	*Central Assistance (Grant)*	*State Share (Grant)*	*HUDCO loan/other financial institution sources*	
A (20,000)	10	4.8	3.2	2.0	20
B (20,000-50,000)	20	9.0	6.0	5.0	25
C (50,000-1,00,000)	35	15.0	10.0	10.0	29
D (1,00,000-3,00,000)	55	21.0	14.0	20.0	36
E (3,00,000-5,00,000)	75	27.0	18.0	30.0	40

The project costs indicated above are based on "Minimum Project Cost" concept, higher project size being conditional on the availability of higher loan /other resources. The objective is to see that the available funds are not spread out too thinly and the desired objectives of developing regional centres of economic growth and employment are achieved. There is need for adopting a comprehensive town and integrated approach of planning.

While there may be a limit on Central assistance, there should be no ceiling on the amounts that can be made available from the state governments/local bodies from their own resources and from institutional financing agencies so as to make the projects viable. Cost recoveries direct and indirect from projects may be pooled up after repayment of loans to constitute a revolving fund at the municipal level. The objective should be to see that bulk of the soft money from the Central and state governments flow back to the fund for taking up infrastructural development works on a continuing basis. The state governments/Union Territory administrations may identify the financial institutions that have expressed interest in funding the loan components of the proposed investments and send their financial appraisal reports to the Sanctioning Committee for the Scheme. The Committee could be constituted at the Central or state level preferably at the state level in the spirit of decentralization as envisaged in the Constitution 74th Amendment Act, 1992.

Considering the geographical and other factors in difficult tracts such as Jammu and Kashmir, Himachal Pradesh, Arunachal Pradesh, Nagaland, Manipur, Tripura, etc., the suitable revisions of the criteria as proposed could be made by the Ministry of Urban Affairs and Employment. This could be in consultation with the Planning Commission.

The separate accounts books for Central assistance, state share and for loans from financing institutions should be maintained by the local bodies/agencies in respect of each of the components of the approved programme and these should not be mixed up with any other funds.

In the process of formulation and implementation of the programmes, the state governments and local bodies should involve the private sector or adopt public-private partnerships to the extent possible. The modalities of involvements of the private sector in implementation of the programme could be spelt out in the IDSMT project reports. Private investment could be a substitute to the loan component.

The question is whether the Centre will allocate the cent per cent grants for the Small and Medium towns development under the IDSMT scheme. The states too have shown their anxiety to procure more and more money from the Centre and it seems less bothered in developing small town settlements.

Further, a crucial factor in developing is the land acquisition which involves a cumbersome administrative problems.

The small town settlements can be saved from neglect when industries grow up on being given incentives like cheap land, adequate power supply, long-term loan at low rates of interest and cheap transport network facilities.

For ensuring an effective economic base in small towns, there is an imperative need to promote the small scale industries as they have a larger labour absorption capacity. The small-scale industries in the small towns will have to utilize agricultural surpluses and thereby, transfer the finished manufacturing products in the rural settlements. However, the small town settlements can become meaningful if the local resources are utilized with the application of an appropriate technology.

The potential industries in small towns are sugar industry, match industry, power loom and handloom, handicraft, paper, soap, etc. Besides, the repair of engineering services will have a significant importance in the small town settlements for catering to the needs of rural areas.

For boosting the agro-industrial development, there is need to have a comprehensive survey of small town planning area and embodying the village clusters. The demographic and public utility services and industrial establishments, needs have to ascertain the present and future perspective planning of the small town and rural settlement pattern. However, it would be worthwhile to assess the demand and supply of consumer and industrial goods requirements in the small towns. Especially, the economic interdependence has got to be streamlined in terms of agro-industrial resource movements in the context of small town planning area.

Industries in Small Town Settlements

The agro-industrial based small town settlements should have suitable industrial structure in line with agricultural development. For such a line of set up, the following are the types of industries which are suggested for broad categorization for promoting employment in small town economy. The industries as specified below, indicate the employment that can be promoted effectively through the application of labour intensive technology. As such, the large scale industries do not have large employment potentials in small and medium towns and therefore, the small scale industries need to be emphasized. The rural areas have excessive resources and their best utilization is dependable on low investment small scale industries.

The type of industries in small and medium town settlements should be established which have the local raw material availability and the advantage of village produced agricultural inputs and equipments. However, the small scale industries which can emerge in the small and medium town settlements are namely, food and sugar industries, wood and furniture, edible oil and vegetable based industries, textile industries and handloom, so on.

The industrial set up in the small town settlement has to visualize the potential exploration of potentialities for vitalizing the economic development. The important perspective in view is not only to have a rapid capital formation, but to utilize in the best possible manner, the agricultural resources energy for promoting the optimal employment prospects.

Planning in a Regional Perspective

For an effective planning of small town, a comprehensive evaluation of demographic and working force needs to be assessed. The resource availability has to be assessed and accordingly the locational based agro-industrial development has to be advocated. However, the landuse potentialities have to be ascertained and thereby the specific locational activity must be emphasized. The land classification in terms of industrial, commercial, residential and recreational purposes must be prepared to provide in the small town settlements an economic and effective spatial development. Thereby, the pace of economic development prospects would vitalize the employment prospects.

There is an important need for developing the small and medium town settlements in a regional perspective. The hierarchial pattern of settlement constituting villages, urban villages, small towns, large metropolitan cities need to be linked with the integrated spatial and economic plan. The appropriate agro-industrial technology needs to be duly emphasized for strengthening the economic base of small town settlements.

The spatial planning has to be specified with reference to the residential, commercial, industrial and recreational uses. The suitable types of industries will have to be selected for specifying the optimal use of local resources. However, the agro-based industries of labour intensive technology will have to be duly encouraged.

With the integrated landuse plan and financial institutions, the small and medium town settlements can be planned effectively with a well regulated transport and marketing network system. One of the vital factors for stimulating the tempo of economic activities in small and medium towns is the regularity of power supply. Further, there is need for ensuring the transformation and transmission lines and generators for power supply from the metropolitan centres to the adjoining small town settlements. The potential agro-based industries should be duly encouraged with incentives of credit, concessions of land and power facilities in the small and medium town settlements. With the effective planning of small and medium town settlements, the economy of rural areas can be strengthened for boosting the optimal production, income and employment prospects. There is imperative need for evolving a decentralization approach of economic policy development.

The rapid process of urbanisation in developed countires and regions in an inevitable phenomenon. First, the high rates of natural increase in the population and secondly, the unending immigration from the country-side. When it is remembered that the crowded cities of India have no industrial facilities for employment for these immigrants, a dark picture of unceasing social tension is uncovered.

There is need for a small town planning as an alternative strategy of urbanization. Put a stop to further growth of metropolitan cities by developing the small towns into centres of industrial growth and bring the adjoining rural areas into the vortex of agro-industrial complexes for the rapid process of development.

The level of economic development should relate to the growth potential of small and medium towns. Accordingly, the industrial location and licensing policy needs to be oriented not only to areas but also for the requirements of a system of human settlements, keeping in view the development of those industries which have the capacity for absorbing the alarming number of labour force.

Industrialization is not necessarily urbanization. Integrated sectoral development with a system of balanced human settlements should be the base for urbanization. The diversification of the industrial base is necessary, so as to accelerate the pace of agricultural development which would strengthen the markets.

There is need for recognition of the informal growth of the economy which absorbs the majority of labour, having neither skills nor capital. However to match it with formal growth of the economy, it would be necessary to take immediate steps for boosting the organized sector. In addition to the location of labour intensive and small industries in small towns there is need for encouraging, reviving and strengthening the small scale and cottage industries in these human settlements. The adequate vocational training facilities should be provided for the improvement of human and technological skills in a big way.

Institution and infrastructure, appropriate technology, diffusion of innovation and energy are the main ingredients for socio-economic change in human settlements. The small and medium town settlements can be made attractive and functional with the comprehensive developments of infrastructural institutions.

The type and level of development and services to be provided in small town settlements may be determined by the choice of appropriate technology. In this context, decentralization of economic and other activities may be instrumental for the effective and efficient use of the appropriate technology. To do so, the political process at district level and below should endeavour to avail local resources, skills, enterpreneurship and investment by diffusion of innovation. The development of small town settlements should take into account the need of a change over from the non-commercial to commercial energy utilization in its optimal achievement.

For the redistribution of population together with decentralization of economic and other activities from large cities and metropolises to small and medium towns and cities, the transportation and communication network does play an important role. A clear policy has to be contemplated for providing the physical linkage to small and medium towns and cities which in turn will be able to develop and strengthen the productive, functional linkages of these human settlements.

The report document of the 'Task Force on Planning and Development of Small and Medium Towns and Cities (Volume I, Government of India) had observed rightly that the Town and Country Planning Department in each state or Union Territory should be responsible for the planning and control of development of small and medium towns and cities. It should first select those small and medium towns and cities which can be developed on a priority basis. The Master Plan should follow the imperatives given in the district and area plans at lower levels. For other small and medium towns and cities, the following are the guidelines for the preparation of Master Plan and Zonal Plans:

(a) Based on forecasting of population and activity growth, a planning area needs to be defined which may extend beyond the municipal area. While it is important to develop existing undeveloped areas within the municipal limits, the proposals in the Master Plan are to be so made as to ensure the feasibility of phasing the development, so that there is a contiguity of development covering ultimately the entire planning area. A land policy should enable quick acquisition of land for development and prevent land speculation. It may be desirable to purchase outright the unbuilt sites proposed for new commercial areas or public or semi-public use.

(b) While the proposal of the Master Plan should be made in order to meet the existing gaps and harness the potentialities for development, these should also recognize the personality of a human settlement which needs to be conserved and enriched by an environmental and cultural setting and ecological balance.

(c) The proposals in the Master Plan should identify the basic urban structure and an attempt should be made to solidify it by a concept. In addition, the urban structure should be such that the systems are functional and economically operative.

(d) Besides supplementing the urban structure and urban systems, the proposed landuse should have sociocultural, economic and environmental relevance. The percentage of landuse distribution for each category should vary accordingly. The proposed landuse should not be ad hoc and unrelated but it should follow a landuse system on the basis of the hierarchy and inter-relation of the activity systems. For optimizing the functional efficiency, economics of land, urban investment and its pay off, the landuse intensity should be important consideration for the landuse system, which in turn should determine the relations between land and bulk of building under each category of landuse as well as overall gross and net densities of population.

(e) The study of selected small and medium towns and cities reveals that the percentage of area developed with or without approach road, water supply, electricity, sewer in a classical book *Agrindus Integration of Agriculture and Industries*, Haim Halperin has rightly observed that the rural family which is larger than the family in the city, has a surplus of labour owing to the absence of agrotechnology and higher levels of productivity. This surplus must find an outlet in other nonagricultural branches of the economy.

The physical proximity of small town settlement has got to be linked effectively with the score of village. This needs to be identified and suitable integrated economic activities should be planned.

One of the vital aspects of small and medium towns is to absorb the rural manpower surplus. The main objective of developing the small towns is to act as countermagnets of urban centres. The specific function of small town can act as a prominent centre of promoting the utilization of local resources and the use of an appropriate technology. The higher economic growth necessitates favourable income returns due to the emergence of a self-reliant tempo of production activity. Boosting the small industries calls for lesser power but has higher employment generating prospects. The agro-industries will be able to play an important role in economic development of small and medium towns for catering the need of adjoining rural to areas. In this process of spatial and economic development the agro-industrial revolution has to be stimulated for attracting the entrepreneurial and technological skill. As a measure of incentive land should be made available on a concessional rate and loan for agro-industries on a cheap term repayment basis.

Further, the landuse planning assumes a significant aspect of small town development with reference to (i) residential, (ii) commercial, (iii) industrial, (iv) recreational, etc. However, the significant land needs to be provided for the industrial estate. The small scale industries have a great scope and potentialities in small town settlements. All out efforts needs to be directed for providing a comprehensive electrification programme while planning the small town settlements.

It is realized that "one of the reasons why small towns have never grown up is the contempt with which state governments have treated smaller municipalities and starved them of funds. Substantial fiscal autonomy should be given to them and assured funds made available for development." The significant attention of administrative machinery with the efficient level of services and industrial growth backed by financial institutions has not been given the due recognition as a policy action for developing the small town settlements.

The small town will have to act as growth centre to a score of villages. The input-output matrix will have to be formulated. Further, the agricultural raw material output flow would induce industrial input within the small settlements. The underlying approach towards small and medium town development is to promote the optimal agro-industrial development. It is pointed out that the small and medium towns have to act as efficient marketing and distribution centre of an urban economy. However, the cold storage facilities in small town will enable farmers within the rural physical proximity an advantageous economic gain. Above all, the small and medium town settlements have to be directed with adequate infrastructural-cum-socio-economic facilitities to grow as viable growth centres. The Five Year Plans perspective has to be directed accordingly.

TABLE 1

Increase/Decrease of Urban Population in each Size/Class: India (1981-91)

Size/ Class of Towns	*1991 Population (in '000)*	*Population Increase/ Decrease 1981-91*		*Contribution to Total Population*		*Decadal Population Growth Centre*	
		Absolute ('000s)	*Percentage*	*1981*	*1991*	*1971-81*	*1981-91*
I-VI	212,867	56.447	100.00	100.00	100.00	46.23	36.09
I	138,803	44,298	+ 78.48	60.42	65.20	54.35	46.87
II	23,309	5,119	+ 9.07	11.63	10.95	55.73	28.14
III	28,079	5,670	+ 10.04	14.33	13.19	30.85	25.30
IV	16,531	1,600	+ 2.84	9.54	7.77	27.54	10.72
V	5,531	–70	– 0.13	3.58	2.60	17.82	– 1.27
VI	613	–170	– 0.30	0.50	0.29	65.73	– 21.70

Note: Excludes Assam and Jammu and Kashmir.

Towns are classified into six population size/classes by the census as follows:

Class I	:	Population of 100,000 or more
Class II	:	Population between 50,000–99,999
Class III	:	Population between 20,000–49,999
Class IV	:	Population between 10,000–19,999
Class V	:	Population between 5,000–9,999
Class VI	:	Population below 5,000

Source: Various publications of the 1981 and 1991 census of India; cited from a Paper of Dr. K. Srinivasan and Dr. Sanjay Kumar, India's Urbanization and Health Conditions: Some Observations.

TABLE 2

Growth in Number of Small and Medium Towns and their Population 1901-1991

Years	*Medium Towns*				*Small Towns*						*Total Small and Medium Towns*	
	Class II		*Class III*		*Class IV*		*Class V*		*Class VI*			
	No. of Towns	*%pop.*	*No. of Towns*	*% pop.*	*No. of Towns*	*%pop.*	*No. of Towns*	*%pop.*	*No. of Towns*	*%pop.*	*No. of Towns*	*%pop.*
1901	44	11.37	144	16.94	427	22.60	771	20.61	503	6.38	1889	77.91
1911	38	9.51	158	18.80	388	20.73	750	20.15	546	7.05	1880	76.25
1921	49	11.21	172	18.19	395	19.18	773	19.36	626	7.51	2015	75.47
1931	59	12.40	218	19.75	479	19.60	849	17.99	580	5.76	2185	75.52
1941	88	12.95	273	18.93	554	17.46	979	15.90	478	3.57	2372	68.13
1951	111	12.20	374	17.79	675	15.00	1195	13.62	628	3.33	2993	61.96
1961	139	12.06	518	19.94	820	14.31	847	8.01	268	1.12	2592	55.46
1971	219	13.48	652	18.28	987	12.80	820	5.67	290	0.82	2968	51.05
1981	270	11.69	743	14.15	1059	9.39	758	3.57	253	0.56	3083	39.57*
1991	345	10.95	944	13.30	1170	7.91	740	2.62	198	0.31	3397	35.09**

*Includes projected population of Assam.

**Population percentage in relation to total urban population.

***Excludes population of Jammu and Kashmir.

Source: Census of India 1971, 1981 and 1991, cited from D.S. Meshram and A. Qaiyum Small and Medium Towns A Weak Link in the Human Settlement System in India, Spatio Economic Development Record, Volume 2, Number 3, May-June, 1995.

TABLE 3
Cumulative Release of Central Assistance and Expenditure Reported Under IDSMT
(From 1979-80 upto 30th December, 1999)

Rs. in Crores

Sl. No.	*State/Union Territories*	*Towns Covered*	*Funds Released*	*Expenditure Reported*
01.	Andhra Pradesh	77	37.85	59.93
02.	Arunachal Pradesh	5	0.94	1.64
03.	Assam	21	6.88	8.69
04.	Bihar	42	11.71	14.75
05.	Goa	6	1.67	1.19
06.	Gujarat	54	24.47	42.73
07.	Haryana	14	2.56	9.99
08.	Himachal Pradesh	7	2.19	4.65
09.	Jammu and Kashmir	8	3.40	6.16
10.	Karnataka	79	28.08	34.49
11.	Kerala	33	14.55	26.34
12.	Madhya Pradesh	75	28.19	33.17
13.	Maharashtra	98	47.10	84.46
14.	Manipur	11	3.46	4.48
15.	Meghalaya	7	2.26	4.48
16.	Mizoram	5	2.33	6.52
17.	Nagaland	7	2.23	4.04
18.	Orissa	42	13.22	18.49
19.	Punjab	27	11.06	22.87
20.	Rajasthan	45	20.94	39.03
21.	Sikkim	5	1.29	2.72
22.	Tamil Nadu	100	33.36	51.72
23.	Tripura	10	3.16	3.84
24.	Uttar Pradesh	89	27.98	41.76
25.	West Bengal	68	24.61	38.67
26.	Andaman and Nicobar Islands	1	0.92	1.24
27.	Dadar and Nagar Haveli	2	1.12	0.16
28.	Daman and Diu	1	0.23	0.00
29.	Lakshadweep	1	0.25	0.00
30.	Pondicherry	6	2.11	1.60
	Grand Total	946	363.10	569.80

Source: Town and Country Planning Organization; Chapter IDSMT Scheme Progress and Achievement (SMT Division) Training Programme Management of Small and Medium Towns 10-14 January, 2000. Reading Material Sponsored by the Department of Personnel and Training and Ministry of Urban Development.

TABLE 4
Number of Towns Covered and Central Assistance Released Planwise Under IDSMT

(Rs in crores)

Plan Period	*Number of Towns*	*Central Assistance (CA) CA Released*
VI Plan	235	63.57
1991-91	77	19.10
VII Plan	145	80.01
1991-92	60	13.44
VIII Plan	387	107.81
1997-98	16	26.02
Grand Total	920	3019.95

Note: The total expenditure reported by State Governments amounts to Rs 91.17 crores for towns covered during the Eighth Five Year Plan period. Thus, the total Central assistance released for 920 towns covered, so far amounts to Rs 309.95 crores against which an expenditure of Rs 465.72 crores was reported by the close of the financial year 1997-98.

Source: D.S. Meshram, IDSMT: Strengthening Infrastructure in Small and Medium Towns, Cited from the document of Town and Country Planning Organization, Training Programme Management of Small and Medium Towns, 1-14 January, 2000 Sponsored by the Department of Personnel and the Ministry of Urban Development, Government of India.

REFERENCES

1. Bhargava, Gopal; Small Town Development Socio-Economic Aspects, *The Economic Times,* April 11, 1992.
2. _____________: Small Towns Still in Doldrums, *The Hindustan Times,* February 22, 1983.
3. _____________: Developing the Small Town Settlements, *Employment News*, April 23, 1982.
4. _____________: Small Town Development Socio-Economic and Spatial Aspects, *The Economic Times*, April 11, 1992.
5. _____________: Small Town Planning, *The National Herald,* September 2, 1983.
6. Eldelman, D.J. and Banerjee, R.: Fifteen Years of the Integrated Development of Small and Medium Towns (IDSMT) in Karnataka—Some Observations, Institute of Town Planners, India, Journal, Volume 14, No. 2 (163-164) September-December, 1995.
7. Ensminger, Doughlas, Growth and Viable Rural Urban Communities, Kurukshetra, October, 1969.
8. Government of India: Task Force on Planning and Medium Towns and Cities, Volume 1, Ministry of Works and Housing.

9. Kulshrestha, S.K.: Neglected Small and Medium Towns, Spatio-Economic Development Record, Volume 2, Number 3, May, 1995.
10. Meshram, D.S. and Qaiyum, A.: Small and Medium Towns, A Weak Link in the Human Settlement System in India, Spatio-Economic Development Record, Volume 2, Number 3, May-June, 1995.
11. Meshram, D.S.: IDSMT: Strengthening Infrastructure in Small and Medium Towns (paper), cited from Town and Country Planning Organization, Training Programme Management of Small and Medium Towns, 10-14 January, 2000, reading material sponsored by the Department of Personnel and Training and Ministry of Urban Development, Government of India.
12. Mohanty, Prasana: Scheme of Integrated Development of Small and Medium Towns—Some Suggestions and Restructuring Spatio- Economic Development Record, Volume 2, Number 3, May-June, 1996.
13. Pandey, H.B.: Small Town Planning Guidelines for Zonal Planning-I, Small Town Planning-II, Factors Accelerating Development, *The Economic Times*, January 28-29, 1983.
14. Riberio, E.F.N., Qaiyum, A. and Nazim, Abu: Role of Small and Medium Size Towns in the Human Settlement System of India, Town and Country Planning Organization, May 1985.
15. Srinivas, K. and Kumar, Sanjay, India's Urbanization and Health Conditions (Paper).
16. Town and Country Planning Organization: Integrated Development of Small and Medium Towns, Retrospects and Prospects, Ministry of Works and Housing, Government of India, 1984.
17. Inaugural address of Advance Course on Management and Development of Small and Medium Towns by J.P. Singh, May 8, 1995.
18. Wishwakarma, R.K.: Integrated Development of Small and Medium Towns: Critical Areas and Issues for Policy Options (Proceedings of the Workshop held on July 14-15, 1981 organized by the Centre for Urban Studies, Indian Institute of Public Administration, New Delhi.

CHAPTER 10

NATIONAL CAPITAL REGIONAL PLAN PROBLEMS AND PROSPECTS

The National Capital Region (NCR), an area comprising 30,242 square kilometres. NCR includes Delhi, Haryana sub-region comprising Faridabad, Gurgaon, Rohtak and Sonepat districts; Rewari and Bawal tehsils of Mahendragarh district and Panipat tehsil; Uttar Pradesh sub-region comprising three districts, namely Meerut, Ghaziabad and Bulandshahr; Rajasthan sub-Region comprising six tehsils of Alwar district, namely Alwar, Ramgarh, Behror, Mandawar, Kishangarh and Tijara.

The NCR Plan is based on the concept of 'developing the region in a balanced manner with optimum growth. It promises to take a multi-sectoral approach, ensuring inter and intra-sectoral integration. The region includes Delhi and parts of Haryana, Rajasthan and Uttar Pradesh. The physiography of the region is characterised by the presence of the Ganga skirting at its eastern boundary. The Yamuna traversing its north-south and forming the boundary between Uttar Pradesh and Haryana and the sand dunes and barren low hills of the Aravalli chain and its outcrops in the west, flat topped prominent and percipitious hills of the Aravalli range enclosing fertile valleys and high table lands in south-west and the rolling plains dominated by rainfed torrents in the south. The east of the region is plain with a general scope of north-east to south-west.

Concentration in Delhi

From being an administrative centre in 1951, Delhi's character in the post-Independence era has changed and become multi-functional. Even today Delhi acts as a powerful job market at the national level. Delhi has been drawing nearly 1.5 lakh migrants every year from the neighbouring as well as far flung states. The city has recorded a growth of 300 per cent between 1951 and 1981. The estimated population in

Area of National Capital Region

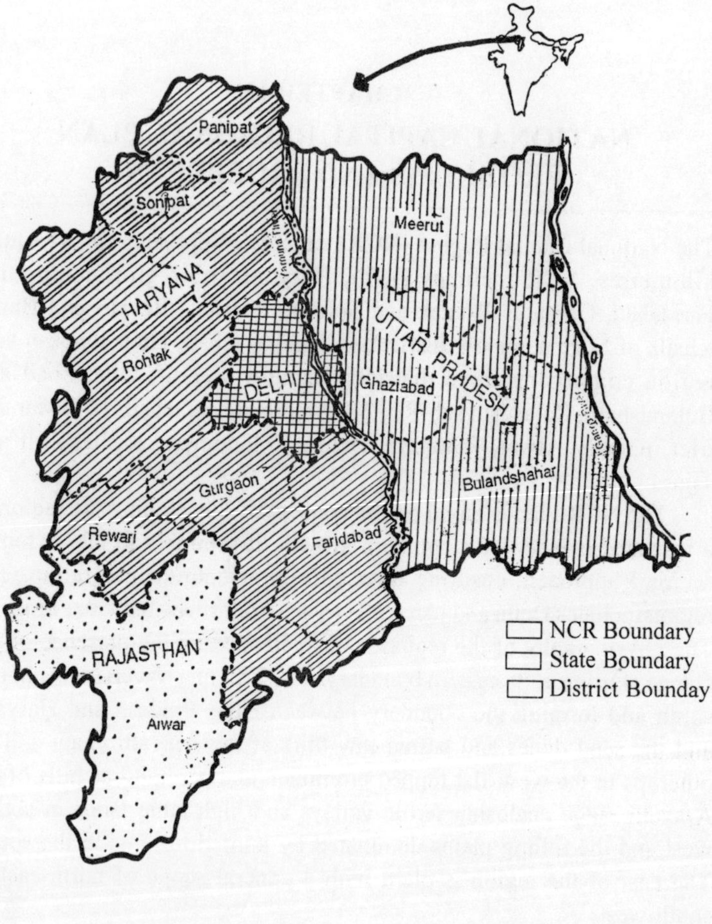

Source : 1. Town & Country Planning Organization, Government of India
2. National Capital Regional Planning Board, Ministry of Urban Development, Government of India.

1997 seems to be more than 96 lakhs in Delhi and if left unregulated, this would reach nearly 125 lakh by 2001. Such an unprecedented population explosion has already imposed a severe burden on the fabric of civic infrastructure and the quality of life in the city of Delhi and will aggravate it further. It is therefore essential that the NCR plan should be implemented expediously to ensure a harmonised and balanced development of the region.

As such, even under the best of planning efforts and circumstances, it is an exceedingly difficult task for providing and managing an enormous population growth year after year in the National Capital—Delhi. People are coming from the adjoining states because there is not adequate work available for them especially to the new entrants of the labour force. And in so far as the creation of employment opportunities is concerned, it cannot possibly be the exclusive concern of the Union Government alone, it is infact the great responsibility of the state governments to create ample and adequate jobs alongwith the minimum acceptable facilities. But, as we know, the record of the neighbouring states of Delhi leaves much to be desired. The absence of a legally enforceable plan for the NCR has led to the developments of areas like Kundli, so many townships around Delhi's southern fringe in Haryana and the next door NOIDA—all of them have added to the problems and vexations of Delhi without any tangible benefits. The adjoining states infact have unabashedly cashed on the of Delhi with the prominence least concern to help mitigate its problems.

In 1962, the Government of India approved the Master Plan for Delhi which recommended a regional approach for the planning of the National Capital. In 1967, a resolution by the high power board to set up a statutory NCR Board was prepared by a special committee. In 1973, the high power board approved the NCR Plan, but this plan was without statutory status. Finally, in 1985, constitution of the statutory NCR Planning Board was possible after the enactment of an Act by the Parliament.

The regional plan stipulates that countermagnet areas to Delhi should be located sufficiently away from the NCR and should have their known established roots and inherent potential to function as viable independent growth foci. Such identified countermagnets would have the attributes of physical, social and economic viability, modality with respect to transportation network and will have the quality of physical linkages in the form of facilities for transportation and communications.

TABLE 2
Population Projections for the NCR by Constituents

		Population		Projected Populations		
Sub-Region	Total	62.2	92.5	132.6	185.1	258.3
Delhi UT*	Rural	4.5	4.4	3.6	2.8	0.7
	Urban	57.7	88.1	129.0	182.3	257.6
Haryana	Total	49.4	62.7	72.1	86.0	96.2
	Rural	37.3	40.3	34.4	28.3	17.9
	Urban	12.1	22.4	37.7	57.7	78.3
Rajasthan	Total	10.6	11.3	11.9	13.0	15.2
	Rural	8.9	8.7	8.5	7.7	6.3
	Urban	1.7	2.6	3.4	5.3	8.9
Uttar Pradesh	Total	69.7	87.6	108.6	147.1	173.7
	Rural	50.2	51.8	45.0	38.8	27.5
	Urban	19.5	35.8	63.6	108.3	146.2
NCR	Total	191.9	254.1	325.2	431.2	443.4
Delhi UT*	Rural	100.9	105.2	91.5	77.6	52.4
	Urban	91.0	148.9	233.7	353.6	391.0

*Projection for Delhi, UT is based on the draft recommendations of the Expert Committee on Population.

Source: Regional Plan: 2001, National Capital Region, National Capital Region Planning Board, Ministry of Urban Development, Government of India.

These countermagnets would play complementary roles in the context of the NCR. First, as the future interceptors of migratory flows which may escalate with the accelerated development of the NCR, would provide a pull to migrants from the less developed adjoining areas, and secondly, as regional growth centres in the region of their setting would help, over a period of time, to achieve a balanced pattern of urbanization.

It is pointed out that development of countermagnet areas would require coordinated efforts of the State and Central Governments and the NCR Planning Board.

In the interest of the balanced directional split, the following centres have been recommended as countermagnets to the NCR for first-stage intervention. Hissar in Haryana in the western region, Patiala in

Punjab in the northern region, Gwalior in Madhya Pradesh in the south-eastern region, Kota in Rajasthan in the south-eastern region and Bareilly in Uttar Pradesh. It is pointed out that development of counter-magnet areas would require coordinated efforts of the State and Central Governments and the NCR Planning Board.

NCR 2001

The development plan for NCR known as regional plan—2001 has been formulated and adopted by the NCR Planning Board and came into operation since January 1989.

The objectives of the National Capital Regional Plan—2001 is to reduce the pressure of population on Delhi and evolve policies for control of landuse and planning infrastructure in NCR, so as to avoid the haphazard process of development.

The Regional Plan—2001 for the NCR seeks a solution through an integrated policy framework relating to the population distribution, settlement system, rural development, regional landuse, environment and ecology, economic activities and infrastructure facilities, both physical and social, including shelter. For application of various policy packages three district policy zones have been identified in the regional plan, they are the Delhi Union Territory for normal growth as projected and rest of the region for induced growth.

The first and foremost is the population distribution policy for the year 2001. If the present growth trend continues, Delhi have a population of about 132 lakhs. Further, it can be limited to about 112 lakhs but by suitably redistributing 20 lakhs population amongst sub-regions. The plan envisages the deflection of Delhi-bound potential migrants to priority towns in the sub-regions selected for induced development by implementation of various policies of the plan. The 20 lakh population would be accommodated in the priority towns—12 lakh in Uttar Pradesh sub-region, 6 lakh in Haryana sub-region and 2 lakh in Rajasthan sub-region. The policy therefore, stipulates, restricting the population size of Delhi Union Territory (UT) to 112 lakh by 2001, and also the population size of Delhi Metropolitan Area, excluding Delhi UT, to 38 lakh by 2001, inducing the growth of selected towns and complexes in the rest of the region for accommodating a population of 8 lakh by 2001 out of 175 lakh.

The next stage of developmental programme is the settlement policy for judicious distribution of population. The policy identifies four hierarchical system of settlements consisting of regional, sub-regional service centres and basic villages. To evolve, the most suitable urban settlement system for the region, different development options were considered and finally, the selection of urban centres as priority towns were chosen as the most appropriate option. These towns through the process of decentralization of economic activities away from Delhi and, through appropriate incentives for the induced development are likely to create the large scale employment opportunities, thereby attracting Delhi-based potential migrants.

An important employment generator is the wholesale and distributive trade of various commodities such as foodgrains, building materials, textiles, chemicals, vegetables and fruits. Out of the total volume of major commodities brought into Delhi for trading more than half is sent outside the city distribution. However, that is why the policy on the abolition of wholesale distribution of trade and commerce in the plan envisages a special advantage of preferential treatment by lower taxes in Delhi. The hazardous and space extensive trades must also be decentralized and located outside Delhi and encouragement thereof must be given emphasis for the development of all types of trades including wholesale markets in Delhi Metropolitan Area (DMA) and the rest of the region.

In the NCR Plan, transport and road planning has got to play an important role for accelerating the rural and urban linkages. The approach of village planning of NCR should be developed with well-planned road and transport planning, so that the easy availability of (i) scientific or agro-industrial know-how, (ii) raw material, (iii) finished goods, (iv) marketing and skilled manpower availability can be made a possibility.

Surprisingly, there is an ineffective transport network system connecting NCR areas with Delhi. The transport facility is also expensive and involves a long travel time. There is an imperative need for planning in NCR with a well-connected transport network system at reasonable rates, so that people are induced to live outiside the city of Delhi.

Enforcement of NCR Legislation

The National Capital Region Planning Board Act, 1985 was to provide for the constitution of Planning Board, the preparation of a plan for the development of NCR, coordinating and monitoring the implementation of such plan and for evolving harmonised policies for the control of landuses and development of infrastructure in the NCR, so as to avoid any haphazard development of the region.

The NCR Planning Board Act, 1985 has the adequate legal provisions which if implemented in letter and spirit would ensure an effective functioning of NCR planning and development. As such, the constitution of the Board itself is a point to be noted. It consists of the highest dignitaries drawn from the Centre and the states. At the official level it has a Planning Committee consisting of top level of officials both from the Centre and the states.

The functions of the Board have been defined in a comprehensive manner. It has been given the responsibility of preparing the Regional Plan and Functional Plans for arranging the preparation of Sub-regional Plans and Project Plans by each of the participating states and the Union Territory and to coordinate the enforcement and implementation of these plans. Further, it also assumes the systematic process of programming by the participating states and the Union Territory of Delhi and for assisting them in project formulation, determination of priorities in the NCR or its sub-regions. The Section 8 of the Act gives adequate powers to the Board to call for reports and information and to review from time to time the work being done in the functioning of NCR plan.

The NCR Planning Board Act, 1985 under Section 7 has spelt out the Board's functions as follows: (i) To prepare the Regional Plan and the Functional Plans; (ii) to arrange for the preparation of Sub-regional Plans and Project Plans by each of the participating states and the Union Territories; (iii) to co-ordinate the enforcement and implementation of the Regional Plan, Functional Plans, Sub-regional Plans and Project Plans through the participating states and the Union Territories; (iv) to ensure proper and systematic programming by the participating States and the Union Territories in regard to project formulation, determination of priorities in the NCR or sub-regions, and phasing of development of the NCR in accordance with states indicated in the regional plans; (v) To arrange for, and promote the financing of selected development projects in the NCR through Central and State Plan funds and other sources of revenue.

Usually, when powers are referred, implied reference is to the 'sanctions' or the authority to impose penalties, the Section 19 and Section 20 of the Act specify that participating states or the Union Territory of Delhi shall finalize the plan or the sub-regional plan "after due consideration of the observations made by the Board". Section 20 rightly places the primary responsibility for the implementation of the sub-regional plan and project plans on the states and the Union Territory.

It is worthwhile to point out that in regard to violation of Regional Plan, the following provisions are spelt out:

> "29 (1) and from the coming into operation of the finally published Regional Plan, no development shall be made in the region which is inconsistent with the Regional Plan as finally published. (2) Where the Board is satisfied that any participating state or the Union Territory has carried out, or is carrying out, any activity which amounts to a violation of the Regional Plan, it may, by a notice in writing, direct the concerned participating State or the Union Territory, as the case may be, to stop such violation of the Regional Plan, within such time as may be specified in the said notice and in case of any omission or refusal on the part of the Union Territory to stop such activity, withhold such financial assistance to the concerned participating State or the Union Territory as the Board may consider necessary".

However, in the extreme cases as an ultimate resort the Board has been given powers under Section 33 "to depute any person generally or specially authorized to enter upon any land or premises and do such things thereon as may be necessary for the purpose of lawfully carrying out any works or for making any survey, examination or investigation, preliminary or incidentally to the exercise of any power or performance of any function by the Board under this Act".

Planning Implications

The NCR Planning Board Act, 1985 has been notified in the extraordinary Gazettee on February 11, 1985. The Board constitutes 21 members and predominant are the Union Minister for Urban Development the Chief Ministers of Haryana, Uttar Pradesh and Rajasthan and other members nominated by the Central Government on the recommendations of the participating states and 11 members of Planning Committee. The administrative structure of NCR Board is constituted with large number of politicians and bureaucrats.

Unfortunately, the document, Regional Plan 2001, National Capital, is biased towards any long-term statistical exposition of the 2001 perspective in terms of (i) demographic profile, (ii) settlement system, (iii) telecommunications and strategies and priority areas for development. The NCR plan should be confined to a Five Year Plan perspective and should be spatially and economically linked with the balanced process of development spatially and economically.

In fact, within a radius of one kilometre on both sides of Delhi border no construction is supposed to take place and the land must be kept vacant. This stipulation is part of Delhi's Master Plan and the NCR concept has been subsequently reiterated.

Similarly, the uninhibited colonization of vacant land on both sides of the border of Delhi has been allowed to take place allegedly with the convenience of the authorities and subsequently has resulted in the mushrooming of large number of residential colonies.

NCR has been conceived to relieve pressure of Delhi which has been witnessing population explosion. Consequently, there has been a rapid growth of slums and *jhuggi-jhompri* clusters with haphazard growth and uncongenial living conditions. Also, the floating population of the same magnitude travel in and out of the National Capital every day either in pursuit of business activities or for professional work.

The civic amenities are far from adequate in terms of water supply, electricity and transport. There is no permanent and lasting solution except to plan the towns and the rural areas of NCR.

Surprisingly, it has been realized that the participating states are not taking the NCR Plan seriously in terms of integrating process of developmental activities. The population explosion in Delhi has to be curbed if it is not to degenerate into one of the world's largest slums. The faster growth of satellite towns is mainly in Gurgaon, the boundary of the Union Territory of Delhi compared to that of the proposed counter-magnets such as Meerut, Hapur, Bulandshahar, Khurja, Panipat, Rohtak, Rewari, Palwal and Alwar.

It is feared that by the time the participating states would get down to implement the NCR Plan in a coordinated manner, the actual population would have far exceeded the projections. The satellite and ring towns are themselves turning into huge, unmanageable agglomerations. Unless the growth of participating states of NCR is not regulated by the State authorities then it would become impossible to relieve the pressure on Delhi, which continues to grow with high rise residential, commercial complexes and expanding trade commerce activities.

For the speedy implementation of the NCR Plan, the other major stumbling block is the lack of resources and political will at the state and Central levels. However, the support given by the Centre for implementing the regional plan is not enough.

The meagre fund allocations, lack of legal, 'teeth' to the NCR Planning Board, a low profile approach within the Government itself and lack of adequate interest amongst the member—states have resulted the NCR concept being a 'non-starter'. As such, the concept of developing satellite towns and countermagnets identified in the NCR plan has remained neglected and thus has added to the multiple growth problems of congestion of Delhi.

While inaugurating the 13th meeting of the National Capital Region Planning Board, Mrs Sheila Kaul, the then Minister for Urban Development, Government of India, had rightly pointed out that the NCR Planning Board should be amended for providing more financial and administrative powers to the Board, so that it can bring about a speedy implementation of the NCR Plan. Mrs Shiela Kaul had also pointed out that the efforts to increase investment for better planning in NCR was mainly directed towards encouraging movement out of Delhi and discourage the movement into it.

The administrative controls in the NCR Planning Board Act has to be amended through the (1) control over Master Plan, (2) shifting of officers and industries, (3) mobilizing the financial resources, (4) Delhi statehood controversy, (5) establishing power authority : role of private sector, (6) housing and squatter settlements, (7) priority and counter-magnet planning dilemma; mini Delhi metropolitan centres. These aspects have to be considered in the context of planning for NCR.

Control Over Master Plans

In an alarming phenomenon, the housing developments are taking place in the peripheral areas of Delhi. The NCR Plan has spelt out a harmonised process of regional development outside the city of Delhi. There has been the large scale conversion of fertile agricultural land for housing developments adjoining Delhi in Palam Vihar and Qutab Enclave, constituting Gurgaon area of Haryana, by private developers on one side and by the Urban Development Authority in Jharsa village on the other. This has led to the distortion of ecological balance and is against the principle of NCR. Surprisingly, the Master Plan of Gurgaon has approved the peripheral development adjoining Delhi by permitting the acquisition of fertile agricultural land. It is against the principle of NCR objective.

Both the Noida and townships of Haryana have taken the benefits of Delhi's proximity, but not contributed to the development of balanced regional objectives as envisaged in the NCR Plan. Even the Ghaziabad Master Plan provides the growth of tall buildings through the participation of governmental housing agencies and private developers without adequate power and other basic public utility amenities. Such a situation has led to the haphazard urban environment and speculation in the building activities as Ghaziabad township is in the periphery of Delhi.

The peripheral growth near Delhi embodying the adjoining states has been contradictory to the NCR Plan. In fact due to lack of legislative controls over the Master Plan of the participating states of the NCR, the Planning Board Act has shown its helplessness. Unless, the NCR Planning Board has no scrutiny over the cities Master Plans of participating states of the NCR, the haphazard developments are likely to emerge in a big way. Even the Delhi Master Plan for 2001, is against the principle of NCR. Therefore, it is suggested that for the effective enforcement of entire Master Plans of NCR urban settlements should compulsorily seek the approval by the NCR Planning Board. However, such a provision should be incorporated in the NCR Planning Board Act.

Shifting Offices and Wholesale Trade

The controversy has arisen concerning the shifting of offices and wholesale trade from Delhi to other viable NCR towns. Surprisingly, no developmental agencies have taken up the responsibility to decongest the city of Dehli and promote thereby the balanced regional development.

There are offices which are not required in National Capital of Delhi and they do not provide the central ministerial linkages. They are listed as "Coast Guard (Headquarters), Research and Development Centre of the Postal Department, National Crime Report Bureau (Home Ministry), Central Institute of Research and Training (Ministry of Labour), Department of Publication, Board of Industrial and Finance Reconstruction. The other list of public sector offices which should be shifted are National Seed Corporation Limited, Central Warehousing Corporation, Food Corporation of India, Vayudoot, Helicopter Corporation of India, National Airport Authority of India, State Trading Corporation, National Power Commission, Bharat Heavy Electricals Limited and Cement Corporation of Delhi".

The Regional Plan, 2001, NCR prepared by NCR Planning Board spelt out two main objectives namely: (i) to achieve a balanced and harmoniously developed region and (ii) to achieve a manageable Delhi by 2001. The plan document has visualized that the objective of Balanced Regional Development of NCR could be achieved by the progressive decentralization of population, offices, wholesale trade and economic activities far away from Delhi and their dispersal to various viable settlements of NCR.

Keeping this objective in view, the NCR Planning Board Act should be given the prerogative powers for shifting the offices and wholesale trade of Delhi in the viable urban areas of NCR. In fact, the developmental authorities of Delhi and participating states should be controlled and regulated in the developmental schemes by the approval of NCR Planning Board. Therefore, there is the need that the Act should provide the suitable provisions for regulating and developing the balanced process of NCR.

Too much legislation has led to discretionary powers causing administrative loopholes. In the context of violation of building byelaws, the Delhi Municipal Corporation Act has used its discretionary powers by demolishing few buildings and not others. Surprisingly, the implication of NCR legislation has become discretionary, thereby giving rise to the serious charges of administrative loopholes by the urban authorities.

Thus, due to the misrepresentation of legislation, the provisions for greater teeth of legal powers are not suggested for the NCR Planning Board. However, the NCR Planning Board Act for an efficient functioning necessitates the awareness, political will and peoples' participation in an effective manner.

Mobilization of Financial Resources

There is an acute scarcity of financial resources for the development of NCR. Yearly, in the budgetary provisions, NCR has been allocated a meagre financial amount, whereas the Delhi annual plans have been provided an enormous amount for public utility services and infrastructural facilities.

Presently, for the NCR developments there is a meagre financial outlay, therefore the NCR Planning Board should be empowered to float bonds on the similar pattern as has been done by the Calcutta Metropolitan Development Authority. Such a provision has got to be supplemented in the NCR Planning Board Act. However, the financial discipline necessitates the application of strict measures while implementation of floating the bonds for mobilizing the financial resources for NCR. Above all, the financial resource mobilization has to be committed for providing the comprehensive power, transport, communication and agro-industrial developmental facilities based on competitive commercial gain prospects.

Private Developers

There has been a widespread offer by colonizers and private developers for unapproved farm houses and housing schemes with swimming pools, golf facilities and other amenities in the location of NCR townships. Thus the private developers and colonizers have collected lakhs and crores of rupees in the unapproved NCR areas. Such examples are the pink city at Noida-Dadri road and Eden farms at Sonepat hill which is an example of exploitation of Aravalli hill ranges. The NCR Planning Board Act should be provided with suitable administrative and legal power for restricting the fraudulent activities of land development of colonizers and private developers.

Delhi Statehood Implications

The concept of statehood for Delhi is politically oriented with the consideration of larger powers to the politicians and enormous demand for respective constituencies. This would lead to the greater financial requirements of housing, transport and security for the ministerial staff. Greater strain on public utility services would also be realized by the Delhi planning and civic authorities. If Delhi acquires a statehood, then obviously, it would loose the National Capital status. Further, there is the possibility of being deprived of Central Government financial assistance and subsidies provided for socio-economic and infrastructural facilities being the National Capital.

Keeping these considerations in view, the NCR Planning Board should oppose the proposal of Delhi statehood. In fact the concept of statehood for Delhi is detrimental to the NCR Plan objectives.

Power Development

Presently, there is an acute shortage of power in the entire rural and urban settlements of NCR. There is an imperative need for providing an uninterrupted power supply in the entire NCR. Therefore the preference and priority in making available the additional power has to be visualized. In this connection, the role of private sector participation will be able to generate electricity both in rural and urban settlements. Such an action programme would boost the agro-industrial developmental prospects in NCR.

The NCR Planning Board should be given the power for establishing an NCR Electrification Authority with the help of the effective and efficient private sector organizations. In this connection, the NCR Board Act should provide the suitable provision of control and regulate the establishment of a Power Authority. However, it should be followed with the appropriate rules and regulations in terms of pricing and meeting the rural and urban power demand requirements in a regular manner. The NCR Planning Board should be authorized for ascertaining the location of power plants and assessments of required installation capacities both in the rural and urban settlements. Further, the financial feasibilities of private sector involvement, pricing of power tariff could be regulated by the NCR Board.

Infrastructural Facilities

The Cooperative Group Housing Societies (CGHS) and squatter settlements have emerged in an alarming proportion in Delhi. To decongest such developments it is imperative that the NCR Planning Board should provide the adequate public utility services and infrastructural facilities in the NCR. The people will be induced to live outside and shelter problem in NCR can be resolved through the inter-regional group housing scheme on a massive scale.

In this connection, the provision of shelter planning for squatter settlements and sources of employment and income prospects should be provided in NCR urban settlements. Such should be the appropriate line of action for the NCR Planning Board.

Counter-Magnet Planning for NCR

As a part of decentralization policy, the Regional Development Plan for the NCR, has, inter alia, recommended development of eight priority towns in the region outside the Delhi Metropolitan Area to accommodate population of 49 lakhs by 2001. These are Meerut, Hapur, Bulandshahr - Khurja Complex, Palwal, Panipat, Rohtak, Rewari Complex and Alwar. Besides Ghaziabad - Loni, Noida, Faridabad Complex, Gurgaon, Bahadurgarh and Kundli are the six ring towns to be developed within the Delhi Metropolitan Area to accommodate a population of 37 lakhs by 2001. The Region is to be planned for a total population of 325 lakhs of which the urban component would be 234 lakhs, with 110 lakhs accommodated in the Delhi Urban Area.

As a general principle, it would be logical to surmise, that the need for a potential countermagnet would be more in districts, or groups of districts, which have shown a higher rate of out-migration of population to Delhi. It is observed that the districts closer to Delhi, even though developed on their own than others located further away, have shown a higher rate of out-migration. This is attributed to the distance criteria, and also to the functional affinity with Delhi. The Development of a countermagnet at a nodal centre in such districts would also help to establish a new alignment for future migratory tendencies from farther districts. However, if a countermagnet is located in the outlying district, bypassing the near districts having higher migration rate, it will have to acquire in the initial stages itself a very strong development base to help reverse the migratory flow away from the strong magnetic pull of Delhi and the NCR.

As such, the development of countermagnets has to be viewed as an integral part of the extended decentralization strategy of the NCR Plan itself. To enable this, sequential development strategy in relation to the priority towns would be necessary. While the countermagnets would have an inherent growth propensity and potential of their own, they should receive additional developmental inputs, only after the first stage of development of the NCR priority towns has been realized and they have been firmly established to fulfil their role. This calls of proper synchronization of investment planning and development programming, both in the priority towns and the countermagnets.

The NCR Planning Board has promoted various residential and commercial schemes in the priority towns, yet the alarming magnitude of migration towards Delhi has not been checked. The objective of priority and countermagnets towns have not been able to ensure a balanced process of development in NCR.

The NCR Planning has to be directed towards promoting the balanced spatial and economic developments by integrating the rural and urban settlements through an effective process of transport network system.

The NCR Plan should aim for identifying the viable physical potentialities of both the rural and urban settlements. As such, greater emphasis has to be laid on the comprehensive development of small and medium town settlements of NCR for checking the alarming trend of migration towards the National Capital-Delhi.

Regularity in power supply should be the watchword of the NCR planning. Further, the planners have to play a significant role for assessing the growth potential prospects of NCR's rural and urban settlements.

Such an action of planning directions would be able to promote a balanced process of regional development in the context of 2001 AD NCR Perspective.

The NCR set up is mainly directed by the high-powered Board constituting of politicians, whereas the planners have become silent spectators. Greater role in NCR development should be given to the planners and their recommendations of planning proposals must be endorsed by the politicians. For an effective implementation of NCR planning, Prime Minister should be the Chairman of the NCR Planning Board. Then only the different states would cooperate in terms of planning and development.

For the decentralization of economic and other activities away from Delhi, the NCR Plan has identified ring towns within the region, so that the prosperity and burdens of development are shared and balanced regional development is promoted. It was proposed to develop the ring towns as self-contained growth centres through an effective programme of integrated process of urban development. However, this needs to be accompanied by the adequate investment outlay in different vital sectors, notably water supply, flood control, transport, power, housing and communication. There is need to relocate the selected Government offices, industries and wholesale trade activities away from Delhi. The overall objectives of Regional Plan has not been achieved due to the existing inadequate investment in different sectors and in the absence of a high powered authority to coordinate the planning and investment decisions by the Central and state agencies in the region.

The spatial and economic development in Delhi has its limitations. The NCR Planning Board with the assistance of a technical committee has to specify the appropriate scale of economic development in a regional perspective. The inter-state approach of planning as embodied in the NCR has to ensure the provision of adequate socio-economic and infrastructural facilities for ensuring the balance spillover of population and economic development. Thus, such an approach should be adopted now, then in 2001 concentration of population in Delhi with its attendant problems can be checked to a considerable extent.

The National Environmental Engineering Institute (NEERI) has developed two scenarios for action. The short-term plan till 2001 includes implementation of the NCR Board's recommendations with a stringent environment plan, with the long-term plan, developed till 2021, calls for radical changes to promote the non-efficient technologies.

Management Structure for NCR Plan Implementation

The NCR Plan needs to be implemented by the participating states and the NCT of Delhi, while schemes falling in the Central sector will be implemented by the concerned Central Ministries.

The existing planning and implementation arrangements however, have a varied pattern in the three participating states and the NCT of Delhi. None of the existing arrangements has been found to be fully compatible to fulfil the needs of taking up the balanced and integrated development of the concerned sub-regions at the field level, which could encompass both the rural and urban settlements for the integrated process of planned development.

Since an integrated approach is crucial for the development of the region, the NCR Planning Board feels that it is of utmost necessity that a suitable organizational set up at the sub-regional level which would have jurisdiction for planning in the entire sub-regional and an overseeing role in the implementation of the NCR objectives and policies. It would be necessary at the sub-regional level to have one plan for the entire sub-region consisting of resources from the NCR Planning Board and the regular schemes of the State Plan.

The NCR Planning Board, though a statutory organization, has still to function as a coordinating and planning agency which endeavours to harmonise the work of the participating governments. The interest of Delhi lies that while activities which create wealth remain within Delhi, the pressure of population is shifted elsewhere. The interests of the neighbouring states should take into consideration the maximum advantage of the "economics of cluster" available in Delhi, with industry and business being located as near Delhi as possible and maximum advantage being taken of the highly developed physical and social infrastructure available in the National Capital - Delhi. The Board has not been able to reconcile these conflicting interests, with the result that the adjoining towns of Sonepat, Ghaziabad, Noida, Faridabad, Gurgaon have developed virtually as extensions of Delhi, whereas the development in peripheral towns has tended to be slow. Unless a regional planning organization such as NCR Planning Board is able to resolve such conflicts, the constituent states will not fall in line and could well pull in opposite direction.

Judging from the fate of these elaborate regional plans prepared, mostly they have remained documents on paper. Even in the case of

NCR Plan which is equipped with a statutory Board and has an approved Plan, the provisions of the Regional Development Plan has either not been translated or not taken note of in the sub-regional plans prepared by the concerned State Governments and in certain major issues conflict with the provision of the Regional Plan.

Policy Guidelines

The NCR concept has shown a new method for inter-state cooperation and regional planning. The NCR Plan and related plans, drawn by the NCR Planning Board, have been excellent exercises in documentation, design and policy formulations. In actual practice implementation has fallen severely short of expectation due to: (a) lack of political will and profile within Government circles; and (b) severe lack of financial resources.

The initiative for the NCR has been confined to official levels and there has been no effort to seek any meaningful participation of the private sector or the people for boosting the process of planning activities.

The development in the sub-regions of the NCR is frequently at variance with the NCR Plan. Consequently, Delhi's urban growth has not been dovetailed into the urbanization of the small towns around it.

Policy for the discouragement in the establishments of Government and public sector offices in Delhi and encouragements for shifting of offices on a selective basis outside Delhi, as well as shifting of industries to conforming locations outside have neither been defined nor undertaken.

The financial strategy for the NCR, including financial contributions and source, needs to be defined and spelt out clearly by the Government. The proposed NCR Funds, consisting of grants and loans from Centre and constituent states, should mobilize additional funds from all-India financial institutions. Agencies like the recently promoted Infrastructural Leasing and Financial Services Ltd. (ILFS) have an important role to play. Special agencies for housing finance including Housing Urban Development Corporation (HUDCO) and HDFC need to assign priority to NCR towns financing of the NCR Plan from the open market (on which there is no bar in the NCR Planning Board Act) needs also to be considered. However, efforts need to be made for mobilizing the foreign capital prospects.

The involvement of private sector is essential in order to enhance financial and managerial resources and expedite implementation in a meaningful manner. An approach of Government's liberalization policy for private sector participation has to be appreciated. The areas for such initiatives are presently housing, including provision of internal and peripheral services, express highways, hospitals, educational institutions and the like. However, the private sector should be allowed to involve itself in the development of the NCR and Growth Centres therein. Enclaves, on large plots, of a massed land could be developed by the private sector, including infrastructural and social development on the pre-agreed terms and conditions. This could be accomplished on the pattern of 'Build', 'Operate' and Transfer, i.e. 'BOT' basis. The private sector should be asked to work as partners in joint ventures for which appropriate Memorandum of Understanding between it and the Government could be signed accordingly.

The NCR Planning Board needs to utilize its powers more actively. Under the NCR Planning Board Act, 1985, it is obligatory for the participant states to implement the plan objectives. The NCR Planning Board should prevail upon the participant states under Sections 19, 22, 29, 33 etc., to frame and implement their sub-regional plans in consistency with the NCR Plan only and assist the NCR Board to realize its objectives.

The hypotheses on which the NCR was initially based are still valid and feasible provided the concept of planned development of Counter Magnets and Ring Towns is in coordination with Delhi, as per the NCR Plan. This needs to be emphasized and implemented with the sense of urgency. The real solution lies in development of towns with a full provision of civic services where people can go for work and live. Telecommunications, transport facilities, social and academic infrastructure, housing so on, need to be upgraded within the sub-regional towns of NCR for inducing the population and industries to move out of Delhi. This requires investment in infrastructure at appropriate locations in keeping with the priorities of the NCR Plan. Moreover, instead of only harping on development of existing towns, which is very expensive beyond a point, some new towns must be created within the NCR. New towns are required to be developed quickly and easily with the involvement of private initiative.

The investment plan for the NCR should provide incentives for dispersal of economic activity into a number of smaller towns where appropriate infrastructure should be developed to start such activity. A three point package for shifting of industries out of Delhi needs to be adopted and nodal agency needs to be designated to undertake the task.

Firstly, the shifting of industrial units may be allotted serviced land at fixed rates; secondly, loan facilities and tax concessions on the lines of those for new units need to be extended. Thirdly, land vacated by the shifting industries should be allowed to be developed by them as per prescribed use under the Delhi Master Plan. The nodal agency could be a Board constituted to control and regulate dispersal of employment generating activity. The Board could monitor the location of trade and industrial activity outside Delhi. The Government offices/Public Sector Undertakings (PSUs) which have no direct work in Delhi, wholesale markets, godowns and warehouses also need to be shifted to the Delhi Metropolitan Area and the NCR. Sustained efforts accordingly need to be made to earmark/allot land for worthwhile, official and non-official institutions in these areas on payment, extending to 3 to 10 years. As such, this will help in diffusing socio-economic activity from Delhi to the Delhi Metropolitan Area and NCR.

For the vigorous development of the NCR, quite a few suggestions have been made like—

(i) Treating the entire NCR as common economic market;

(ii) Rationalization of tax structure (octroi, sales tax, property tax, professional tax, etc.);

(iii) Differential rates for power, water, transport should be worked out in a manner not to accord a privilege position to Delhi. Or, in other words, a system of positive incentives should be devised for preferential development of areas (towns, cities, villages) in the NCR.

(iv) The final set to tie up the various communities—urban and rural - is the communication system and a viable transportation network. To promote accelerated development of the NCR, it is absolutely necessary to develop a comprehensive transportation plan comprising several components: good surface transport with highways, limited access expressways, and well-designed road network. Then to facilitate quick transit, mass transit system need to be developed improving accessibility in between the towns and cities within and outside the NCR.

Delhi and other towns in the NCR need to enforce urban discipline and contain unplanned growth firmly. The squatter settlements, ribbon development on roads coming into Delhi from Haryana and Uttar Pradesh etc., have become the rule rather than exception. Unless such contraventions are dealt with firmly, the need to move out to the NCR would be neither created nor felt.

The NCR concept, even otherwise, cannot blossom merely through official efforts. The task is so colossal with so many imponderables that unless the beneficiaries of the programme get actively involved, it cannot move forward. Real success would come only when an enlightened public opinion is formed and the NCR emerges as a people's movement.

The distributive trades can adjust from traditionally core area integrated locations of storage, commodity handling, transactions, road and rail transportation to identified peripheral locations—thanks to rail saturation as also limited inner city road capacities. Their location outside the Union Territory, however, to other parts of the NCR is subjected to a variety of conflicting taxation policies and this brings into focus the need to make the NCR one zone for the free movement of people and goods and transactions, given proper telecommunications and integrated transportation systems. The NCR Board would no doubt give priority to this issue in view of several gains for the common good—the most important of which would be the channelization of heavy truck movements with their physical and social costs, away from the core.

The investment plan for NCR should provide incentives for dispersal of economic activity into a number of smaller towns where appropriate infrastructure should be developed to start such activity. A three part package for shifting of industries out of Delhi needs to be adopted and a nodal agency needs to be designated to undertake the task. Firstly, shifting industrial units may be allotted serviced land at fixed rates, secondly, loan facilities and tax concessions on the lines of those for new units need to be extended; and thirdly, land vacated by the shifting industries should be allowed to be developed by them as per prescribed use under the Delhi Master Plan. The nodal agency could be a Board constituted to control and regulate dispersal of employment generating activity. The Board could monitor the location of trade and industrial activity outside Delhi. An alternate nodal agency could be DSIDC Government offices/ PSUs which have no direct work in Delhi, wholesale markets, godowns and warehouses also need to be shifted to the Delhi Metropolitan Area and the NCR. Sustained efforts according to the need should be earmark/ allot land for worthwhile official and non-official institutions in these areas on payment, extending to 3 to 10 years. This will help in diffusing socio-economic activity from Delhi to the Delhi Metropolitan Area and the NCR.

REFERENCES

1. Batra, B. and Johri, O.K.: NCR Plan in Doldrums, Estate December 17, 1988.
2. Bhargava, Gopal: Action Plan for NCR, *The Hindustan Times,* August 18, 1986.
3. _____________: Making NCR Work, *The Hindustan Times,* November 18, 1987.
4. _____________: National Capital Regional Plan Limitation of Promises.
5. Dave, P.K.: Interview 'NCR Plan to get a Boost', *The Hindu,* May 20, 1993.
6. Document of Punjab, Haryana Chamber of Commerce, New Delhi, 1992: National Capital Region—A Critical Review.
7. Estate June 17-30, 1989: An Analysis of the NCR Plan.
8. Government of India, National Capital Region Board, Ministry of Urban Development, 1988: Regional Plan 2001, National Capital Region.
9. Gupta, R.C.: Countermagnets Development Approach to Metropolitan Region Planning, *Delhi Vikas Varta*, Journal, Volume 1, No. 2, July-September, 1990.
10. Kumar, Rahul: National Capital Region, Still on Paper, *The Economic Times,* Supplement, Data Bank, 1989.
11. Ribeiro, E.F.N.: 'Planning for Capital' in Environmental Concern, edited by S.C. Bhatia, published by Centre for Adult Continuing Education and Extension, University of Delhi, supported by Department of Environment, Government of India, 1983.
12. __________. The National Capital Region : The Framework for Coordinated Growth, Cyclostyle paper.
13. Sinha, R.L.P.: Regional Development and Planning in India: Need for an Organizational Structure, paper presented at the Regional Planning Symposium organized by the Institute of Town Planners, India.
14. Singh, B.N.: Special Presentation by the NCR Board, Seminar on National Capital Region—Need for a Critical Reappraisal organized by PHD Chamber of Commerce and Industry, 1992.
15. Singh, Dhamandeep: Quality of Life in NCR on the Decline, *The Indian Express,* January 30, 1997.
16. Shafi, Sayed S.: National Capital Region : The issues, *Delhi Vikas Yatra,* Journal, Volume 1, No. 2, April-June, 1990.
17. The Gazettee of India, Extraordinary Part II. The National Capital Region Planning Board Act, 1985, No. 2 of 1985.

CHAPTER 11

REGIONAL PLANNING AND DEVELOPMENT POLICY PERSPECTIVE

India stands politically divided and every state is functioning as a separate entity. As a result of political restrictions the states have remained backward and do not have the effectiveness in economic developmental programmes. No single state has the adequate natural resources for producing everything as is indicated by all India riverine, agricultural, industrial and forest maps. However, the development of each state in isolation is not justifiable from the planning perspective. The present inter-state river water disputes and lack of resource movements have been responsible for hindering the economic development. As such, in the 21st century perspective, there is an imperative need for coordinating the different states into a single unit of market mechanism in terms of resource movement. Such a concept of regional identity would be able to vitalise the economy of planning areas.

The approach of Regional Planning should be emphasized, so as to prevent the excessive process of urban development at the cost of rural settlements. A proper balance between town and country should be achieved within the framework of a inter-state regional perspective.

In a country of continental dimensions like India, with an amazing diversity in natural factors, planning cannot be carried at one level. Thus, it has to be decentralized for a specific developmental purpose. It has become a vital necessary for the fullest utilization of national resources of the country.

The political barriers in different areas of the states can be removed if a joint planning council is constituted. The mutual inter-state economic benefits would enable a regional plan for achieving its objective of balanced development and thereby ensure the national economy with a steady and progressive growth of self-reliance. Therefore, the technique of regional approach to planning necessitates for the removal of political pressure tactics. In this connection, the techno-economic-cum-political experts of different states may constitute a regional inter-state organizational set up for promoting an effective process of planning and development.

Defining a Region

A region indicates a physical uniformity or homogenous characteristics. The view of a region as a natural homogenous area is based on the idea that the separate spatial units can be linked together on the ground that they would be able to exhibit certain uniform characteristics like similar production structures, homogenous patterns of consumption and like occupation distribution of the labour force or they might reflect the geographical factors such as the unequity of a dominant natural resource, or a similar topography or climate, or they might include the non-economic variables such as uniform social attitudes, a regional identity or a similar political outlook.

More rational concept of region is that of planning or programming a region. This is defined in terms of the coherence and unity of economic decision making. The implementation of a regional policy demands a capacity for action and this depends on the effective role of the governmental action. However, it might be argued, therefore, that regions need to be defined as having the coordinated unity within the political and planning jurisdiction.

Power Development

Though the Five Year Plans of India have aimed at regional development and regional balances, we are still at the stage of project planning. We have, no doubt, some notable examples of multipurpose river valley projects in the form of (i) Damodar Valley Corporation, (ii) Rajasthan Canal Project, (iii) Dandakaranya Scheme, and (iv) Kosi Project, etc. However, it is doubtful whether they are comprehensive enough to be termed as regional planning and development in their true sense. Many regional scientists have expressed a serious doubt whether a watershed region or river valley region will have the necessary economic base and ecological equilibrium to be considered as an entity for planning, except for floods, irrigation and hydel power generation.

The river valley projects are being initiated in India for the development of hydro-electric power as well as the industry as a whole. However, these projects are concerned with the creation of necessary barriers, channels and accordingly the projects are justified and therefore, the consideration of programmes often stops soon after the canal is dug or the last power unit is commissioned. It seems that the comprehensive development of the river valley areas is generally ignored. Further, the question arises as to how the direct benefits conferred by the river valley projects are to be utilized and subsequently how these benefits can be maximized from the point of view of social technology is a missing link, so far as the comprehensive and planned development of resources of a valley is concerned.

The development of hydro-electricity is based on the limited regional considerations for the supply of electric power, irrigation, water and navigational facilities in case of places situated over a larger area; but it stops short of taking into consideration the human side of the problem. Although there is some planning of electric power development in the region, however, it is not a comprehensive regional planning and that is why no socio-economic prosperity of the region had followed the implementation and construction of hydro-electric projects.

Five Year Plan Perspectives

The first Five Year Plan had made only an indirect reference to the need for examining the physical setting, while the Second Plan gave a definite lead by emphasizing the need for minimizing the regional disparities. The Third Plan considered regional and national development as two different facets of a common objective. In fact, the preparation of State Plans and the block development programme for village groups are some of the attempts made towards an area approach for planning, if not a systematic regional approach.

The policy of the country in regard to regional development needs to be reviewed to assess the progress.

In the First Plan there is a mention about the need for constant consultation with States Planning at different levels. Emphasis has been placed on the need for regional planning primarily with a view for mobilizing local resources and also involving the peoples' participation. There was no expression of any objectives in terms of achieving a balanced process of regional development.

The Second Plan had specifically recognized the question of regional disparities. While it was considered that the pattern of investment must be devised for promoting a balanced regional development, it was expressed that the problem is particularly difficult in the early stages when the total resources available are unsatisfactory. With the object of making every effort towards the spatial and economic balanced development in different states, the considerations for developing a balanced economy while deciding on location of new enterprises and organized schemes of labour migration settlements from less developed area to a more developed area was highlighted. Further, the continuous study of the problem of regional disparities was assessed. The greatest contribution of Second Plan was the multi-level planning and the delineation of appropriate functions for various spatial levels of the country.

In Third Plan the balanced regional development was expressed as a specific objective. The plan had emphasized that the development of less developed areas was really significant in regard to the State Planning. For instance, it emphasized that through the State Plans, the improvements in the living conditions of weaker sections of the community and less developed areas is likely to be achieved. Eventually, the Third Plan had dealt at length the problems of an overall economic development vis-a-vis the balanced approach towards planning.

According to the plan objective for securing the fullest possible utilization of the resources of each region it can contribute its best to the national pool and take its due share from the benefits accruing from national development. The major problem of reconciling the economic utilization of resources of each region and the equitable distribution of benefits is not ascertained. The Third Plan had envisaged the preparation of long-term plan for the country for 15 years based on resources of various regions.

Unfortunately, the Fourth Plan had not contained any detailed discussion on the problem of balanced regional development. The Fourth Plan had taken the cognizance of the fact that in the past there has been natural tendency for new enterprises and investments to gravite towards the already overcrowded metropolitan centres. The plan document describes the problem as highly complex and explains that the differences in the levels of development between the states had given rise to the variations in activity in three sectors, namely cooperative, private and public. It is expressed that the availability of resources with the governments of states is an uphill task accomplish. Implicitly, the role of Central Government would be limited in its functioning.

In the Mid-term Appraisal of the Fourth Plan, a clear mention was made that the problem of inter-district disparities is essentially the responsibility of the states. However, the various measures for reducing regional disparities had been clearly specified and the need for district and regional planning emphasized.

The Regional Planning starts with the basic assumption of the existence of political, geographic, economic, and social regions within a nation or a group of nations. The climatic and soil differences are pronounced in different parts of the country demanding the different level of economic and social developmental achievements. Historical reasons, political situations, language differences, ethnic diversities and most important, the economic considerations all dictate that we choose a smaller area and decide the optimum planning strategy. In the beginning it may appear that this policy of treating a portion of the space (district, metropolitan area, river basin, state or a combination of states, etc.) as the proper planning unit, goes against the very formulation of overall national plans and the concept of national unity. But this does not have to be that way.

A national plan cannot take into account the best possible strategy for regional development in its broad framework. On the other hand, the regional plan by its very definition poises some question of an inter-regional conflict. Whereas, these conflicts are often over-emphasized and used against the concept and implementation of regional plans, enough is not said about how we can resolve these conflicts through interregional cooperation and at the same time maximize the potentialities of development of respective regions. It is true that the benefits of this type of cooperation is often preached by the politicians in different regions. But in reality it is seldom pursued primarily due to the absence of scientific studies which can show how this cooperation will lead to increase benefits for the interested regions and nation as a whole.

At present, the states of India are serving as 'planning regions' only as a name sake. But the question is whether the present administrative political boundaries of the states are suitable for regional planning or a drastic realignment of their boundaries is required to bring them within the conformity of economic regions.

The question of effectiveness of state as planning region is closely connected with that of the pattern of economic regionalization of entire country for the purposes of planning. Economic regionalization has as its main objective, the full-utilization of the natural and manpower resources of the region. As such, the structure of productive activities gives the specialized character of a region, the programme for regional development has got to be centred around the specialized economic activities of an inter-state regional identity.

The State Planning regions should conform to the principle of minimum disparity within and maximum disparity from outside. Such regions must be homogenous and they must take into account the agricultural specialization and accordingly be based upon physico-natural regions.

The constituents states in a regional perspective should be financially viable, so that they are able to meet their administrative expenditure as well as development needs without the undue and heavy reliance on the Centre. Further, they must have enough manpower and technical resources, so as to establish an independent and competent planning authority. Several states are now demanding a restructuring of the balance of power between the Centre and the state. The integration of the state economics has taken place and the tendency towards regionalization has been strengthened.

The region being a link between the nation and the local community provides a suitable frame and reference for a balanced integration of developmental projects of national significance with those earmarked for planned and executed on local initiative. Above all, the political boundaries should become coterminous with regional boundaries. As such, there is need for a cooperative approach towards the comprehensive planning, rather than limited to the boundaries of any single authority.

The Planning Commission has divided the country into 15 regions and 61 divisions for the coordination of physical features, agricultural specialization and availability of mineral resources. Here again the "resource development regions" conform to the inter-state boundaries.

At present states are the only level at which regional planning in the sense of subnational spatial planning is being done. But the economists and the geographers aiming at the optimum utilization of national resources and rapid rate of growth would like to discard the existing state boundaries and subsequently emphasize the role of physical and economic factors in regional developmental perspective. Therefore, it would be the responsibility of the Regional Planner to convince the political leadership that such a type of reorganization would be in the national interest. However now the existence of the states has to be accepted by the economic planners as a political reality which cannot be ignored.

Why Regional Planning?

Keeping the present inter-state river water disputes and restrictions in the flow of resource movements, it is imperative for emphasizing an appropriate strategy for regional planning and development. R. Balakrishna in his book *Regional Planning in India* observes that in India, the claim for regional development is based on several considerations. Geographically, the country comprises a vast area with significant variations in its natural endowment. As such, the climatic

INDIA PLANNING REGIONS

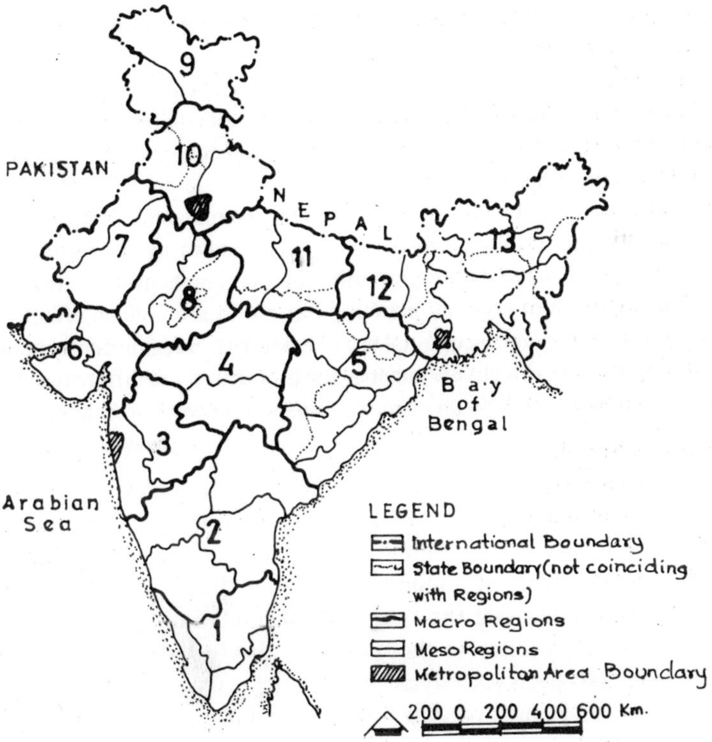

MACRO REGIONS

1. South Peninsular
2. Central Peninsular
3. Western Peninsular
4. Central Deccan
5. Eastern Peninsular
6. Gujarat
7. Western Rajasthan
8. Aravali Regions
9. Jammu & Kashmir & Ladakh
10. Trans Indo-Gangetic Plan & Hills
11. Ganga-Yamuna Plains
12. Lower Ganga Plains
13. North Eastern Region

Source: Town & Country Planning Organization, Government of India Regional Planning Efforts in India a monograph, December, 1982.

and social differences are very pronounced in different parts of the country demanding different patterns of economic development. From the economic standpoint, the factors of production are not equally distributed. Capital and enterprises are available in large measures in certain provinces enabling them to be ahead of the others in exploiting the available resources.

There are glaring differences in respect of social welfare, as the total quantum of the socially necessary work is not equitably distributed over the entire country due to the unevenness of its economic development. Therefore, a regional approach seems to be the only device for addressing the oddities as far as nature would permit. Such a phenomenal economic characteristic can minimize disparities among states by promoting an effective type of industrial programming in a comprehensive manner.

The approach of regional planning has got to promote an effective space development and the optimal use of resources. A region conforming a planning area can effectively enhance the productivity of different space based locational points by an efficient transport network workability.

Economic Stability

If we have to promote economic stability in the context of national developmental programmes, then it is imperative to have the regional framework. It indicates the conformity of planning areas and the rural-urban interdependence of resource mobilization.

It is visualized that the inter-state formulation in its regional framework can accelerate the tempo of production, income and employment prospects embodying the developmental areas. However, at present such a planning process is not functioning and that is why the adequate resource exploration has not been achieved in a significant possible manner. Subsequently, the marketable and exportable surplus has not generated a self-sustained growth of capital formation.

Objectives of Regional Planning

It is worth noting that Professor Ashish Bose in a paper "Some Economic Aspects of Urban Redevelopment" presented at the State Planning Official Conference had rightly pointed out the objective of regional planning should be to avoid the development of towns at the cost of the rural masses and to develop the region economically by bringing about a proper balance between the town and country.

The regional growth dynamics in India, presupposes the underdeveloped areas linked with an effective infrastructural and socio-economic facilities. Thus, the regional approach to planning can promote the optimal financial gains in production, income and employment prospects.

For an effective process of Regional Planning and development, there has to be the determinates which must ascertain the locational suitability in terms of cooperation of agriculture with industry and the linkages of rural with urban settlements. The evaluation of economic activities of the inter-state regions must be assessed by the planners and the coefficients of the incurrence of advantages and disadvantages in terms of cost benefits of different projects and its possible applicability has to be worked out in a comprehensive manner. Such an approach of regional planning needs to be given a top priority in the 21st century.

Spatial Considerations

The locational based spatial considerations assume importance in the context of regional planning and development. It is understood that till now the planning problems of India have been considered mainly on fiscal resources—capital formation, national income, increasing labour productivity and generating more saving and better returns, creating thereby an impression that these are arranged in right proportions and everything else will follow automatically. However, as yet there has not been any provision in the Planning Commission or elsewhere at an appropriate level for an organization or a methodology for coordinated effect pertaining to the locational aspects.

The potentialities of natural resources and the locational developmental advantages must accord the planning areas conformity within the inter-state approach of regional framework. In the past, the vested oriented state policies have not promoted the free flow of resource movements and benefits of economic activities based on locational advantages. The inter-state regional planning needs to be administered with the integrated resource flow movement and an effective transport and market network mechanism. Accordingly, the balanced regional developmental prospects can be achieved.

With the excessive process of urbanization, the adequate attention has not been given for the development of growth centres embodying the small town and rural areas in a comprehensive statewise perspective. Consequently, the advantageous potential based areas were unable to explore the agro-industrial development.

In so far as there exists a system of economic planning in a country, a clear direction should normlly be available for the level and pattern of investments, the spatial implications of which must be worked out and arranged in a manner that ensure their efficient landuse achievements.

The coordination of spatial with economic planning will then add a second sting to the bow.

There is close interaction between spatial and economic developments. In a paper 'Economic Development and Spatial Planning in India' J.P. Sah and S.S. Dutta in Ekistics have rightly observed that by and large the planning of the physical environment still remains in India apart and aloof from the mainstream of national and state economic planning process. The physical plans lack the adequate backing of economic analysis and development orientation. The physical planning is not imbued with the philosophy of economic and social development, nor does the practitioners seem to be fully conscious of their social responsibility.

Most of the physical plans, surprisingly for our cities and towns represent an outmoded western approach, namely, of pathological treatment of micro environment. These plans are mainly preoccupied with the internal problems of towns and cities, quite often severely confined to the formal city limits alone. Within the background of its region or hinterland needs to be emphasized. There hardly exists any framework for the coordinaion of such plans with each other and with economic development at the local regional, state or national level. However, the spatial planning activity is haphazard and seems to be devoid of any direction and perspective which, in fact, the economic development plan embodies and therefore, the areas potentialities have been overlooked in respect of locational advantageous and its physical characteristics.

The diachotomy of space and economic gap has resulted within inter-state areas the low level of developmental prospects. However, the one sided spatial sprawl groth has been responsible for urban industrial complex growth within the nuclei of a region. There has not been a suitable coordination within the agricultural and industrial areas either within or outside the boundaries of the state. Certain parts of the state areas have experienced the optimal utilization of industrial developments with the larger availability of financial resources. The under-developed areas are conditioned with the low capital, income and high degree of unemployment, but paradoxically there has been the rising trend of prices of the various commodities.

The spatial unbalanced growth without the emphasis of balanced regional development has led to the slow progress of agricultural and the industrial sectors in the context of India's Five Year Plan perspectives. Due to the negligence of regional inter-state development the resource mobilization has not been effective for boosting the tempo of India's economic developmental prospects.

Moreover 'space is understood to represent a settlement pattern—an orderly and discrete hierarchy down from villages and country side to town and cities often measured in terms of their location, size density, forms etc., necessitating an integrated comprehensive approach of regional planning.' For realizing an effective level of spatial and economic development in India, there has to be the inter-flow of factors of production from an economically developed state to the under-developed areas of the adjoining state.

The demand and supply of goods and services within the regional planning areas would have to be identified, so as to achieve an optimum rate of economic growth. Such a phenomenal achievement can be attained, when political barriers among the different Indian states are integrated as a single viable economic identity.

Spatial based locational developments of inter-state framework in the country has to be formulated in terms of the availability of men, material and machinery. The region having the growth potentialities within and outisde the Indian states has to be assessed through a comprehensive survey based analysis.

Growth Centre Strategy

There is need for evolving an effective economic policy for accelerating the pace of developmental activities within the viable growth centres. Therefore, in a comprehensive manner the effective process of industrialization is required for gearing an effective tempo of production, income and employment prospects within the growth centres of small town and rural settlements in a regional perspective. The inter-state linkages spatial and economic factors would lead to a balanced regional development. The agro-industrial production prospects has to be boosted with an effective resource flow of movement in a regional inter-state framework.

In India, the inter-state distribution of regional input and output inter flows as per the requirements of planning areas is a prerequisite factor for ensuring a balanced regional development. An effective regional administration and market system assumes a great importance. The emphasis should be given for ensuring the skilled manpower which can meet the adequate productivity requirements of a region.

Output-Input Flow Mechanism

An agro-industrial project in one state can be the output for the project in another state. Thus, the inter-dependence and inter-relationship of input-output requirements of planning areas has to be ascertained. Then only in India the Regional Planning will be able to function a demand and supply equilibrium in the context of inter-state planning areas.

For assessing the effectiveness of input-output flows of resources movements in planning areas, the studies of linear programming and cost benefit analysis will have to be undertaken. However, the former study in its regional perspective visualizes for minimizing production. The application of this planning technique can enable the optimal use of resources in its economic functional characteristic ouput into flows of raw material, and commodity flows would be able to accelerate the market sales prospects. As such, the planning areas in its regional framework must ensure the combination of factors for boosting the regional economy. The application of cost benefit analysis needs to be assessed in terms of cost of projects and its benefits with reference to the regional perspective. Further, such a plan approach would largely benefit the Indian regional communities.

The industrial projects of planning areas within states must minimize the cost of production and promote subsequently the optimal use of productive installed capacity. Moreover, the demand and supply of inter-state regional economic needs should have a comprehensive assessment in the 21st century perspective. When the planning areas are made conducive to accord the equilibrium position in demand and supply within the rural and urban areas, then the balanced spatial and economic development could be achieved in a regional scenario.

Balanced Development Policy

The approach of balanced regional development should be emphasized by integrating the resource availability and technical know-how. In a paper 'Towards Regional Balance in India, Reality and Strategy' K.V. Sundaram has rightly pointed out that the efficient allocation of scarce resource will contribute to regional balance to the extent that part of the investment is concentrated according to some suitable and discriminating geographically decentralized pattern. Such a policy implies a highly selective method of allocating investment in the context of growing points, particularly in the relatively backward regions.

A selective concentration policy of investment seeks to create through intensive conscious efforts. "Investment clusters" of various levels endowed with varying degrees of external economies, complementary infrastructure, trained labour force, social amenities, industry tailored to local resources, productive agriculture and so on. When a number of such "investment clusters" are developed, they tend to become the growth centre for the region and their influence areas tend to flow into one another and work to eliminate the peripheral areas of backwardness. In such a strategy, 'local' is perceived as vital variable of economic development and is conceived as tool for stimulating the process of growth in a regional perspective. It is necessary that this process of selective concentration should be built into the national economic development framework.

There is requirement for adopting a legal action policy for checking the haphazard growth of cities. Moreover, the industries, socio-economic activities, infrastructural and administration of urban set up should be decentralized in the viable growth centres of small town settlements for boosting the rural economy. Thus, the rural-urban integration has got to be planned in an inter-state regional perspective in India's 21st century Five Year Plans.

The "planning at regional level, unless conceived in the context of whole economy, will lack a sense of direction and may not even be compatible with the pace of national economic development progress. In so far as there exists a system of economic planning in a country, which India has, a clear direction should normally be available for the level and pattern of investment, whose spatial implications must be worked out and arranged in an effective manner that ensures their efficient fructification. The coordination of spatial with economic planning will then add a second string to the bow".

Metropolitan Planning for Regional Development

The urban living problems in India are acute. There exist slums in the metropolitan and large cities. Further, there is lack of housing accommodation, a long queue in public hospitals, there is traffic and transportation bottlenecks, only limited seats are available in educational institutions. Indian urban centres like Ahmedabad, Bangalore, Calcutta, Chennai, Mumbai, Pune, Kanpur, there has existed demographic agglomerations of the development requirements.

The immediate need in urban planning is to adopt a regional developmental framework, particularly in the context of metropolitan cities. A plan to develop city of Delhi has been formulated, making effort to integrate the planning areas of three states, namely, Rajasthan, Uttar Pradesh and Haryana, within a regional framework. It has been found that the problem of the growth of a metropolitan city cannot be satisfactorily solved, if planning confines itself only to the area within its administrative boundary. Therefore, it is increasingly becoming necessary to go beyond the city limits and to have a resort to regional planning". The socio-economic inter-dependence of the metropolitan core and its periphery of small towns and rural areas assumes a great importance in a balanced regional development.

While considering the planning of Delhi, the development of its periphery the ring towns like Ghaziabad, Faridabad, Meerut, Gurgaon and Rohtak has to be kept in view. Delhi has witnessed an excessive growth of population and consequently, there has been an acute scarcity of public utility services. The Calcutta Basic Development document of the Metropolitan District, though a tentative physical and socio-economic plan, it is not a compact specified regional plan. It emphasizes the regional developmental prospects with reference to the adjoining states of Bihar and Orissa. However, it does not coordinate the spatial and socio-economic planning mechanism suitably for the workability of an inter-state regional perspective framework. Thus, there is need for developing the comprehensive small town and rural settlements of the Calcutta Metropolitan District. Thus, the alarming migration to Calcutta city from rural areas can be checked by adequate provisions of employment opportunities.

The city of Mumbai has a life of its own where slums are an up-coming phenomenon. The twin city project had envisaged the utilization of the locational advantage to the maximum extent, so as to accelerate the tempo or production and employment prospects. Chennai, which was once a beautiful city has now become over-crowded and migration into the city has increased in an alarming proportion. Slums have grown in unmanageable numbers. So, any plan to develop Chennai must be oriented to the development of small towns in a regional development framework.

Similarly, Kanpur can be developed keeping in view the agro-industrial potentialities of the region. In this connection, the small towns and viable rural settlements will have to assume an important role by providing the adequate infrastructure and the socio-economic planning in a regional development perspective.

The development of small towns should envisage promoting balanced process of regional developmental possibilities by boosting the economic potentialities in the rural and urban settlements. Therefore, the proper emphasis has to be laid on the provision of adequate infrastructural and socio-economic facilities within the comprehensive urban peripheral areas. The inter-state cooperation and coordination is a vital need for planning the regional development.

Regional Planning Administrative Machinery

The establishment of a Regional Council is of vital importance for economic development within the planning areas, such an administrative set up would be able to ensure an effective resource mobilization for an effective flow of men, material and machinery. However, such a structural behavioural pattern of planning areas would ensure the coordinated planned inter-state regional efforts of economic development and planning.

The raw material, manpower, scientific-cum-technological know-how and administrative efficient machinery is a vital necessity for gearing the effectiveness in a regional framework of developmental planning.

Further, the supervision of Regional Plan necessitates a Chief Administrator, representative of the planning areas of inter-states having town planners, engineer planners, industrial planners and geologists. These experts of inter-state planning areas of a region must specialize in the modernized technique of planning and must also have a thorough knowledge of their respective state areas. The regional developmental framework has to be viewed in the context of the Indian national planning perspective. Accordingly, the administrative set up has to be oriented for boosting the marketable and exportable prospects. Further, the self-sustained growth of capital formation, has to be emphasized in the context of the Indian economic planning and programming framework. As such, a regional plan should be devised to explore the economic unity of viable inter-state settlements.

The need is that if a project comes up in Bihar, it should also benefit the people and economy of Uttar Pradesh. However, this has to abide to the physical proximity within the influential planning inter-state areas having the inter-dependence of economic activities. Such a framework is one of the vital factors of regional planning characteristics. The objective has to be realized by exploring the optimal resource-based agro-industrial potentialities and to generate the tempo of production, income and employment prospects.

Regional Policy

There is an imperative need that the Indian Government should formulate the regional developmental policy with a 21st century perspective for integrating the economic programmes. This has to be linked with an effective administrative-cum-techno-economic set up in respect of exploring successfully in its optimality the agro-industrial potentialities. Thus, the urban periphery identified in its regional framework is expected to ensure an optimal production and income and have an advantageous finance prospect through the multiple economic activities. With the adequate infrastructural base it would be able to absorb the surplus manpower and rural resources. At present, there is lack of economic viability in the small towns, therefore, the rural migrants have been attracted towards the industrial urban centres for income and employment opportunities. Thus a regional planning framework within the present states framework has to be formulated.

It is also observed that the industrial urban centres of India have not contributed significantly during the past seven plans in respect of value-added output for the national economy in terms of money for ensuring the self-sustained growth prospects. Therefore, the need of the hour in national planning is to induce the adequate infrastructural and socio-economic opportunities in the growth centres of small towns and rural areas to boost the agro-industrial possibilities. By integrating the rural urban settlements, the balanced regional development would be feasible.

In the Indian context a suitable policy is required that the financial resources are linked with economic rationally rathar than on political bargaining capacity as has been existing in different states. Thus, the locational factors and effective investment flows is a consideration of regional planning decision for boosting the economic developmental prospects.

It is interesting to learn from the Report of the Consultative Assembly on Regional Planning, published by the Council of Europe which observes that any regional planning policy claiming to be progressive must have two-fold considerations. Firstly, it must plan new structures inside towns and restore healthier living conditions to heavily urbanized areas by reviving ancient town centres and creating green areas. Secondly, the open spaces need to be equipped in such a way as to be suitable for new recreational and leisure activities, in addition to the land used for farming, which is going to cover an ever-shrinking area and providing fewer jobs.

Accordingly, the regional planning policy will have to be directed ›r providing infrastructure equipment and employment in modernizing ıe agricultural methods and in encouraging industrialization, rbanization and decentralization. Such a policy is to some extent a oordinated one and is based on the idea of regional development.

It is learnt that throughout the country the objective of regional lanning is to ensure conditions that are specifically favourable to man's ıll development in today's progressive society. In other words, diffusion f knowledge, expansion of society, search for well-being and, to enable ıe regional and national community the happiness of economic prosperity f an optimal production, income and employment possibilities. In the ndian economic planning context, there is an urgency to have a ecentralized urban policy to shift industries to the growth centres of mall towns and rural areas. These growth centres must be provided vith the adequate socio-economic and infrastructure facilities to gear ıe effective process of balanced regional development.

REFERENCES

. Bhargava, Gopal: Effective Resources Mobilization Through Inter-State Regional Planning, *Young India,* Volume 1, No. 15, March 18, 1971.

. Chatterjee, M.: Regional Planning National Development and Conflict Resolution, paper presented in the North-East Section meetings of Pace Science Society.

. Gupta, Sen P. and Dasyuk, G.S.: Paper, Economic Regionalization in Regional Development in India, presented at the Seventh Regional Science.

. Gupta, Shefali Sen: A Note of Regionalization and Regional Development in India presented at the Seventy Regional Science.

Paper on the Spatial Dimension in National Planning, presented at the Symposium organized by the Association of Scientific World.

. Qaiyum, A: Regional Development Planning in India—A Retrospect, *Journal of Institute of Town Planner,* India, Volume 1, Numbers 1 and 2 (112-113), 1982.

. Rao, V.L.S. Prakash and Bhat, L.S.: A Regional Framework for Resource Development (mimeograph), Indian Statistical Institute, Regional Survey Unit, New Delhi.

. Reddy, Y. Venu Gopal: Paper on Regional Planning of Utilities and Resources.

. Richards, H.W.: Regional Economic Location Theory, Urban Structure and Regional Change, Weidenfeld and Nocolson, London.

0. Seminar on 'Regionalization for Planning', organized by the Institute of Town Planners, Indian Council of Geographers and School of Planning and Architecture, New Delhi.

1. First, Second and Third Five Year Plans, Planning Commission, Government of India.

2. Shreevastava, M.P.: Paper submitted for the seminar on Regionalization and Regional Development, held at Delhi..

APPENDIX I

Regional Planning Activities in the States Legend

1. MAHARASHTRA
   1. Mumbai Metropolitan Region
   2. Poona Metropolitan Region
   3. Nagpur Metropolitan Region
   4. Nasik Agro-Industrial Region
   5. Kolhapur-Khalkaranji Agro-Industrial Region
   6. Sangli Miraj Agro-Industrial Region
   7. Jalgaon Agro-Industrial Region
   8. Aurangabad Jalna Agro-Industrial Region
   9. Chandrapur Resource Region
   10. Ratnagiri Resource Region
2. TAMIL NADU
   1. Chennai-Chenglipet Region
   2. Vellore-Dharmapure Region
   3. Salem-Cuddalore Region
   4. Coimbatore Nilgiris Region
   5. Tiruchirapalli-Thanaja Region
   6. Madurai Region
   7. Ramanathapuram Region
   8. Tirunelvelli-Kanyakumari Region
3. ANDHRA PRADESH
   1. Rayalaseema Region
   2. Telengana Region
   3. Coastal Andhra Region
4. UTTAR PRADESH
   1. Meerut-Bulundshahr Region
   2. Banda-Hamirpur Region
   3. Gorakhpur-Deoria Region
   4. Raibareli District Region
   5. Mirzapur Rihand Region
   6. Saharanpur-Dehradun Region
   7. Saharanpur-Muzaffarnagar Region
   8. Agra-Mathura Region
   9. Jhansi-Lalitpur-Jalaun Region
   10. Allahabad-Fatehpur Region
   11. Jaunpur-Balia-Ghazipur Region
   12. Barabanki-Faizabad Region

13. Basti District Region
14. Hardoi-Sitapur Region
15. Bareli-Pillibhit Region
16. Kumayun Region
17. Garhwal Region

5. MADHYA PRADESH
   1. Gawalior Agro-Region
   2. Bhopal Capital Region
   3. Indore Agro-Industrial Region
   4. Narmada Tapti Region
   5. Forest and Ferrous Mineral Region
   6. Jabalpur Forest Resource Region
   7. Bhilai Region
   8. Korba Non-ferrous Mineral Resource Region
   9. Bundelkhand and Bagelkhand Region
   10. Bastar Tribal Region
6. KERALA
   1. Greater Cochin Region
   2. Trivandrum Region
   3. Calicut Region
   4. Malapuram District Region
   5. Quilon District Region
   6. Cannanore District Region
   7. Iduki District Region
   8. Kottayam District Region
7. PUNJAB
   1. North Western Region
      (a) Gurdaspur-Pathankot Sub-Region
      (b) Hoshiarpur Sub-region
      (c) Ropar Sub-region
   2. Central Region
      (a) Amritsar Sub-region
      (b) Jullundhar Sub-region
      (c) Ludhiana Sub-region
      (d) Patiala Rajpura Sub-region
      (e) Chandigarh-Mohali Sub-region
   3. South-West Region
8. GUJARAT
   1. Ahmedabad Metropolitan Region
9. WEST BENGAL

1. Hill Region
2. South Eastern Region
    - (a) Northern Sub-region
    - (b) Sunderban Sub-region
    - (c) Rest of the South Eastern Region
3. South-Western Region
4. City and Metropolitan Region
    - (a) Calcutta Metropolitan District
    - (b) Asansol Durgapur Region
    - (c) Silliguri-Jalpaiguri Region
    - (d) Haldia Region

10. KARNATAKA
    1. Krishna Valley Region
    2. Tungabhadra Valley Region
    3. Western Ghats Region
    4. Bangalore Metropolitan Region
    5. Cauvery Valley Region

11. BIHAR
    1. North Gangetic Plain
        - (a) Tirhut-Agro-Industrial Region
        - (b) Kosi Plain Agricultural Region
    2. South Gangetic Plain
        - (a) Magadh Agro-Industrial Region
        - (b) Lower Son Valley Agro-Region
    3. North Chotanagpur Plateau
        - (a) North Chotanagpur Plateau-Industrial Region
    4. South Chotanagpur Plateau
        - (a) Pattland and Ranchi Plateau Region
        - (b) South-East Chotanagpur Plateau Industrial Region

12. RAJASTHAN
    1. Rajasthan Canal Region

Source: A. Qaiyam, Regional Development Planning in India—A Retrospect, Journal of Institute of Town Planners, India, Vol. 1, Numbers 1 and 2 (112-113) 1982.

BIBLIOGRAPHY

1. Ahmedabad Municipal Corporation Department, document, Ahmedabad.
2. Baig, S.P.; Fire Risk Management with an approach on Statutory Requirements, Civic Affairs, Volume 34, Number 2, September 1986.
3. Batra, B.K. and Johri, N.B.: NCR Plan in Doldrums, Estate, December 17, 1988.
4. Bepin, Behari: Energy Needs of Rural Development, *The Financial Express,* June 11, 1986.
5. ___________: Rural Industrialization in india, Vikas Publishing House, New Delhi.
6. Bhargava, Gopal: Pressures on Cities of the Future, *Business,* November 13, 1980.
7. Bhargava, Gopal: Socio - Economic and Legal Implications of Urban Land (Ceiling and Regulation) Act, 1976, published by Abhinav Publisher Private Limited, New Delhi, 1983.
8. Bhargava, Gopal: Housing the Urban Poor, *Evening News, The Hindustan Times,* June 1, 1995.
9. Bhargava, Gopal: Rehabilitation Programme Should Be Well Planned, *Real Estate,* November, 1985.
10. Bhargava, Gopal: Slum and Squatter Settlements of Urban India, *Real Estate,* June 1989.
11. Bhargava, Gopal: Urban Slums: Planning and Policy Perspective, *The Financial Express,* January 2, 1992.
12. Bhargava, Gopal: Environmental Challenges and Ecological Disaster : Global Perspective, Mittal Publisher, New Delhi, 1992.
13. Bhargava, Gopal: Pollution and its Control, published by Mittal Publisher, New Delhi, 1992.
14. Bhargava, Gopal: Role of Government in Informal Sector, *Manpower Journal,* Volume XXIX, No. 3, October - December, 1993.
15. Bhargava, Gopal: Effective Resource Mobilization through Inter-

State Regional Planning, *Young Indian,* Volume I, Number 15, March 18, 1971.

16. Bhargava, Gopal: Screenplay it fits more Towering Infernos, *The Economic Times,* June 29, 1997.
17. Bhargava, Gopal: Small Town Development, Socio-Economic Aspects, *The Economic Times,* April 11, 1992.
18. Bhargava, Gopal: Small Towns still in Doldrums, *The Hindustan Times,* February 22, 1983.
19. Bhargava, Gopal: Developing the Small Town Settlements, *Employment News,* April 23, 1983.
20. Bhargava, Gopal: Small Town Development, Socio-Economic and Spatial Aspects, *The Economic Times,* April 11, 1982.
21. Bhargava, Gopal: Small Town Planning, *The National Herald,* September 2, 1983.
22. Bhargava, Gopal: The National Capital Region : The framework for Coordinated Growth, cyclostyle paper.
23. Bhargava, Gopal: Action Plan for NCR, *The Hindustan Times,* August 18, 1986.
24. ________: Making NCR Work, *The Hindustan Times,* November 18, 1987.
25. __________: National Capital Regional Plan; Limitations of Promises, *The Hindu,* January 9, 1987.
26. _________: Enforcement Powers for NCR Planning Board - Administrative and Legal Provisions, papers presented at seminar 'National Capital Region-Need for Critical Appraisal' organized by PHD Chamber of Commerce and Industry in collaboration with Ministry of Urban Development and NCR Planning Board, held on May 16, 1992, New Delhi.
27. _________: More Teeth to State Rent Laws, *The Economic Times,* March 2, 1997.
28. __________: Local Self-Government in Doldrums, Anomalies of Constitution Seventy Fourth Amendment Act, 1992, *Quarterly Journal of Local Self Government,* Volume LX VII, No. 1, January - March, 1997.
29. __________: Putting the Master Plan to Practice, *Observer of Business and Politics,* July 19, 1996.
30. _________: Urban Land Ceiling Act has Failed Viewpoint, *Patriot,* December 3, 1985.
31. __________ Need to Amend Urban Land Ceiling Act, *The Evening News, The Hindustan Times,* August 3, 1992.

32. Bhargava, Gopal and Batra, B.K.: Make Space for Immigrants in Plans, *The Economic Times,* May 3, 1992.

33. ___________ Delhi's Squatter Settlements, The Evening News, *The Hindustan Times,* August 17, 1993.

34. ___________ Yet Another Problem, *The Hindustan Times, Sunday Magazine,* December 26, 1993.

35. Bhattacharya, K.P.: Housing in India—Observations on Governmental Intervention Policies, Edited by Gil Shidlo published by Roitlege, London, 1980.

36. Birdi, H.D.: Slum Law and Urbanization, Vidhi Publishing House, New Delhi, 1985.

37. Biswas, Dilip and Dutta, S.A.: Vehicular Pollution; Combating the Smog and Noise in Cities, *The Hindu,* Survey of the Environment, 1994.

38. Buch, M.N., Towards A National Urban Policy, *Journal of the Institute of Town Planners,* India, Number 83, November 1974.

39. Buchanan, Golin: Cities in Crisis : An Overview, *The Planner,* The Journal of the Royal Institute of Town Planners, Volume 61, July–August 1975.

40. Census of India, 1971: Number 1, Birth Place Migration in India, Special Monograph.

41. Chatterjee, M.: Regional Planning National Development and Conflict Resolution, paper presented in the North-East Section meetings of the Pace Science Society International.

42. Dave, P.K.: Interview 'NCR Plan to get a Boost'. *The Hindu,* May 20, 1993.

43. Delhi Development Authority document cyclostyle 'Role of Private Developers in the context of Delhi, 2001'.

44. Editorial, Urban Development, *The Economic Times,* February 5, 1981.

45. Editorial, Move on Slums, *Civic Affairs,* Volume 32, No. 7, February 1985.

46. Editorial, Urban Planning and Development, *Journal of the Institute of Town Planners,* India, No. 90, 1976.

47. *Economic and Political Weekly,* Volume X, Number 4, January 25, 1975, Social Development and Strategy for Urbanization: Absence of a Positive Approach to Urbanization.

48. Eldelman, D.J. and Banerjee, R.: Fifteen Years of the Integrated Development of Small and Medium Towns (IDSMT) in Karnataka —Some Observations, Institute of Town Planners, India, Journal,

Volume 14, Nos. 1 and 2 (163-164) September–December 1995.

49. Ensminger, Doughlas: Growth and Viable Rural—Urban Communities, Kurukshetra, October, 1969.
50. Estate, June 17-30, 1989. An Analysis of the NCR Plan.
51. Expert Group on National Planning Organization held on January 28, 1975, New Delhi—National Urbanization Policy.
52. Federation of Indian Chambers of Commerce and Industry, background paper, seminar on Housing and Urban Development February 5, 1996, New Delhi.
53. Federation of Indian Chamber of Commerce and Industry—Meeting of Committee on Housing and Public Works held at Madras on February 16, 1992, Item Number 1 Agenda Draft Memorandum on the Urban Land (Ceiling and Regulation) Act, 1976.
54. Gambir, J.C. and Narayan, Prakash: Planning for Development (including redevelopment) of Cities, Review of the Master Plan, Concept paper presented at the National Workshop on Master Plan Approach—Its Efficiency and Alternatives organized by the Ministry of Urban Development, Government of India.
55. Ghose, S.: No. Sign Yet of Urban Strategy, *The Economic Times*, October 6, 1991.
56. Government of India: Document Task Force on Housing and Urban Development.
57. Government of India: Planning Commission, First, Second, Third, Fourth, Fifth, Seventh and Eighth Five Year Plans.
58. Government of India: Report of National Commission on Urbanization, Interim Report, January, 1987. 159. *The Statesman*, June 20th, 1997.
59. Government of India: Report of National Commission for Urbanization, Volume I, August 1998.
60. Government of India: Ministry of Urban Development, 1992 National Housing Policy.
61. Government of India: Ministry of Urban Development, Town and Country Planning Organization, Industrial Profile of Haryana Sub-Region of National Capital Region, Document.
62. Government of India: Ministry of Urban Development, Seventy Fourth Amendment Act, 1992 on Municipalities.
63. Government of India: Ministry of Urban Development, Power to the People, Booklet.
64. Government of India: Ministry of Urban Development, Agenda Notes : Conference of Ministers of Local Self Government and

Urban Development States and Union Territories, held on 17-18 January, 2000 at New Delhi.

65. Government of India: Ministry of Urban Development, National Capital Region Planning Board, December 1988, Regional Plan 2001, National Capital Region Document.
66. Government of India: Ministry of Housing, Task Force on Planning and Development of Small and Medium Towns and Cities.
67. Goyal, A.K. and Shorey, S.P.: Master Plan Approach, Hyderabad experience, Spatio-Economic Development Record, Volume 2, Number 2, March–April 1995.
68. Gupta, J.K.: Economic Institutions and Employment Generation in Rural Areas, Agenda for Action, paper presented at the 44th National Town and Country Planners Congress, Planning for Rural Development.
69. Gupta, M.M.: Regional Demographic Situation in India, paper presented in the seminar, Regional Dimension of India's Economic Development, held at Nainital April 22-24, 1982.
70. Gupta, R.C.: Management of Urban Development: Issues and Imperatives, paper presented at 43rd Annual Town and Country Planning Seminar, February 3, 1995.
71. ___________: Counter Magnets Development Approach to Metropolitan Region Planning, Delhi Vikas Varta, Journal, Volume 1, No. 3, July - September 1990.
72. ___________: Rural Development Planning, Journal of Institute of Town Planners, India, Volume 1, Number 2 (144), January 1991.
73. Gupta, Shefali Sen: Note of Regionalization and Regional Development in India, presented at the Seventh Regional Science Seminar, organized by the Centre for the Study of Regional Development, Jawaharlal Nehru University and Regional Science Association, India.
74. Indian National Group of the International Association for Bridge and Structural Engineering, Delhi–National Conference on Tall Buildings, January 22-24, 1973.
75. Indian Society for Agro-Asian Studies, Foundation Day–Seminar held at New Delhi on February 23, 1992, Paper–Problems of Urban Governance in a Comparative Perspective.
76. Inaugural address of Advance Course on Management and Development of Small and Medium Towns by J.P Singh, May 8, 1995, organized by the Town and Country Planning Organization.
77. Institute of Town Planners, Indian Council of Geographers and

School of Planning and Architecture, New Delhi–Seminar on Regionalization for Planning.

78. Jagmohan: Delhi 2000, *National Herald*, October 2, 1983.
79. ____________: Challenges of Our Cities, Vikas Publishing House, New Delhi.
80. Jagmohan: Cities and Civilizations, Delhi : A Case Study, *The Hindustan Times,* March, 1995.
81. Javed, Qamar, A.: For the People by the Government, *The Hindustan Times,* December 14, 1995.
82. Jha, Gangadhar: The Seventy Fourth Constitution Amendment and the Empowerment of Municipal Government : A Critique, Urban India, Volume XII, No. 2, July-December, 1993.
83. Joshi, Prabha: Slum Improvement in Greater Bombay–seminar paper presented at the centre of Urban Studies, Institute of Public Administration, New Delhi, March, 1979.
84. Joseph, D.T. and Pathak, V.K.: Flexible Planning and Innovative Development Management, Spatio-Economic Development Record, Volume 2, No. 2, March–April, 1995.
85. Kaul, Shiela: Need for Adaption of Mixed Landuse Planning Approach (Inaugural Address at the National Workshop on Master Plan Approach, its Efficacy and Alternatives, February 24-25, 1995 organized by the Ministry of Urban Development, Government of India.
86. Kochatta, R.C.: Fundamental of Rent Control Legislation in India, Indore, 1983.
87. Krishnan, Jairam: Urban Ceiling Law Proves Counter Productive, *The Economic Times,* September 6, 1985.
88. Kulshrestha, S.K.: Neglected Small and Medium Towns Spatio-Economic Development Record, Volume 2, Number 3, May, 1995.
89. Kumar, Rahul: National Capital Region Plan, Still on Paper, *The Economic Times,* Data Bank, 1989.
90. *Link,* India 2001, November 10, 1985, The Urban Scenario.
91. Lok Sabha Bill No. 56 of 1998 Introduced in Lok Sabha, June 11, 1998 : The Urban Land (Ceiling and Regulation) Repeal Bill, 1998.
92. Mayur, Rashmi: A Presage of Urban Decay, More Less Life, Femina, January 28–February 10, 1977.
93. Mayur Rashmi: Urbanization in India in the year 2000 A.D. (Cyclostyle paper) May 21, 1974.
94. Mayur Rashmi: Man, City and Future, Civic Affairs, Volume 27, Number 6, January 1980.

95. Mazumdar, Atreyi: Problems of Urbanization in India by 2001 AD, Demographic View, paper presented in the seminar organized by the National Institute of Urban Affairs and Town and Country Planning Organization, New Delhi.
96. Mahapatra, Satyen: Delhi 2001, Delhities Gasping for Breath, *The Hindustan Times,* September 27, 1991.
97. Mohanty Manoranjan: Expanding Million Cities and Urban Future of Cities by 2000 AD. Problems and Prospects in book, India's Land Policy and Development Finance, edited by R.C. Sharma, published by Seema Publications, Delhi, 1988.
98. Maudgal, S.: An Outlook for India's Future (2000 AD) Interim Report on Urbanology (National Committee on Science and Technology), Government of India, September 15, 1975.
99. Mehta, Jaswant B.: High Rise Buildings, published by Skyline publisher, Bombay, 1978.
100. Mehta, Meera: Housing in Delhi Squatter Settlements Increase, Development Alternatives, Newsletters, Volume 4, Number 4, May, 1994.
101. Meshram, D.S. and Bansal, R.P.: Legal Provisions for Public Participation with Reference to 74th Amendment Act, 1992, Institute of Town Planners Journal, Volume 12, Number 1 (155), September, 1993.
102. ________: Town and Country Planning Legislation—Some Basic Issues, Journal of the Institute of Town Planners, India, Volume No. 11, Number 4, June, 1993.
103. Meshram, D.S. and Qaiyam, A.: Small and Medium Towns—A Weak Link in Human Settlement System in India, Spatio-Economic Development Record, Vol. 2, No. 3, May-June, 1995.
104. Meeting of Committee on Housing and Public Works—Madras, Item No. 1, Agenda Draft Memorandum on Urban Land (Ceiling and Regulation) Act, 1976, organized by Federation of Indian Chambers of Commerce and Industry, Coimbatore, February 16, 1992.
105. Menezes, Louis: An Approach to Urban Land Policy, Social Action, 1982.
106. Mohanty, Prasanna K.: Scheme of Integrated Development of Small and Medium Towns—Some Suggestions for Restructuring Spatio—Economic Development Record, Volume 2, Number 3, May-June, 1996.
107. Murthy, M. Krishna: Alternate Building Technologies and

Materials for Housing, paper presented at the International Symposium on Housing, Energy and Environment, organized by Shelter Promotion Council, India, held at New Delhi, during January 27-29, 1996.

108. Nangia Sudesh: Slums of Urban India: Planning and Policy Actions, The Civic Affairs, December, 1987.

109. Ordinance Promulgamated to Repeal ULCRA, *National Herald,* January 13, 1999.

110. Pandey, H.B.: Small Town Planning Guidelines for Zonal Planning-I, Small Town Planning II, Factors Accelerating Development, *The Economic Times,* January 28-29, 1983.

111. PHD Chamber of Commerce and Industry—seminar on National Capital Region—Need for a Critical Reappraisal, organized by PHD Chamber of Commerce and Industry in collaboration with Ministry of Urban Development and NCR Planning Board, New Delhi, held on May 16, 1992.

112. Panicker, Rita: The Urban Poor can stand on their Own, Social Welfare, Volume XXIX, Number 3, June, 1982.

113. Papola, T.S.: Urban Informal Sector in a Developing Economy, Vikas Publishing House Private Limited, New Delhi.

114. Prasad, D. Ravindra and Ganeshwar: Seventy Fourth Constitution Amendment Act: Conformity Legislation in Andhra Pradesh, Urban India, Volume XV, January-June, 1995.

115. Pratap, Krishan: Alternative Models for Assemblage of Land for Development of the NCR Towns, Spatio-Economic Development Record, Volume 1, Number 5, November-December, 1994.

116. Puri, M.M.: Hazards of Automobile Emissions, *Link,* February, 17, 1991.

117. Qaiyum, A.: Regional Development Planning in India, A Retrospect, Journal of Institute of Town Planners, India, Volume No. 1, Numbers 1 and 2 (112-113), 1982.

118. __________: Rural Development Efforts in India, +14XJournal Institute of Town Planners, India, 1993.

119. Qaiyam, A. and Nasim, Abu: Role of Small and Medium Size Towns in the Human Settlement Systems of India, Town and Country Planning Organization, May, 1985.

120. Raj, Deva: Some Factors in National Urbanization Policy, Nagarlok, Volume VII, Number 19, January-March, 1975.

121. Rao, B.V. Venkata: Rural Development, To the Editor, *The Hindu,* February 9, 1996.

122. Rao, M. Koteswara: Trends and Patterns of Urbanization in India, The Civic Affairs, April, 1989.
123. Rao, V.L.S. Prakash and Bhat, L.S.: A Regional Framework for Resource Development (Mimeograph) Indian Statistical Institute, Regional Survey Unit, New Delhi.
124. Reddy, V. Venugopal, paper submitted for the seminar on Regionalization and Regional Development held at Delhi.
125. Riberio, E.F.N., Review of the Provision of Infrastructure in Slum and Squatter settlements in Urban India (paper).
126. ________: Planning for the Urban Poor: Basic Needs and Priorities, Social Action, Volume 32, April-June, 1982.
127. ________: Planning for Capital, Environmental Concern edited by S.C. Bhatia, published by Centre for Adult Continuing Education and Extension, University of Delhi, sponsored by the Department of Environment, Government of India, 1983.
128. ________: The National Capital Region: The Framework for Coordinated Growth (cyclostyle paper).
129. Richards, H.W.: Regional Economic Location Theory, Urban Structure and Regional Change, Weidenfeld and Nocolson, London.
130. Risbud, Vijay D.: Alternative Approaches to Master Plan, presented in the Settlement Planning Concepts and Systems, Technical papers of 40th Annual Town and Country Planning Seminar, Pune January 15-17, 1992.
131. Sadhu, Arun: Bombay the Big Cities in a Big Mess, *The Sunday Statesman,* November 29, 1981.
132. Saha, Swati, Practice of Master Planning Approach in West Bengal: A Critical Study, paper presented in 40th Annual Town and Country Planning Seminar, January 15-17, 1992.
133. Sarin, Madhu: The Informal Sector Regional Planning and National Research Project, financed by grant from Overseas Development Administration, Britain.
134. Sen Gupta, B.K: Financial and Technological Innovations for Cost Optimised Housing, key note address for presentation in the International Symposium on Housing, Energy and Environment Organized by Shelter Promotion Council (India), held at New Delhi during January 27-29, 1996.
135. Savitha, G.L.: Moving Shop, Stock and Barrel, *The Times of India,* March 8, 1998.
136. Shah, S.M.: Urbanization: Emerging Problems, Journal of Institute of Town Planners, India, Number 83, November 1974.

137. Sharma, D.P., and Desai V.V., Rural Economy of India, Vikas Publishing House, New Delhi, 1980.
138. Sharma, R.C., edited India's Urban Land Policy and Development Finances, Seema Publications, Delhi.
139. Shafi, Sayed S.: National Capital Region: The Issues, *Delhi Vikas Varta,* Journal, Volume 1, Number 2, April-June, 1990.
140. Shetye, Madhu: Bombay Slum Underworld remains a Challenge, *Patriot*: January 15, 1985.
141. Singh, Damandeep, Quality of Life in NCR on the Decline, *The Indian Express,* January 30, 1997.
142. Singh, B.N.: Special Representation by the NCR Board, Seminar on National Capital Region—Need for a Critical Reappraisal, organized by PHD Chamber of Commerce and Industry, 1992.
143. Singh, Radha Raman: Studies in Regional Planning and Rural Development, Associated Book Agency, 1982, Patna.
144. Singh, Shamsher: 74th Constitution Amendment Implications for Urban and Regional Planning Policies, Institute of Town Planners, India, Journal, Volume 12, Number 1 (155), September 1993.
145. Singh, Lalitha and Singhal, J.C.: Fire Water Supply System in High Rise Buildings, Civic Affairs, Volume 33, Number 11, June 1986.
146. Sinha, R.P.L.: Regional Development and Planning in India Need for an organizational Structure, paper presented at the Regional Planning Symposium, organized by the Institute of Town Planners, India.
147. Siddiqui, Agha M.A.: Rural Roads Planning Vis-a-Vis Rural Development, Journal of Institute of Town Planners, Volume 13, No. 2 (160), December, 1994.
148. Spatio-Economic Development Record, Volume 2, Number 2, March-April, 1995.
149. Suresh V.: Strategies and Solutions for Squatter Settlements, Shelter, Volume 1, Number 3, July-September, 1998.
150. Srinivas, K. and Kumar Sanjay: India's Urbanization and Health 129 Industrial Area (cyclostyle paper).
151. Tandon, S.K.: Anand Parbat Industrial Area (cyclostyle paper).
152. Tewari, V.K.: Urbanization in India, Patterns and Perspective, presented at National Seminar on Future Cities—Urban Vision, 2021, October 6-7, 1977, organized by the Ministry of Urban Affairs and Employment, Government of India.
153. __________: Rent Control in India, Research Study Reports Part

V, Report of the National Commission on Urbanization, Volume V, August 1988.

154. *The Economic Times,* The Challenges of Urban Slums, November 14, 1993.

155. _______: New Urban Land Ceiling Act to reclassify towns, to cover only cities with population of over 10 lakh. Thrust on Development of vacant Land not Acquisition, June 5, 1997.

156. *The Economic Times:* Tall Claims that can lead Delhi in a Mess, March 8, 1998.

157. *The Financial Express,* Check the Hazardous Pollution, May 10, 1994.

158. The Gazette of India Extraordinary Part-II, The National Capital Region Planning Board Act, 1985, No. 2 of 1985.

159. *The Hindu*: Meeting the Challenge, October 6, 1991.

160. *The Statesman*: June 20, 1997.

161. Town and Country Planning Organization, Ministry of Urban Development, Informal Sector in Metropolis: Case Study of Delhi: Industrial Informal Cluster, Anand Parbat.

162. _________: Integrated Development of Small and Medium Towns, Retrospects and Prospects, Ministry of Works and Housing, Government of India, 1984.

163. _________Workshop, Master Plan Approach, Its Efficacy and Alternatives, 1995.

164. Town Planning Departments, Government of Karnataka, Town Planning Department, Government of Uttar Pradesh, Town Planning Department, Government of Orissa.

165. Urban Informal Sector: Concept Policy Issues and Measure, Urban Affairs, Quarterly Centre for Urban Studies, Indian Institute of Public Administration, Volume XII, Number 1, 1980.

166. Urban India, Volume XV, January-June, 1995, special number on the Seventy Fourth Constitution Amendment and the Conformity Legislation.

167. United Nations, Economic and Social Commission for Asia and the Pacific, Guidelines for Rural Centre Planning, New York, 1979.

168. Vagale, L.R.: State Capital of India: Planning Imperative for Sustainable Development, paper presented at 45th National Town and Country Planners Congress on Planning and Development of State Capitals, held at Thiruvananthapuram and organized by the Institute of Town Planners, India.

169. __________: Decentralized Regional Development Process by

Multi-Level Planning, The District, Metropolises and Urban Areas as Planning Identities, Soveneir, 43rd Annual Town and Country Seminar January 30–February 3, 1995, Emerging Dimensions of Regional Development Planning, organized by the Institute of Town Planners, India.

170. Varashar, Pradeep: Slums in Delhi, *Delhi Vikas Varta,* Volume 5, Number 2, April-June, 1992.

171. Wishwakarma, R.K.: Integrated Development of Small and Medium Towns: Critical Areas and Issues for Policy Options (Proceedings of the Workshop held on July 1981, organized by the Centre for Urban Studies, Indian Institute of Public Administration).

172. ________Informal-Formal Sector Linkages: Its Implications for Development Policy, Manpower Journal, Volume XXIX, Number 3, October-December, 1993.

173. Zakaria, Rafiq: Urban Chaos, *The Illustrated Weekly of India,* Volume XCV (27), September 1, 1974.

174. Zaidi, S.T.H.: Urban Planning and Development, Civic Affairs, Volume 26, Number 8, March, 1979.

INDEX

O

R

S

T

U

V

W

Y

Z